ONE UP ON TRUMP

How You Too Can Make Real Estate $$$ Millions in the New R.E.O. Market And Keep It!!

Stephen Murphy
with Dr. Stanley Reyburn

ACFH

Published by **American Capital Foundation for the Homeless, Inc.**
330 Washington Boulevard, Penthouse Suite
Marina Del Rey, California 90292
(310) 822-0005

Library of Congress Cataloging-in-Publication Data

Murphy, Stephen J.
    One Up on Trump: How You Too Can Make $$$ Millions in the
    New REO Market, and Keep It!

By Stephen Murphy with Dr. Stanley Reyburn

ISBN: 1-883077-00-1

Printed in the United States of America

* * * * *

SPECIAL ANNOUNCEMENT

(Tax Deductible, Charitable Donation to the Homeless)

100% OF THE PROCEEDS FROM THIS BOOK WILL FUND AND SUPPORT THE INITIATIVES OF THE PRIVATE, NON-PROFIT AMERICAN CAPITAL FOUNDATION FOR THE HOMELESS, A CALIFORNIA, NON-PROFIT CORPORATION. YOUR PURCHASE OF THIS BOOK IS A 100% TAX DEDUCTIBLE, CHARITABLE DONATION TO THIS FOUNDATION. THIS ORGANIZATION IS COMMITTED TO PURCHASING REO HOMES AND APARTMENTS ACROSS AMERICA, TO PROVIDE HOMES AND NEW LIVING REHABILITATION PROGRAMS FOR THE MANY THOUSANDS OF AMERICANS WHO ARE OFTEN FORGOTTEN BY SOCIETY, AND OFTEN BESET BY THE DISEASE OF DRUG/ALCOHOL ABUSE. WE BELIEVE THAT THE BEST INVESTMENT THAT WE CAN MAKE IS IN OUR OWN PEOPLE. WE ARE HONORED AND PRIVILEGED TO HAVE THIS RESPONSIBILITY.

AMERICAN CAPITAL FOUNDATION FOR THE HOMELESS HAS ALREADY PURCHASED TWO HOMES IN LOS ANGELES, CALIFORNIA AND NEW HAVEN, CONNECTICUT, AND HAS DONATED THE USE OF THEM TO HOMELESS VIETNAM VETERANS.

AMERICAN CAPITAL FOUNDATION FOR THE HOMELESS
330 WASHINGTON BOULEVARD, PENTHOUSE SUITE
MARINA DEL REY, CA 90292
(310) 822-0005

To Order:
(800) 959-6544
Credit Cards
Accepted

FORWARD

Excellence, according to Webster is "a fact or condition . . . or superiority; surpassing goodness, merit, etc.," and "something in which a person or thing excels." Aristotle once said, ". . .to enjoy the things we ought and to hate the things we ought has the greatest bearing on excellence of character. . ." When one thinks of the definition in these terms, certain names come to mind:

- The "Hallmark" of quality.

- At "Zenith" the quality goes in before the name goes on. Zenith means the highest point, a peak — you're at the top of your game.

These exemplary human beings in the arena of life have no peers — they represent the highest standards of excellence, integrity, and achievement:

> **Donald J. Trump** has no peer. His degree of excellence embodies one who has gone above and beyond the call of duty to a higher plane, surpassing all others in the process in levels of achievement. He typifies one that commands our respect and admiration.
>
> **Edward R. Murrow** had London in our living rooms during World War II and a television audience in the living rooms of the rich and famous thereafter.
>
> **Winston Churchill** went beyond grit in his dogged determination and the ever familiar "V" for victory sign that he gave during the second World War.

Webster defines *oneupmanship* as, ". . . the practice of, or skill in, seizing an advantage or gaining superiority over others. . ." In other words, you're just practicing Gresham's Law of Primacy — He who gets there firstest gets the mostest — although this advantage, or edge, if you will, is only temporary unless one continues to pursue excellence and remain on the leading edge in the process. IBM is a classic example of this. Others are Title Insurance and Trust Company that was absorbed by Chicago Title in January, 1991. They used to have close to 100% of the title business in Los Angeles County and at their demise had less than 10%.

Donald J. Trump is a very respected standard for financial success in the real estate world. He, like other great developers of worldwide stature got caught up in the buying frenzy of the '80s where laws of supply and demand seemed temporarily suspended, resulting in the biggest commercial real estate debacle in the history of the U.S. economy. For a general frame of reference, imagine that the stock market — now worth about $3.8 trillion — was to decline in value by approximately 30%, a loss of $1.1 trillion. This is exactly what happened in the commercial real estate market and most of the active and visible players were on 80% margin. No wonder a huge credit crunch ensued resulting in serious, but not fatal financial reversals for these well known developers.

Buying low and selling high was and is the most basic fundamental premise of business success. But during the 1980s a lot of developers got caught in a buying frenzy, because the required money was always available, and emotions ruled over intelligence. As Bernard Baruch once said, ". . . Timing is everything — the difference between salad and garbage is timing as well." J. Paul Getty quoted in his autobiography stated, ". . . if you want to make money, really big money, do what nobody else is doing. . . Buy when everyone else is selling and hold until everyone else is buying." This is not merely a catch slogan. It is the very essence of successful investing." And it is the motto of American Capital Investments, Inc.

ONE UP ON TRUMP teaches you how to follow J. Paul Getty's advice, and avoid the pitfalls of the eighties. It shows you in simple straight-forward language, how small and big investors alike, can participate in the upward cycle of commercial real estate. It outlines how investors in American Capital Investments, Inc. partnerships have purchased more than $50,000,000.00 of prime commercial property in selective areas of America, for $.22 to $.56 on the dollar, with amazing cash returns of 16% to 50%. ACIs simple secret formula of proven methods of business negotiation and due diligence are shared with you in this very special edition. American Capital Investments has created the most exciting, and profitable financial investment since the post-depression 1940s. Its clients have enjoyed amazing profits of 135% to over 200% annually, and are proud to offer you proof in their testimonials.

But make no mistake about it. Many entrepreneurs, like my mentor, Donald J. Trump, who have suffered temporary financial setbacks are leaner, meaner, and wiser today, and are just some of our exciting competitors in the explosive and profitable REO (Real Estate Owned) market.

To all those who dare greatly and have the courage to remain persistent and one up!

Stephen Murphy

Hear the Praise Clients Have for Stephen Murphy and American Capital Investments, Inc.

"For the first time investor, it is important that one chooses a company he can trust. American Capital Investments Inc,. had made good on their word and are genuinely concerned about their clientele."

— John Armstrong

"I was very impressed by the performance of my initial investment with American Capital in the Orlando project. To make 50% in 3 months is almost unheard of with any investment vehicle, and they showed me it was possible with their REO projects."

— Nick Di Paolo

". . . Mr. Murphy is the kind of guy that makes things happen. I had to cash in some of my investments to participate, but I have never looked back and have been kept apprised of the actions and potential for new investments."

— R. Al Morrison

"American Capital Investments, Inc. has with careful research, good judgment, and timeliness, purchased outstanding undervalued commercial Real Estate, resulting in excellent financial returns. A company in the right place at the right time."

— Betty Smay

"ACI is a hard working team that provides true leadership in seeking financial opportunities in today's commercial real estate market. They provide a realistic degree of capital and profit protection, incorporating a traditional environment of honesty and integrity."

— Wil Burkhart

"Stephen Murphy has increased my investment as quickly as he promised. Small investors should join the American Capital Investments team!"

— G. A. Tobey

". . . Since I have been invested with American Capital Investments, I have been involved in two of their projects, one of which paid 135% profit . . . and the other pays 16% annualized, paid monthly. If you're looking for investments or a place to roll over your IRA — give these guys a try."

— Larry Finan

Investing in Real Estate never looked better — especially with the business expertise and personal attention shown to the investor, like myself, by Mr. Stephen Murphy, President of ACI, Inc. My retirement this year, from a financial standpoint, looks a helluva lot better than it did just six months ago. Thanks, Steve. 1993 — Here we come!"

— Bill Newman

"I invested in REOs with Steve Murphy and made 150% return. This was accomplished in a shorter period of time than any other investment I've made. His savvy insight and uncanny perception of timing and real estate opportunities has made me a much wiser and richer investor."

— Marc Tanner

"Steve Murphy and American Capital Investments is the most incredible success story I've seen in 30 years in the Real Estate Investment business."

— Mike Stabach

"As investors in American Capital, we highly recommend it to others. Expecting only a 50% return on our first investment, we were pleased with an initial 135% return, enjoy 16% annual interest, and expect additional gain."

— John and Elaine Rohr

"Since I met Steve Murphy, he has shown me how to make more money than I ever had imagined possible with REOs. He is truly today's MAVIN of Real Estate. He has shown a great concern for fellow mankind and is a real HAMISHAH MENTSCH. If not for his CHUTZPAH, his investors would have to settle for today's CD rates and not benefit from the WHOLESALE Real Estate purchases he's made. What he's done for his clients in an absolute MITZVAH. I would give him an honorary membership in our TRIBE. He is an adept investor, great teacher and truly remarkable individual. I hope to be able to continue earning and learning with him in the years ahead."

— Alan Ramer

"Investors in Steve Murphy's American Capital benefit from his ability to find, negotiate, buy, manage — and ultimately sell — commercial real estate. As one of them myself, I recommend his talents as 'visionary,' and I rarely use that word. Some smart money is riding his coattails."

— Mike Geller

"UNEQUALED EXCELLENCE!" Stephen Murphy has combined wit, talent, tenacity and a never say die attitude toward the pursuit of financial stardom. Relentless efforts have garnered admiration amongst his peers. The right deals just seem to be landing in his lap, and he knows just what to do with them. His genuine concern for his investors puts him a cut above the rest. And his heartwarming rise from adversity makes him truly one of a kind. If more people gave back to society what this man has, our world would be a much better place for all."

— Jeff Solomon

Acknowledgements

The efforts of many are required to produce any great achievement. I am especially indebted to the following person(s) for their own direct or indirect contributions to this book.

To Donald J. Trump, my mentor, a man I admire tremendously for his courage, determination, ambition, and character, for as Martin Luther King, Jr. so eloquently said, "The ultimate measure of any man is not where he stands in moments of comfort and convenience, but where he stands at the times of challenge and controversy."

To Harry Helmsley and Larry Wien, my mentors also, whose vision, persistence, and creativity accomplished for them in the '40s, '50s, and '60s, what American Capital is accomplishing today.

To my mom and dad, who taught me the value of hard and careful work, and provided me a wonderful foundation of positive mental attitude and spiritual beliefs.

To my children, Michelle and Mai Ly, whose love for each other and for me has meant so very much.

To my colleagues at American Capital Investments, Inc., whose extra efforts have made American Capital's performance possible but who have received none of the favorable publicity.

To Holy God for all the incredible blessings I have been given in my lifetime.

To John Keaveney, whose spiritual presence and privileged friendship, is a genuine inspiration to me.

To my great friends and colleagues, Jeff Solomon, Major League Properties, real estate broker par excellence; and Cindy Watkins, the best attorney in the United States; without their assistance, American Capital's achievements and success would not have been as great.

To the friends and residents of New Directions, an organization that inspires me daily to care for and always lend a helping hand to the less fortunate among us, homeless Vietnam veterans.

To John Yzurdiaga, whose high standards of integrity and character served as a very positive influence on me at the crossroads of my life - Thanks.

To the Boy Scouts of America, who provide a wonderful training environment for the next leaders of our country.

And last, but not least, to the United States of America, the greatest democratic country in the world, that provides a free entrepreneurial atmosphere for all Americans to be the best that they can be.

Dedication

DEDICATED TO THE FORESIGHTEDNESS, CONVICTION AND COURAGE OF ALL MY MANY, MANY INVESTORS IN AMERICAN CAPITAL INVESTMENTS, INC., WHO HAVE ENTRUSTED THEIR SAVINGS TO ME AND WHO HAVE SENT HUNDREDS OF LETTERS AND MADE HUNDREDS OF CALLS COMPLIMENTING ME ON OUR HARD WORK AND VERY PROFITABLE RESULTS. GOD BLESS YOU.

One Up On Trump

CONTENTS

INTRODUCTION

"If a little knowledge is dangerous, where is the man who has so much as to be out of danger?" Those very prophetic words came from the pen of Thomas Henry Huxley in his **On Elementary Instruction in Physiology** written in 1877. Time has done nothing to reduce the sagacity of Mr. Huxley's remarks.

In our complex society dancing to the final melodious strains of the 20th century, tremendous technical advances have been evidenced. Everything from the Wright Brothers first successful plane flight in 1903 at Kitty Hawk to modern rocketry all have occurred within this hundred year span. In the same way, how man utilizes land resources has changed in this same era. We have seen the gradual conversion from an agrarian economy where many of our citizens lived off the land to a highly industrialized and service oriented economy geared toward consumption. How one looks at real estate as an investment vehicle has changed along with all of the other technological changes that have taken place.

As our society has rapidly adapted to an urban oriented culture, commercial and industrial properties have taken a large role in our leading cities. Depending upon the nature of the locale, this role may be a major or minor one.

Within the pages of this text, the potential investor will discover the options available to devote capital expenditures to the optimum degree. In any investment, there must be a proper **yield**, combined with a reasonable degree of **safety** containing adequate **liquidity** to satisfy individual investment objectives. The following pages will serve as an investment road map leading one to the ultimate destination of considering commercial/industrial properties as a potential syndication device.

In particular the availability of investment in commercial/industrial property through the use of trained and experienced negotiators, such as American Capital Investments, Inc., as the means of obtaining proper sales terms, leverage and tax advantage to wind through the maze of real property analysis to identify the opportunities is explored.

As the reader will note in perusing the information in the text, selection of a proper investment vehicle requires considerable due diligence. This extensive time consuming process is usually a luxury that most investors cannot afford. This is the reason why they rely on the experts to assemble attractive investment packages for their consideration.

The book will also indicate that real estate investment in certain areas is not for the tyro. A certain degree of sophistication is required for those who would devote a portion of their capital to ventures involving office buildings and shopping centers, as opposed to the more familiar residential properties. It's a matter of where the investor's comfort zone lies in dealing with the former properties.

Real estate is unique, since there are no two parcels on earth that are exactly alike. If nothing else, they don't share the same location. This seems incongruous with the statement that homogeneity is important when considering a real estate investment. Not so. Properties might not share the same location, but being in an area where land use is compatible is one way of stabilizing and preserving value. Value and potential to any real estate investor is high on the priority list.

With this thought in mind, several areas of the country will be indicated as locations which show excellent future potential to out-perform the economy in general. The data presented on these areas should be studied carefully.

It is our sincere desire that this book will be informative in the respect that the entire investment process involves considerable research before any recommendations are made relative to the devotion of dollars seeking adequate sheltered return with proper return on the risk undertaken. The presentation of knowledge in this book is designed to take the investor out of Mr. Huxley's danger zone.

1
PAST DECISIONS CREATE PRESENT OPPORTUNITIES

THE 1980s CREDIT CRUNCH

Bartletts attributes to France's Alex De Tocqueville the following:

"America is a land of wonders, in which everything is in constant motion and every change seems an improvement. The idea of novelty is there indissolubly connected with the idea of amelioration. No natural boundary seems to be set to the efforts of man; and in his eyes what is not yet done is only what has not been attempted to do."

The thrift industry of our country took De Tocqueville's words to heart. They felt their quest for increased profits was connected to being able to their ability to directly compete with their banking counterparts. When things got a little tight for them, their powerful lobbying arm was putting the pressure on Congress to do just that.

What the entire financial community failed to realize was the fact that, if they kept their investment and lending houses in order, financial institutions had a legislatively guaranteed profit under the former Federal Reserve Regulation Q, which set a ceiling on interest rates that financial institutions could pay depositors. For years, characteristically, thrifts would set an approximate 2% margin between the cost of money and mortgage rates as their profit margin with consumer type financing for home improvements and construction financing being the frosting on their return on equity cake.

During the 1970s, however, a new word creeped into the vocabulary of financial institutions — "disintermediation." The unpardonable had happened. Depositors were no longer satisfied with the regulated interest rate ceilings in their savings accounts. They were no longer satisfied with no return on sizeable checking account balances. As a result, depositors started withdrawing in droves to seek higher yielding instruments such as treasury bills, commercial paper, bonds, trust deeds, common stocks and the like. This came as a shock to this staid industry who prided itself in the "one stop service" facilities, particularly in commercial banks. Commercial banks used to have trust capabilities, escrow facilities, lending officers and the like at every location. It was a far cry from the centralized operations we experience in today's "lean and mean" world.

The lobbyists protested that they needed some sort of financial instrument to compete with their customers who were no longer using them as an investment conduit, rather they just dealt directly with the investment source leaving the financial community out in the cold. Succumbing to the pressure of the financial community, legislation was passed allowing the first indexed savings account labeled **the treasury bill account**. This account was geared to treasury bill rates with savings and loans having a one quarter of one percent higher interest rate ceiling above nine percent than banks while being on par with their competitors below the nine percent rate. Herein lies the first chink that was to expand in the balance sheet armor of the thrift industry. The mainstay of savings and loans had been **fixed** rate financing on residential properties. It had been their bread and butter item since the 1800s. Now their liabilities were starting to be priced at **variable** rates.

One might envision the savings and loan industry as a large rubber band that had continued to expand during the post-war years of the 50s and 60s. Now the 70s had arrived with slackened demand and increasing interest rates. As the interest rate escalator began to climb (Note Illustration 1-1), borrowers quickly perceived the advantages of maintaining existing lower rate mortgages as opposed to the ones available in a rising rate market. Their quest was fueled by a landmark California decision in a 1978 case entitled Wellenkamp v. Bank of America. In the **Wellenkamp** case the so-called "due on sale" provision placed in trust deeds and notes by financial institutions was effectively put on hold. This was a provision that if the property was sold, the institution had the right to call the loan. The court in the Wellenkamp case said, as long as the institution could not prove that the borrower was going to trash the property or that they did not have the qualifications to adequately service debt, the existing lien could be taken over by a new purchaser. The only segment of the industry **not** effected by this decision were the federally chartered thrifts due to the case of Glendale Federal v. Fox. This was a case where the real estate commissioner of the state of California was sued by the thrift for failure to approve their documentation for financing a new subdivision which contained a "due on sale" clause. The court held for the thrift, thus insulating them from the problems of the state chartered associations and all of the banking fraternity in that regard. This caused a spate of requests by state associations, generally stock-owned for conversion the federal charters, which were mutual (owned by depositors). The reason was very simple. The escalation of the cost of deposit acquisition was teetering painfully close to their return on assets. In some cases the red ink had already begun to flow from hapless operating statements.

The early 1980s, as Illustration 1-1 vividly points out, saw interest rates escalate to unprecedented levels. At one point in time the banks' prime lending rate reached a record level of twenty one and one half percent! This was a severe blow, particularly to mature savings and loans. Some still had four percent fixed rate Veterans Administration guaranteed loans on their books. This meant that their average return on assets might be in the eight to nine percent range with their cost of money somewhere in the ten to twelve percent range. Any way you look at it, this represented deep losses incurred by most of these institutions during that trying period. Strangely enough, a spate of applications for new bank charters occurred during the same period. The rationale behind these new institutions was the fact that they did not have the lower cost burdens of existing portfolio to erode their profits. They could lend at the higher rates creating an adequate profit margin in the process.

Again the lobbying wheels began to grind out an all-too-familiar story concerning the plight of the banks and thrifts that were burdened with a majority of fixed rate paper while having to deal with rates paid depositors that no longer had the comfortable ceiling cushion of Regulation Q that had protected their bottom line for many years. Their lobbying efforts were finally rewarded with the passage of the **Garn - St. Germain Depository Institutions Deregulation Act of 1982**. In the case of some, the damage caused by the hemorrhage to their balance sheets was irreparable. Illustration 1-2 notes the reduction of savings institutions in the years 1985 to 1989 which were a direct result of the inflationary spiral of the early 1980s. By this time the well stretched rubber band of expansion in the thrift industry, once the largest provider of funds for permanent loans on single family residences, had snapped!

One Up On Trump

Illustration 1-1

Money Market Interest Rates and Mortgage Rates: 1970 to 1990

[Percent per year. Annual averages of monthly data, except as indicated. See also *Historical Statistics, Colonial Times to 1970*, series X 444-453]

TYPE	1970	1980	1981	1982	1983	1984	1985	1986	1987	1988	1989	1990
Federal funds, effective rate [1] . . .	7.18	13.36	16.38	12.26	9.09	10.23	8.10	6.80	6.66	7.57	9.21	8.10
Commercial paper, 3-month [1][2] . . .	(NA)	12.66	15.33	11.89	8.88	10.10	7.95	6.49	6.81	7.66	8.99	8.06
Prime rate charged by banks	7.91	15.27	18.87	14.86	10.79	12.04	9.93	8.33	8.21	9.32	10.87	10.01
Eurodollar deposits, 3-month	8.52	14.00	16.79	13.12	9.57	10.75	8.27	6.70	7.07	7.85	9.16	8.16
Finance paper, 3-month [2][3] . . .	7.18	11.49	14.08	11.23	8.70	9.73	7.77	6.38	6.54	7.38	8.72	7.87
Bankers acceptances, 90-day [2][4] . .	7.31	12.72	15.32	11.89	8.90	10.14	7.92	6.39	6.74	7.56	8.87	7.93
Large negotiable CDs, 3-month, secondary market . . . . [2]	7.56	13.07	15.91	12.27	9.07	10.37	8.05	6.52	6.86	7.73	9.09	8.15
Federal Reserve discount rate [5] . .	5½ -6	10-13	12-14	8½ -12	8½	8-9	7½ -8	5½ -7½	5½ -6	6-6½	6½ -7	6½ -7
Taxable money market funds [6] . . .	(NA)	12.68	16.82	12.23	8.58	10.04	7.71	6.26	6.12	7.11	8.87	7.82
Certificates of deposit (CDs): [7]												
6-month	(NA)	(NA)	(NA)	(NA)	(NA)	9.99	7.83	6.51	6.47	7.18	8.34	(NA)
1-year	(NA)	(NA)	(NA)	(NA)	(NA)	10.37	8.29	6.75	6.77	7.47	8.41	(NA)
2 1/2-year	(NA)	(NA)	(NA)	(NA)	10.06	10.82	9.00	7.13	7.16	7.77	8.33	(NA)
5-year	(NA)	(NA)	(NA)	(NA)	(NA)	11.25	9.66	7.60	7.66	8.11	8.30	(NA)
U.S. Government securities: [8]												
3-month Treasury bill	6.39	11.43	14.03	10.61	8.61	9.52	7.48	5.98	5.77	6.67	8.11	7.50
6-month Treasury bill	6.51	11.37	13.80	11.07	8.73	9.76	7.65	6.03	6.03	6.91	8.03	7.46
1-year Treasury bill	6.48	10.89	13.14	11.07	8.80	9.92	7.81	6.08	6.32	7.13	7.92	7.35
Prime 1-year municipals [9]	4.35	6.25	7.92	7.88	5.29	6.05	5.12	4.33	4.44	5.15	6.11	(NA)
Home mortgages: [10]												
HUD series: [10]												
FHA insured, secondary market [11]	9.03	13.44	16.31	15.31	13.11	13.82	12.24	9.91	10.16	10.49	10.24	10.17
Conventional, new-home [12][13]	8.52	13.95	16.52	15.79	13.43	13.80	12.28	10.07	10.17	10.30	10.21	10.08
Conventional, existing-home [12]	8.56	13.95	16.55	15.82	13.45	13.81	12.29	10.09	10.17	10.31	10.22	(NA)
Conventional, 15 yr. fixed [7] . . .	(NA)	(NA)	(NA)	(NA)	(NA)	(NA)	(NA)	10.05	10.04	10.14	10.05	(NA)

NA Not available. [1] Based on daily offering rates of dealers. [2] Yields are quoted on a bank-discount basis, rather than an investment yield basis (which would give a higher figure). [3] Placed directly; averages of daily offering rates quoted by finance companies. [4] Based on the most representative daily offering rates of dealers. Beginning Aug. 15, 1974, closing rates were used, and from Jan. 1, 1981, rates of top-rated banks only. [5] Federal Reserve Bank of New York, low and high. The discount rates for 1980 and 1981 do not include the surcharge applied to frequent borrowings by large institutions. The surcharge reached 3 percent in 1980 and 4 percent in 1981. Surcharge was eliminated in Nov. 1981. [6] 12 month yield for period ending December 31. Source: The Donoghue Organization, Inc., Holliston, MA, *IBC/Donoghue's Money Fund Report*, weekly (copyright). [7] Annual averages. Source: Advertising News Service, Inc.; North Palm Beach, FL, *Bank Rate Monitor*, weekly (copyright). [8] Averages based on daily closing bid yields in secondary market, bank discount basis. [9] Averages based on quotations for one day each month. Source: Salomon Brothers, Inc., New York, NY, *An Analytical Record of Yields and Yield Spreads*. [10] HUD=Housing and Urban Development. [11] Averages based on quotations for 1 day each month as compiled by FHA. [12] Primary market. [13] Average contract rates on new commitments.

Illustration 1-2

SAIF¹—Insured Savings Institutions: 1980 to 1989

Institutions
Number (in thousands)

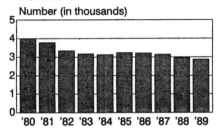

Mortgage Loans Foreclosed²
Percent

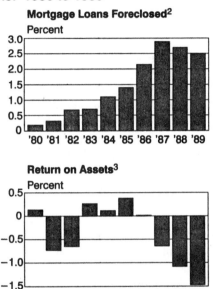

Net Income After Taxes
Billions of dollars

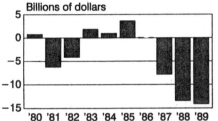

Return on Assets³
Percent

¹Savings Association Insurance Fund. ²Based on amount of mortgages foreclosed.
³Net after-taxes income to average assets.
Source: Chart prepared by U.S. Bureau of the Census. For data, see tables 816, 819, and 820.

THE GARN - ST. GERMAIN BILL - OPENING THE FLOODGATES OF SPECULATION

With the long sought after opportunities to increase bottom line performance sought by the thrifts, the Depository Institutions Deregulation Act of 1982 (Public Law 97-320) became law on October 15th, 1982. Thrifts were major beneficiaries of this sweeping legislation designed to breathe new life into an industry that was sinking rapidly.

One hole in their punctured dike of profitability that was shored dealt with the "due on sale" clause. The legislation provided a "window period" until October 15th, 1985 for allowing buyers to take subject to existing financing containing that clause as long as it conformed, in California at least, to the guidelines outlined in the **Wellenkamp** decision. After the latter date, thrifts could then enforce the "due on sale" provisions of their loan documentation allowing them to negotiate with borrowers at prevailing rates or to negotiate variable rate financing which would adjust to the dictates of the market place.

The bill also provided for weakened thrifts to be taken over by institutions (including banks) with stronger financial backing. Additionally the bill provided for propping up weak institutions with "net worth certificates" to shore up their balance sheets. The so-called certificates were also exempt from taxation. As previously noted, the bill also allowed conversion by state chartered associations to a federal charter.

The **key** provisions of this bill, which actually turned out to be the death knell for the thrift industry and its powerful lobbying clout, were in these areas:

- Dollar loan limits on single and multi-family residential lending were lifted.

- Non-home and nonprincipal residence loans were allowed with loan to value ratios in excess of 90% with Board of Director approval.

- Single and multi-family loan to value ratio ceilings were lifted to 90% of value.

- Commercial loans were permitted to 100% of value (construction financing was included in this category) with commercial mortgages allowed up to 40% of the thrift's assets, as compared to the previous 20% allowance.

- Federally chartered thrifts were allowed to make loans up to 100% of the appraised property value.

- Both thrifts and banks (with enabling state legislation) were allowed to pursue joint venture opportunities in land development.

Particularly with the last conferred authority, thrifts entered the joint venture field with a vengeance gobbling up vacant land like it was going out of style. One of the factors that precipitated this major change in asset concentration was the fact that many of the thrifts came under control of real estate developers. Probably one of the most prominent of these was Charles Keating and the well-publicized Lincoln Savings debacle. He was just one of a legion of developers who gravitated to this position of being the proverbial fox in charge of the hen house. Again that rubber band of opportunity was stretching its wings into Mr. De Tocqueville's uncharted horizons.

The primarily single family residential lending experience of thrifts was put to the test relating to their new found abilities to make commercial and industrial loans. It was a totally uncharted territory with no managerial rudder to guide it. The industry's answer to this perplexing question was to find the talent necessary to establish a viable commercial lending activity. The obvious conduit for personnel to establish this activity is the commercial banking fraternity. Bank lenders were recruited in droves to establish commercial lending centers for the purpose of making unsecured loans and attracting healthy corporate deposits in the process. They were to be disappointed in the results of their efforts. Just as the introduction of the treasury bill account was felt as a means of attracting new deposits, the thrifts were disappointed in that effort by the fact that depositors were merely transferring deposits from lower rate savings accounts into the new account with few new depository dollars resulting, just a higher cost of doing business. In the same fashion, commercial lending provided additional costs to the bottom line without the attendant profits and new balances expected. It was soon learned that the type of borrower that was being attracted to the savings and loan commercial lending activities turned out to be the one that was always being rejected by the commercial banker as an unacceptable credit risk.

As the industry charged into another spate of rising values, speculation in the market place, development of marginal properties, questionable appraisal practices, fraudulent transactions fueled by unrealistic appraisals, a continuous fueling of the money supply, rapid expansion of the national debt and the euphorious feeling that the economic expansion would last forever - finally reality set in. Suddenly home sales started to slacken. Office, retail and industrial vacancies started to soar. The geometric effect of this slackening in a market that often represents ten percent of all economic activity in this country again caused alarm within our legislative ranks.

What nobody had figured into the economic equation was the fact that the dizzying '80s also represented a cacophony of corporate mergers and consolidations. The byproduct of this activity was using the acquired company's liquidity as part of the down payment with leverage in the form of a heavy debt load representing the balance of the purchase price. The principal orchestrator of this financial symphony of doom was the well-publicized Michael Milken of Drexel, Burnham and Lambert. He, directly or indirectly, is responsible for a substantial reduction in net worth of many major corporations and their stockholders. Some of the first players to step on to Mr. Milken's bandwagon of corporate legerdemain were the thrifts, eager to increase the yield at any price. One need only be reminded of the Columbia Savings and Loan Association's boast of being "the best run thrift in the country." They had fallen for the junksterism of Mr. Milken in a big way and fattened their investment portfolio with junk bonds. Meanwhile the financing needs of purchasers of single family residences were being ignored in the process. Mr. Milken's activities created the proximate cause of the demise of the real estate market during the late 1980s, since the mergers and consolidations created an economic "ripple effect." As companies merged and consolidated, thousands of jobs were lost in the process, particularly at the middle management level. Reorganization became a way of corporate life. As management levels continued to be pared, full-time employees with benefits began to be replaced by part-time workers with no benefits. Older obsolescent facilities were replaced by newer, more efficient plants, retail outlets, and offices. The tremendous debt load created by the paper pyramid involved in effecting corporate takeover was taking its toll.

As the lawsuits and scandals started to surface, the Federal Home Loan Bank Board finally recognized that there had been some abuses of the powers conferred to thrifts and, to some extent, by banks in the expanded lending powers conferred. One of the principal offenses appeared to be in the abuse of the appraisal process creating a means of lending money on collateral which, in many cases, was far in excess of its true value. For this reason, the Board issued is R41b and R41c rulings relating to standards and practices of appraisers dealing with thrifts. It was too little - too late. The damage had been done. Thrift portfolios were becoming burgeoned with non performing assets caused by irresponsible commercial lending activity, failure to understand the commercial/industrial lending market. The latter performs in a completely different manner than the residential market and lending at 80 and 90 percent of value is unrealistic if the net income before debt service is not adequate to service the debt. Thrifts were being consolidated, merged or closed at an alarming rate by regulators due to unsafe and unsound lending practices. It was time for congress to again act in order to stem the tide of abuses that had permeated a once vital industry. Again that pliant rubber band had snapped due to its inability to cope with the powers conferred under the Garn-St. Germain bill in a responsible manner. It was obvious that curative legislation was required to stem the rampant abuse of proper standards and practices exercised by lending institutions in their insatiable quest for profits. The dividends of this form of fiscal intoxication was the accumulation of "scheduled assets" (those that were either non-performing or which had been acquired through foreclosure) of unprecedented proportions. The escalator of nonperforming assets continued to go up with no ceiling in sight. Congress with prodding from the regulators got down to business with the passage of FIRREA in August of 1989. Through the passage of Public Law 101-73 formally known as the Financial Institutions Reform, Recovery and Enforcement Act of 1989, a monumental restructuring of the thrift industry was to take place creating unprecedented opportunities for real estate investors with the adequate capital and the foresight to recognize windows of opportunity throughout the country.

FIRREA — LENDER'S DISTRESS — PAINFUL REAL ESTATE VALUE ADJUSTMENTS

With the inception of FIRREA, the thrift industry encountered dramatic changes from an operational and supervisional standpoint. The Federal Savings and Loan Insurance Corporation, virtually decimated from paying off depositors of failed thrifts, was folded into the Federal Deposit Insurance Corporation, the banks' deposit insurer, who assumed the additional burden of thrifts in addition to certain thrift and loans who qualified for insurance. The added burden of the thrifts has placed this insurance fund in the precarious position of having to increase their assessment to individual banks and thrifts as a means of replenishment of their depleted resources trying to keep up with the added demands on its resources.

The Federal Home Loan Bank Board was supplanted by the Office of Thrift Supervision which took over the regulatory powers originally exercised by its predecessor.

The highly restrictive provisions of FIRREA relative to minimum capital requirements for thrifts virtually eliminated them from lending in the commercial/industrial real estate lending market and severely limited their construction and joint venture activities with the latter area becoming almost non-existent. This did not rectify the substantial portfolios of commercial/industrial loans that had been originated by thrifts or huge undeveloped land inventories created by abortive joint venture activities. These mounting problem assets created a need for some form of a liquidation device over and above the Federal Deposit Insurance Corporation which would normally have supervised this activity for the thrifts as they have for the banks in the past.

FIRREA solved the liquidation problem by creating the unique agency of The Resolution Trust Corporation (RTC). The mission statement for this organization was to acquire all bankrupt banks and savings and loan associations, reorganize them, and dispose of their foreclosed properties or other "scheduled items" (such as real estate owned for development, etc.)

An initial commitment of $164 billion was made for what has been termed to be "the savings and loan bailout." By early 1990 there were more than 300 institutions under RTC control. Today that number has increased considerably.

The RTC is designed to be a self-liquidating organization with a strategy to liquidate all properties within a five year period. Non-profit and low income purchasers are being encouraged to take advantage of these properties that are being sold on an "as is" basis with particular priority given to liquidation of properties located in Texas and Arizona, which were particularly hard hit initially by hard economic times. Terms are offered on a cash basis with the purchaser being responsible for obtaining the necessary financing to accommodate acquisition. As we enter into the 1990s, rays of economic sunshine are starting to bathe those aforementioned areas while selective clouds of gloom gather at California's sunny shores. Also the liquidation strategy of the RTC has changed somewhat. In an effort to accelerate property disposition, blocks of properties are being offered to well capitalized bidders at highly attractive prices in an effort to reduce the huge property inventory presently managed by the agency. The burdens of property management have created logistical problems of incredible magnitude in addition to increased criticism by Congress as well as the General Accounting Office (GAO) concerning their administration of the property disposal program.

Assisting RTC in this mass disposition effort are a wide range of consultants ranging from CPAs and attorneys to appraisers, property managers and property liquidators to assist them in their liquidation projects and the prosecution of offending borrowers in fraudulent loans.

This massive regulatory activity has made the existing financial institutions painfully aware of their need to avoid unsafe and unsound lending practices. As a result, conservative lending practice has become the standard in both the banking and thrift industry since they now share examinations by FDIC examiners in both industry groups.

Characteristic of the throwing of the baby out with the bath water philosophy that pervaded during the hectic 1980s, FIRREA addressed the problem of appraisals that plagued the industry during the overheated inflationary period that fueled the real estate market during those times, namely the appraisal process.

Title XI of FIRREA specifically addresses the appraisal process and the abuses that occurred during the 1980s where reports were rendered on the basis of arriving at a predetermined valuation conclusion irrespective of the true value of the property. Under the aforementioned title, requirements for each state to establish a licensing process for appraisers which provided for two fully qualified categories of certified residential appraiser for residential properties and certified general appraiser qualified to appraise all types of real property including residential. In addition an appraisal advisory board was established for the purpose of establishing Uniform Standards of Professional Appraisal Practice (USPAP) governing the conduct of appraisers in the future.

The response of the states in establishing an appraisal licensing program and the necessary criteria for licensing has been an extended one. The state of California due to its size and number of appraisers needed to be examined has been one of the states where this process has become a long and arduous one starting initially with AB 527 which was the enabling legislation to put the program in place. California is one of the last states to be required to have licensed appraisers to perform appraisals on "federally related" transactions. This means that if an appraisal is being performed for an institution that is federally insured or if the loan is to be sold to a secondary market source that is backed by the federal government or if the loan has FHA insurance or a VA guaranty, dependent upon loan amount, a licensed appraiser qualified in that type of property must be used for the appraisal. This action is a direct result of the unprofessional conduct exhibited by a small group of appraisers in the early and mid-1980s.

Today the cycle of distress in the real estate market continues. RTC finds itself with a continually expanding inventory of properties as it tries to dispose of existing inventory. The logistics of managing these properties as an absentee landlord are overwhelming even with the assistance of professional management in these activities. Within this huge inventory of properties is a significant amount of commercial and industrial structures which hold significant potential for the future and, in many cases, have not reached their full potential.

Additionally, financial institutions that have not been taken over by RTC trusteeship also find themselves with unwanted commercial and industrial properties acquired by foreclosure that are subject to strict regulatory scrutiny. There is a pressing need on their part to dispose of these properties. Sophisticated buyers with cash can structure extremely creative purchase transactions that allow positive cash flow on buildings which may only enjoy as little as 50% occupancy.

Today we are on the cutting edge of opportunity for real estate investors who have the ability to acquire income producing properties at rock bottom prices while having the potential for considerable upside improvement in the process.

The following chapters will provide the potential investor with a road map showing a proven route involving today's prudent purchase to lead to tomorrow's success.

O. Henry once said:

"East is east, and West is San Francisco, according to
Californians. Californians are a race of people; they are
not merely inhabitants of a state."

As the reader of this text will learn in later chapters, O. Henry didn't know what a pundit he was turning out to be, as San Francisco's opportunities will be revealed in Chapter Four.

2
MAKING THE REAL
ESTATE CYCLE WORK
FOR YOU

THE ROLE OF REAL ESTATE
WITHIN THE BUSINESS CYCLE

> "East Side, West Side, all around the town,
> The tots sang ring-a-rosie, London Bridge
>   is falling down,
> Boys and girls together, me and Mamie
>   O'Rourke,
> Tripped the light fantastic on the sidewalks
>   of New York."

This familiar ballad from the pen of James W. Blake is atypical of the attraction of "The Big Apple" to immigrants during the formative years of our country. New York served as a magnet with Ellis Island being the first sight to meet Europeans anxious to taste the fruits of freedom offered them by our country. Being new to the land they were also willing and eager to obtain jobs at any price leading to accusations of "scab" labor by the unions and job riots in some instances. The same type of phenomena is now taking place on the Pacific Coast area of the United States and the so-called "sunbelt" states which have attracted large numbers of immigrants from the Pacific Rim as well as Mexico, Central and South America. As with the influx of cheap labor created unrest in the Eastern part of the United States, this situation of immigration has placed a certain degree of pressure on the west. For example, one-fourth of the population in California as of the 1990 census had a Spanish surname. The hispanic influence as well as its heritage has placed a great burden upon employers and educators to meet the challenge of this dramatic impact on population. Factors of population, employment and income statistics which are key economic components play a large part in the formation and duration of business cycles. The understanding of the role of real estate within the cycle can form the basis for realistic decision making on the part of a wise investor. Timing is as important in real estate investment as the investment itself.

In order to understand the nature of a business cycle one must first analyze its components. Illustration 2-1 is a graphical display of the peaks and troughs as well as the intermediate stages of the cycle. As the illustration notes there are four basic components:

- The **peak** represents the highest level of business activity where employment and plant capacity is fully utilized - The mid-1980s is a case in point.

- **Contraction** results from weakened demand, business reduction in force, weaker companies being forced out of business, retail and home sales declining and a general weakness displayed by the economy - three quarters of no growth in the Gross National (Domestic) Product is symptomatic of what we refer to as a recession. The late 1980s and early 1990s are characteristic of this phenomena. Illustration 2-2 shows trends in the Gross National (Domestic) Product as well as how it performed componentially by industry in the 1980s.

- The **trough** represents the early 1990s where a series of events created massive unemployment nationwide, numerous fiscal crises at the municipal, state and federal levels combined with erosion of our financial institutions created by lending excesses of the 1980s. In the instant case one of the underlying factors is the fact that our economy has relied heavily on the military/industrial complex as a means of sustaining health in the economy. The so-called "peace dividend" with the erosion of communism reducing the threat of war has created a rippling effect on all defense-related industry which is frantically scampering for a survival plan in this new environment. At this point the nadir of business activity has been reached with business failures, unemployment, bankruptcies, loan delinquencies and the like being at their highest levels. As the 1992 trends show in Illustration 2-3, our country was trending toward the trough in February of that year. The trend continued well into October of that year, the latter month appearing to be nearing the bottom of the cycle. **It is at this point that the greatest opportunity for prudent real estate investment affords itself.**

Illustration 2-1

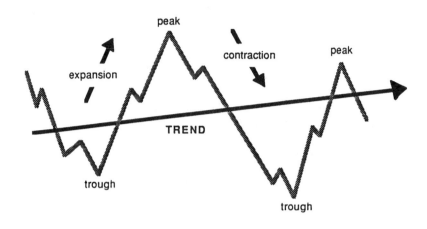

peak

contraction

peak

expansion

TREND

trough

trough

BUSINESS CYCLES

One Up On Trump

Illustration 2-2

Gross National Product, by Industry, In Current and Constant (1982) Dollars: 1980 to 1988

[In billions of dollars, except percent. Data include non-factor charges (capital consumption allowances and indirect business taxes, etc.) as well as factor charges against gross product; corporate profits and capital consumption allowances have been shifted from a company to an establishment basis. These data are not fully consistent with other GNP tables because they do not yet incorporate source data used in the July 1990 revisions of the National Income and Product Accounts]

SIC[1] code	INDUSTRY	CURRENT DOLLARS			CONSTANT (1982) DOLLARS				Average annual percent change	
		1980	1985	1988	1980	1985	1987	1988	1980-1988	1987-1988
(X)	Gross national product......	2,732.0	4,014.9	4,880.6	3,187.1	3,618.7	3,853.7	4,024.4	3.0	4.4
(X)	Domestic industries (gross domestic product).........	2,684.4	3,974.1	4,847.3	3,131.7	3,581.9	3,827.2	3,996.3	3.1	4.4
(X)	Private Industries	2,357.3	3,502.2	4,266.3	2,742.8	3,200.1	3,443.8	3,609.8	3.5	4.8
(A)	Agriculture, forestry, and fisheries .	77.2	92.0	99.8	76.4	95.8	104.4	94.5	2.7	-9.5
(B)	Mining	107.3	114.2	80.4	143.5	139.0	125.5	127.3	-1.5	1.5
(C)	Construction.	137.7	186.6	232.6	153.3	166.3	175.4	176.9	1.8	0.9
(D)	Manufacturing[2]	581.0	789.5	948.6	673.9	779.2	849.7	927.5	4.1	9.2
(X)	Durable goods[2]	351.8	458.8	530.3	408.5	471.5	517.4	583.2	4.6	12.7
24	Lumber and wood products.....	18.7	22.2	29.6	21.3	19.8	24.2	25.7	2.4	6.2
25	Furniture and fixtures.......	8.6	13.6	15.3	10.4	12.1	12.8	12.3	2.2	-3.6
32	Stone, clay, and glass products ..	19.0	24.8	28.3	21.3	22.2	24.9	25.2	2.2	1.5
33	Primary metal industries	44.3	34.8	46.8	48.2	32.7	34.6	37.9	-3.0	9.6
34	Fabricated metal products	46.0	57.8	64.0	53.7	56.2	58.4	63.2	2.1	8.3
35	Machinery, except electrical ..	76.9	82.7	93.1	86.1	124.2	140.7	170.5	8.9	21.2
36	Electric and electronic equipment.	55.0	82.2	91.1	63.3	74.3	78.3	88.1	4.2	12.5
371	Motor vehicles and equipment...	26.7	53.7	55.1	35.2	50.3	46.4	51.7	4.9	11.5
38	Instruments and related products.	19.0	25.8	31.5	21.9	24.2	26.7	31.5	4.6	17.9
(X)	Nondurable goods[2]	229.2	330.8	418.3	265.5	307.7	332.2	344.3	3.3	3.6
20	Food and kindred products.....	52.2	69.8	83.3	59.8	64.8	66.5	67.8	1.6	2.0
21	Tobacco manufactures.......	7.3	12.2	15.5	9.6	6.2	5.6	4.7	-8.5	-15.6
22	Textile mill products..........	15.0	17.1	20.3	16.4	15.6	17.3	16.8	0.3	-3.0
23	Apparel and other textile products	17.1	20.6	24.6	21.1	20.1	22.7	23.2	1.2	2.3
26	Paper and allied products......	23.1	33.1	45.8	25.8	30.2	33.8	34.9	3.8	3.3
27	Printing and publishing	31.6	52.5	64.4	37.0	42.5	43.6	45.5	2.6	4.4
28	Chemicals and allied products...	45.5	63.8	92.1	50.0	59.1	68.2	74.2	5.1	8.8
29	Petroleum and coal products....	16.8	32.2	39.5	22.9	39.4	42.6	44.6	8.7	4.7
30	Rubber and misc. plastic products	16.8	25.9	29.4	18.6	26.6	29.3	29.8	6.1	1.7
31	Leather and leather products. .	3.9	3.4	3.2	4.3	3.2	2.8	2.9	-4.7	3.1
(E)	Transportation and public utilities[2]	240.8	374.1	441.4	294.0	331.4	373.6	392.0	3.7	4.9
(X)	Transportation	105.8	137.5	163.2	117.1	132.4	147.4	150.0	3.1	1.8
40	Railroad transportation.....	20.8	21.7	21.1	22.8	23.5	25.4	26.5	1.9	4.6
41	Local and interurban passenger transit ...	5.4	7.4	9.2	6.4	6.5	6.2	6.1	-0.4	-0.6
42	Trucking and warehousing	44.0	58.6	69.6	49.9	60.9	65.3	65.5	3.5	0.4
44	Water transportation	7.1	7.9	8.3	8.2	3.5	3.7	3.7	-9.4	0.9
45	Transportation by air	18.1	27.1	37.1	17.3	23.2	31.5	31.1	7.6	-1.0
46	Pipelines, except natural gas....	4.7	4.8	4.3	5.3	4.7	4.6	5.4	0.3	17.3
47	Transportation services	5.8	10.0	13.7	7.2	10.0	10.9	11.6	6.1	6.3
48	Communications	66.6	109.5	129.3	79.5	89.8	104.4	107.6	3.9	3.1
481	Telephone and telegraph	60.2	98.3	114.3	71.4	81.7	95.1	98.0	4.0	3.0
483	Radio and television broadcasting	6.3	11.2	15.0	8.1	8.1	9.3	9.7	2.2	3.9
49	Electric, gas, and sanitary services .	68.4	127.0	148.8	97.3	109.2	121.7	134.3	4.1	10.4
(F)	Wholesale trade	193.9	280.8	326.1	200.1	267.1	289.4	296.8	5.1	2.6
(G)	Retail trade	245.0	377.4	454.7	281.7	354.4	370.0	397.1	4.4	7.3
(H)	Finance, insurance, and real estate .	400.6	639.5	830.3	468.9	528.3	564.7	583.7	2.8	3.4
60	Banking	51.1	79.4	99.2	56.7	61.5	62.8	62.4	1.2	-0.6
61	Credit agencies other than banks . .	5.5	11.6	21.3	5.2	7.0	8.3	8.4	6.0	0.6
62	Security and commodity brokers, and services.............	9.7	24.1	40.3	11.2	18.8	29.9	33.6	14.7	12.2
63	Insurance carriers.........	37.0	40.7	68.0	38.7	39.5	38.8	41.1	0.8	6.0
64	Insurance agents and brokers, and services.............	14.4	22.4	32.2	15.9	18.0	18.7	18.8	2.1	0.4
65	Real estate	281.5	449.0	554.6	335.0	374.5	395.3	408.0	2.5	3.2
67	Holding and other investment companies	1.3	12.3	14.7	6.3	9.0	10.9	11.5	7.9	5.5
(I)	Services[2]	374.0	648.1	872.5	450.9	538.6	591.4	613.9	3.9	3.8
70	Hotels and other lodging places ...	18.9	30.4	40.9	22.3	26.0	28.4	30.1	3.8	5.8
72	Personal services...........	18.8	29.7	36.9	22.3	25.2	26.4	27.2	2.5	3.3
73	Business services...........	68.8	145.8	200.3	83.9	120.8	139.7	147.2	7.3	5.3
75	Auto repair, services, and garages .	21.1	33.2	41.8	24.8	28.7	28.9	29.5	2.2	2.3
78	Motion pictures	5.0	9.0	12.2	5.7	7.5	8.1	8.4	5.0	3.6
79	Amusement and recreation services	12.4	19.9	26.5	13.4	17.5	19.6	21.1	5.9	7.5
80	Health services	108.1	184.6	248.5	133.8	148.6	158.7	159.9	2.3	0.8
81	Legal services.............	23.3	46.3	67.4	30.6	33.5	36.8	39.6	3.3	7.6
82	Educational services........	16.0	25.8	33.1	18.9	22.1	23.1	23.8	3.0	3.3
83&86	Social services and membership organizations	26.3	38.3	50.1	30.2	33.3	35.9	38.0	2.9	6.0
88	Private households...........	6.6	9.0	9.4	7.4	8.8	8.8	8.8	2.3	0.8
(J)	Government and government enterprises	322.1	476.7	570.6	382.8	400.5	414.8	422.2	1.2	1.8
(X)	Federal...................	114.7	171.0	187.6	138.3	146.2	148.6	150.8	1.1	1.5
(X)	State and local	207.4	305.7	383.0	244.5	254.3	266.2	271.4	1.3	1.9
(X)	Statistical discrepancy	4.9	-4.8	-9.6	5.9	-4.3	-4.1	-8.0	(NS)	(NS)
(X)	Rest of the world.............	47.6	40.7	33.3	55.5	36.9	26.6	28.1	-6.2	5.8

NS Not significant. [1] 1972 Standard Industrial Classification code; see text, section 13. [2] Includes items not shown separately.
Source: U.S. Bureau of Economic Analysis, *Survey of Current Business*, January 1991.

Illustration 2-2 (cont.)

GNP Components—Average Annual Percent Change in Current and Constant (1982) Dollars: 1970 to 1989

[In percent. GNP = Gross national product. Minus sign (-) indicates decrease. For implicit price deflators and fixed-weighted price indexes, see table 779, section 15]

ITEM	1970-1980	1980-1989	1981-1982	1982-1983	1983-1984	1984-1985	1985-1986	1986-1987	1987-1988	1988-1989
CURRENT DOLLARS										
Gross national product....	10.4	7.4	3.7	7.6	10.8	6.4	5.4	6.7	7.9	6.7
Personal consumption expenditures	10.5	8.0	7.1	9.0	8.8	8.2	6.4	7.6	7.6	6.5
Durable goods............	9.9	9.0	5.3	14.4	16.0	10.9	9.1	4.3	8.1	3.7
Nondurable goods	9.7	5.8	4.1	5.9	6.2	5.1	3.4	6.3	5.9	6.6
Services.................	11.3	9.3	9.9	9.9	8.8	9.6	7.7	9.3	8.6	7.3
Gross private domestic investment	11.4	6.5	-13.2	12.3	32.4	-3.3	2.5	6.1	6.8	3.2
Fixed investment	11.8	5.9	-4.0	8.0	17.2	5.8	3.3	2.9	7.4	3.1
Nonresidential	11.9	5.3	-0.7	-2.7	16.6	6.5	-1.7	2.2	9.8	4.8
Residential............	11.7	7.3	-14.1	45.1	18.8	4.3	15.1	4.1	2.7	-0.6
Exports of goods and services..	17.7	6.6	-5.5	-2.6	8.8	-3.3	6.9	13.4	22.8	13.4
Imports of goods and services..	18.1	8.6	-3.8	6.9	23.3	1.5	10.0	14.3	11.0	7.4
Government purchases of goods and services	9.3	7.6	9.1	5.2	9.0	11.5	6.3	5.6	4.5	6.6
Federal	7.7	7.5	12.6	4.0	9.5	14.4	3.2	4.0	-0.3	5.2
State and local	10.4	7.7	6.7	6.1	8.6	9.5	8.6	6.8	7.8	7.4
CONSTANT (1982) DOLLARS										
Gross national product....	2.8	2.9	-2.5	3.6	6.8	3.4	2.7	3.4	4.5	2.5
Personal consumption expenditures	3.0	3.2	1.3	4.6	4.8	4.7	3.9	2.8	3.6	1.9
Durable goods............	4.2	6.4	0.8	12.0	14.1	9.9	8.3	1.8	6.8	2.3
Nondurable goods	1.9	2.1	0.9	3.8	3.2	2.6	3.6	1.7	1.9	1.2
Services.................	3.6	3.1	1.8	3.5	3.5	4.7	2.7	4.0	3.8	2.4
Gross private domestic investment	2.9	3.9	-18.0	12.7	30.6	-3.3	0.4	4.6	5.5	1.6
Fixed investment	3.3	3.3	-9.6	8.2	16.8	5.3	1.0	1.9	5.6	1.6
Nonresidential	3.7	3.3	-7.2	-1.5	17.7	6.7	-3.3	2.6	8.3	3.9
Residential............	2.3	3.5	-16.9	42.1	14.5	2.0	12.2	0.4	-0.8	-4.1
Exports of goods and services..	8.1	4.8	-7.8	-3.8	6.8	-1.2	8.1	13.8	18.3	11.0
Imports of goods and services..	4.8	7.7	-2.3	9.7	23.8	3.4	11.8	8.2	7.1	6.0
Government purchases of goods and services	0.8	2.8	1.9	1.1	4.4	7.9	4.2	2.3	0.2	2.3
Federal	-0.8	3.4	5.0	0.9	5.7	12.1	2.5	1.6	-3.4	2.1
State and local	2.1	2.4	-0.3	1.3	3.5	4.7	5.5	2.8	2.9	2.4

Source: U.S. Bureau of Economic Analysis, *The National Income and Product Accounts of the United States, 1929-82*, and *Survey of Current Business*, July issues.

No. 701. Gross National Product, by Type of Product and Sector: 1970 to 1989

[In billions of dollars]

ITEM	1970	1975	1980	1983	1984	1985	1986	1987	1988	1989
Gross national product....	1,015.5	1,598.4	2,732.0	3,405.7	3,772.2	4,014.9	4,231.6	4,515.6	4,873.7	5,200.8
BY MAJOR TYPE OF PRODUCT										
Goods..................	467.8	714.7	1,174.9	1,396.1	1,581.4	1,641.2	1,686.7	1,788.4	1,935.1	2,072.7
Services	441.1	725.2	1,265.0	1,682.5	1,813.9	1,968.3	2,119.3	2,292.4	2,488.6	2,671.2
Structures	106.5	158.5	292.0	327.1	377.0	405.4	425.6	434.8	450.0	456.9
BY SECTOR										
Business	856.3	1,341.2	2,306.8	2,866.6	3,201.5	3,412.8	3,599.9	3,844.9	4,147.8	4,418.1
Households and institutions	32.4	52.0	89.3	122.9	132.7	142.3	153.5	169.9	187.3	203.6
Government	119.5	187.7	288.3	366.4	390.6	419.0	443.8	471.9	505.1	541.6
Rest of the world	7.3	17.5	47.6	49.9	47.4	40.7	34.4	29.0	33.5	37.6

Source: U.S. Bureau of Economic Analysis, *The National Income and Product Accounts of the United States, 1929-82*, and *Survey of Current Business*, July issues.

Illustration 2-3

EMPLOYMENT, UNEMPLOYMENT, AND WAGES

In February, civilian employment fell 74,000 and unemployment rose 315,000.

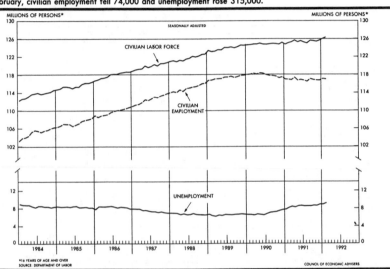

MILLIONS OF PERSONS* / MILLIONS OF PERSONS*

SEASONALLY ADJUSTED

CIVILIAN LABOR FORCE

CIVILIAN EMPLOYMENT

UNEMPLOYMENT

1984 1985 1986 1987 1988 1989 1990 1991 1992

*16 YEARS OF AGE AND OVER
SOURCE: DEPARTMENT OF LABOR

COUNCIL OF ECONOMIC ADVISERS

[Thousands of persons 16 years of age and over, except as noted; monthly data seasonally adjusted except as noted by NSA]

Period	Noninstitutional population including resident Armed Forces NSA	Resident Armed Forces NSA	Labor force including resident Armed Forces	Employment including resident Armed Forces	Civilian labor force	Civilian employment				Unemployment		Civilian	
						Total	Agricultural	Nonagricultural		Total	15 weeks and over	Labor force participation rate (percent) [2]	Employment/population ratio (percent) [2]
								Total	Part time for economic reasons [1]				
1982	173,939	1,668	111,872	101,194	110,204	99,526	3,401	96,125	5,852	10,678	3,485	64.0	57.8
1983	175,891	1,676	113,226	102,510	111,550	100,834	3,383	97,450	5,997	10,717	4,210	64.0	57.9
1984	178,080	1,697	115,241	106,702	113,544	105,005	3,321	101,685	5,512	8,539	2,737	64.4	59.5
1985	179,912	1,706	117,167	108,856	115,461	107,150	3,179	103,971	5,334	8,312	2,305	64.8	60.1
1986*	182,293	1,706	119,540	111,303	117,834	109,597	3,163	106,434	5,345	8,237	2,232	65.3	60.7
1987	184,490	1,737	121,602	114,177	119,865	112,440	3,208	109,232	5,122	7,425	1,983	65.6	61.5
1988	186,322	1,709	123,378	116,677	121,669	114,968	3,169	111,800	4,965	6,701	1,610	65.9	62.3
1989	188,081	1,688	125,557	119,030	123,869	117,342	3,199	114,142	4,657	6,528	1,375	66.5	63.0
1990	189,686	1,637	126,424	119,550	124,787	117,914	3,186	114,728	4,860	6,874	1,504	66.4	62.7
1991	191,329	1,564	126,867	118,440	125,303	116,877	3,233	113,644	5,767	8,426	2,323	66.0	61.6
1991:													
Feb	190,717	1,602	126,669	118,539	125,067	116,937	3,237	113,700	5,685	8,130	1,985	66.1	61.8
Mar	190,703	1,460	126,710	118,294	125,250	116,834	3,124	113,710	5,760	8,416	2,144	66.2	61.7
Apr	190,836	1,456	127,100	118,844	125,644	117,388	3,187	114,201	5,791	8,256	2,180	66.3	62.0
May	190,980	1,458	126,717	118,188	125,259	116,730	3,256	113,474	5,697	8,529	2,213	66.1	61.6
June	191,173	1,505	127,029	118,414	125,524	116,909	3,286	113,623	5,469	8,615	2,488	66.2	61.6
July	191,443	1,604	126,808	118,333	125,204	116,729	3,244	113,485	5,660	8,475	2,355	66.0	61.5
Aug	191,589	1,616	126,620	118,100	125,004	116,484	3,254	113,230	5,710	8,520	2,417	65.8	61.3
Sept	191,746	1,624	127,214	118,713	125,590	117,089	3,283	113,806	6,040	8,501	2,422	66.1	61.6
Oct	191,903	1,614	127,122	118,481	125,508	116,867	3,204	113,663	6,055	8,641	2,570	66.0	61.4
Nov	192,057	1,605	126,979	118,377	125,374	116,772	3,272	113,500	6,123	8,602	2,623	65.8	61.3
Dec	192,209	1,604	127,223	118,332	125,619	116,728	3,183	113,545	6,084	8,891	2,843	65.9	61.2
1992:													
Jan	192,358	1,599	127,645	118,716	126,046	117,117	3,166	113,951	6,429	8,929	3,059	66.1	61.4
Feb	192,469	1,585	127,872	118,628	126,287	117,043	3,232	113,811	6,213	9,244	3,204	66.2	61.3

[1] Persons at work. Economic reasons include slack work, material shortages, inability to find full-time work, etc.
[2] Civilian labor force (or employment) as percent of civilian noninstitutional population.

* Data beginning January 1986 not strictly comparable with earlier data because of change in estimation procedures.

Source: Department of Labor, Bureau of Labor Statistics.

Economic activity does not run a smooth orderly course. There are several factors that create aberrations in cyclical activity. There are four basic fluctuations that represent these aberrations:

Periodic and Predictable - For example, Palm Springs cannot expect an exodus of visitors from approximately May to September due to weather conditions in the area. Thus many businesses in the area actually close shop until the "season" of the fall and winter months comes around again. Likewise, if you do business near the ocean, the summer months create the highest level of business activity for these resort areas.

- **Irregular but Predictable** - The Olympics staged in 1992 in Barcelona, Spain was a predictable economic "boom" for that area on a one-time basis. This activity would not be expected to be maintained over time even though there might be some residual effects for a few months after the events. Some Olympic sites, such as the Coliseum in Los Angeles continue to attract visitors to sporting events and, in fact, hosted two Olympics, in 1932 and 1984. Real estate speculation in a situation such as this is a highly risky endeavor.

- **Random and Unpredictable** - Hurricane "Andrew," The Landers and Big Bear Earthquakes and other natural disasters or epidemics are totally unpredictable, but likely events to happen. If history is any example war always seems to be part of the equation. The only question involved in the scenario is where and when. Even with the peace accords of the early 1990s, nations eager to sell their goods continue to provide other emerging countries with the weaponry to engage in the eternal quest for power and dominion over other nations. There will always be a Saddam Hussien in the world seeking to exercise authority beyond his shores.

- **Cyclical but Unpredictable** - The final category best expresses the description of the **business cycle,** since the predictability of such an event defies even the most expert of economic forecasters. One of the reasons for this is the fact that various decisions made independently by our government and the business sector may lead the economy in opposite directions. 1992 is a classic example of this strategy. While government through the auspices of Mr. Greenspan and the Federal Reserve try desperately to stimulate demand through artificially lowering interest rates to stimulate borrowing by business and consumers, businesses were scampering towards retrenchment and operating "lean and mean." House sales sagged and vacancy rates soared (see Illustration 2-4).

In analyzing the business cycle some observations can be made.

1) Each of the four segments will come into play.
2) Some measurement can be made after the fact (see Illustration 2-5).

Those who take advantage of the trough, once factors comprising that are recognized, can effect prudent real estate investments which can yield excellent future dividends.   The unusual nature of the trough that has developed during 1992 is the fact that one of the key factors in recovery, unemployment, is of the type that will take an extended period of time to rectify.   One of the residual effects of the merger, consolidation, junk bond riddled 1980s, was the disappearance of mid-sized business firms (those with $50,000,000 to $100,000,000 in annual sales) who were usually the victims of merger mania.   This mid-philosophy has now spread to middle management.   One of the efficiencies of merger is that due to size, less managers are required at all levels of the merged enterprise.   Management has now extrapolated the experience of the merger area to totally reorganize corporate structures in a majority of the major industrial firms of this country.   The net result of these reorganization techniques is to compress management levels, thus squeezing many highly educated well compensated middle managers out of these positions either by demotion or layoff with very few opportunities for upward mobility. The redeployment of these individuals will be the ultimate challenge of the 1990s. Many of these numbers, who are classified as **structurally unemployed**, have either an extensive period of unemployment facing them or must opt to survive entrepreneurially through self-employment.   This is the hardest type of unemployment to rectify because of its long term nature.   These individuals may remain unemployed even during periods of economic recovery.   Not only is this trend prevalent in manufacturing, service industries such as banking and insurance are following the same reorganizational practices as a way of paring expenses and maximizing sales dollars. The long-term trend that will develop from this change in management culture is the prospect that median family income nationwide may reduce in the next decade after adjustment for inflation. Understanding what these trends mean in the way of the real estate market and where windows of opportunity may exist even in down markets separates the wise investor from the speculative one.

Illustration 2-4

NEW CONSTRUCTION

[Monthly data seasonally adjusted]

Period	Total new construction expenditures	Private					Federal, State, and local	Construction contracts [3]	
		Total	Residential		Commercial and industrial [2]	Other		Total value index (1987=100)	Commercial and industrial floor space (millions of square feet)
			Total [1]	New housing units					
			Billions of dollars						
1983	294.9	231.5	125.5	94.6	57.7	48.2	63.5	75	756
1984	348.8	278.6	153.8	113.8	74.0	50.8	70.2	83	955
1985	377.4	299.5	158.5	114.7	89.8	51.3	77.8	91	1,097
1986	407.7	323.1	187.1	133.2	84.4	51.6	84.6	96	1,016
1987	419.4	328.7	194.7	139.9	84.0	50.1	90.6	100	1,019
1988	432.3	337.5	198.1	138.9	88.0	51.5	94.8	101	973
1989	443.4	345.3	196.6	139.2	94.3	54.5	98.1	105	961
1990	442.1	334.2	182.9	128.0	96.4	54.9	107.9	95	783
1991	401.0	290.7	157.8	110.6	77.0	55.8	110.2	90	545
			Annual rates						*Annual rates*
1991: Aug	404.8	291.8	161.5	114.4	74.0	56.3	113.1	ʳ93	507
Sept	406.0	293.6	164.2	117.1	72.9	56.5	112.4	ʳ90	408
Oct	406.1	291.7	164.7	117.5	70.1	56.9	114.4	98	625
Nov	401.2	288.3	164.5	118.0	67.4	56.4	112.9	ʳ81	474
Dec	398.7	287.4	164.1	118.3	67.3	56.0	111.4	98	479
1992: Jan	407.1	292.5	169.5	122.0	65.8	57.2	114.6	96	472
Feb	411.8	294.8	169.8	123.3	66.7	58.3	117.0	102	563
Mar	421.5	301.1	172.7	125.9	69.1	59.4	120.4	98	497
Apr ʳ	427.6	309.8	182.6	128.8	65.9	61.2	117.8	98	499
May ʳ	428.0	307.0	182.9	128.1	63.6	60.5	121.0	89	423
June ʳ	426.7	312.2	184.6	128.7	66.8	60.7	114.5	93	525
July ʳ	427.5	308.1	183.2	127.5	63.1	61.8	119.4	91	482
Aug ᵖ	424.0	304.4	186.8	130.2	55.9	61.8	119.6	91	515
Sept ᵖ								89	438

[1] Includes residential improvements, not shown separately.
[2] Includes hotels and motels.
[3] F.W. Dodge series.

Sources: Department of Commerce (Bureau of the Census) and McGraw-Hill Information Systems Company, F.W. Dodge Division.

NEW PRIVATE HOUSING AND VACANCY RATES

[Thousands of units or homes, except as noted]

Period	New private housing units				Units authorized	Units completed	New private homes			Vacancy rate for rental housing units (percent) [2]
	Units started, by type of structure						Homes sold	Homes for sale at end of period [1]		
	Total	1 unit	2-4 units	5 or more units						
1982	1,062.2	662.6	80.0	319.6	1,000.5	1,005.5	412	253		5.3
1983	1,703.0	1,067.6	113.5	522.0	1,605.2	1,390.3	623	301		5.7
1984	1,749.5	1,084.2	121.4	544.0	1,681.8	1,652.2	639	353		5.9
1985	1,741.8	1,072.4	93.4	576.1	1,733.3	1,703.3	688	346		6.5
1986	1,805.4	1,179.4	84.0	542.0	1,769.4	1,756.4	750	357		7.3
1987	1,620.5	1,146.4	65.3	408.7	1,534.8	1,668.8	671	366		7.7
1988	1,488.1	1,081.3	58.8	348.0	1,455.6	1,529.8	676	368		7.7
1989	1,376.1	1,003.3	55.2	317.6	1,338.4	1,422.8	650	365		7.4
1990	1,192.7	894.8	37.5	260.4	1,110.8	1,308.0	534	321		7.2
1991	1,013.9	840.4	35.6	137.9	948.8	1,090.8	509	283		7.4
		Seasonally adjusted annual rates								
1991: Aug	1,053	881	41	131	940	1,051	522	292		
Sept	1,020	864	28	128	974	1,193	499	292		7.6
Oct	1,085	887	49	149	994	1,073	526	289		
Nov	1,085	907	33	145	979	1,021	578	286		
Dec	1,118	972	46	100	1,073	1,021	578	283		7.3
1992: Jan	1,180	989	28	163	1,106	1,043	667	281		
Feb	1,257	1,109	24	124	1,146	1,097	627	269		
Mar	1,340	1,068	53	219	1,094	1,127	555	277		7.4
Apr	1,086	933	27	126	1,058	1,067	546	274		
May	1,196	1,019	33	144	1,054	1,204	ʳ554	272		
June	1,147	999	40	108	1,032	ʳ1,184	ʳ583	ʳ272		7.7
July ʳ	1,100	956	25	119	1,080	1,221	613	271		
Aug ᵖ	1,239	1,056	31	150	1,076	1,132	623	268		
Sept ᵖ	1,256	1,071	31	154	1,125		617	267		7.3

[1] Seasonally adjusted.
[2] Quarterly data entered in last month of quarter. Series beginning 1989 not comparable with earlier data.

NOTE.—Beginning 1984, units authorized are for 17,000 permit-issuing places; for 1978-83 data are for 16,000 places.

Source: Department of Commerce, Bureau of the Census.

Illustration 2-5

Business Cycles 1919-1980s. The figure below can be interpreted as follows: March 1919 is a trough. An expansion begins and lasts 10 months, followed by a contraction that lasts 18 months to the trough of July 1921. The last trough shown is November 1982. As of November 1987, expansion had continued for 60 months. Only two other expansions during this 60 year period lasted longer, those beginning in 1938 and 1961.

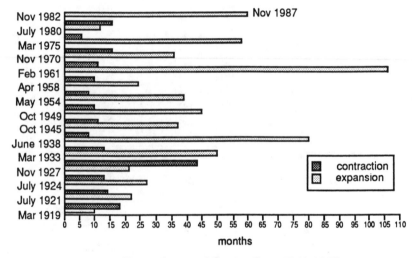

Expansions and Contractions 1919-1987

Real estate is a unique commodity within itself. For this reason, **it has its own cycles which may not necessarily be in concert with the general business cycle.** Activity within the real estate arena is dependent upon a variety of factors including the fact that, unlike stocks and bonds, real estate is a heterogeneous product, and not homogeneous. There are no two parcels on the face of the universe that are alike. If nothing else, they will vary as to location, let alone the improvements that are situated on the site. It is important to examine the components of supply and demand in order to determine the opportune time for investment entry into the market place. The understanding of the interaction of supply and demand components will serve the prudent investor well in predicting the course of the market place in the long term. Long term prospects are a critical factor in making real estate investment decisions, particularly with respect to commercial and industrial properties.

INTERACTION OF THE POLITICAL AND STOCK MARKET CYCLES

Political historian Arthur M. Schlesinger, Jr. has clearly delineated alternative periods of political conservatism and liberalism in his **The Cycles of American History.** Prognosticators of cyclical behavior economically have the advantage of history in observing the interaction of the movements in the political arena and stock market activity over time. Use of stock market indices started shortly after the Civil War, and thus those who study this phenomena have considerable historical data to back up any observations. Any investor wishing to devote capital to some enterprise must gain an understanding of these movements in order to determine the best possible vehicle to expand an investment base over time. To this end, it is important to study how political activity impacts the stock market. There are four phases of political activity that impact the stock market:

- **THE CONSERVATIVE PHASE (Post War Recovery)** - This type of leadership tends to decentralize government, reduce costs of governing, stresses the work ethic, encourages saving and exercises trickle down economics by favoring the rich to regenerate the economy. This phase represents a U shaped curve that shows a high in the stock market after a war has been settled (World War I, World War II and the Vietnamese Peace Pact being examples), then fear of a recession sets in driving stock prices down until recovery takes place allowing prices to rise once again.

The optimum time for investing is in the trough of the U, when pessimism is at its highest.

- **THE POPULIST PHASE (Prosperity)** - This is the time when the wealth actually starts to trickle down. In recent history the years that this phase started were 1924, 1950 and 1982. During this period small investors enter businesses and the business ethic becomes somewhat jaded. During these periods, investors should just ride the escalator of the stock market upward unless the price of the stock in question becomes far greater than its intrinsic worth. In 1992 we are at the end of the populist era and now are about to enter the next phase.

- **THE LIBERAL PHASE (Peaceful Reform)** - During these periods, social responsibility is high on the agenda. This entails periods of civil disobedience, pursuit of a variety of causes for the "betterment of society" and other attempts to revamp the basic social structure of the country. During these times, big business usually gets the proverbial "black eye" and numerous purges and investigations are undertaken in that regard. The most recent period in history was 1961 to 1966 where this phase was evident. During these periods only short-term trading for special situations with no long term market commitment is a proper investment strategy. Prudent real estate investment for the long term can be quite beneficial during these times. 1992 marks the year of entry into this political phase.

- **THE EXTREMIST PHASE (Violent Reform)** - During the years of 1966 to 1973, the last time period for this phase, extremist opinions accentuated with violence become more evident. This phase usually involves a period where our Nation is at war. It was during this last period that Vietnam and the Civil Rights movement became rallying points for this extremist activity. It did not end until after the Vietnam Peace Pact was signed. The stock market takes on a **V** shape during these periods (all war time). A similar strategy for stock market investment that is followed during the liberal phase is in order. Again, those who retained real estate ownership during these periods found themselves ahead of the game by purchasing at war's height and holding on for appreciation.

Each of the four observed phases that have been tracked from 1865 to date follow in the order shown above with the average time periods for each being as follows:

- **Conservative - 8 years**
- **Populist - 14 years**
- **Liberal - 10 years**
- **Extremist - 4 years**

THE ELLIOTT WAVE THEORY

R. N. Elliott, a retired California accountant developed a theory to predict stock market changes that is roughly equivalent to the observations shown above. His theory was based upon the belief that the stock market exhibited a standard repetitive cycle. This cycle consisted of three upwaves and two down; followed by a corrective cycle of two down and one up. The combination of four upwaves and four downwaves completed the full cycle. The theory also applies a factor of the ratio of 1.618 to describe the amplitude of the waves. This "magic number" is derived from a ratio discovered by Fibonacci, an Italian mathematician, during the 13th century. It was discovered by a sequence of numbers starting at one and adding the previous number to the next thusly:

1, 2, 3, 5, 8, 13, 21, 34, 55, 89, 144, etc.

Once one has passed the first two numbers in sequence any number divided by the previous number yields 1.618.

Elliott has had a number of supporters in this theory, in particular Robert Prechter, publisher of the **Market Timing** newsletter who accurately predicted the dramatic stock market change in 1987 using Elliott's hypothesis. Just as any other theory, it has its detractors as well.

WHERE WE STAND IN THE EARLY 1990s

Whether one ascribes to Elliott's Wave or the politicism of the stock market, investment vehicles change over time. Timing is the key to any investment, whether it be the stock market or real estate. We are now definitely into one of the most unique phases ever encountered in cyclic behavior, since it appears with the Clinton administration that liberalism will be smattered with conservatism. The principal item on the president's agenda for the four years between 1992 and 1996 will be the creation of jobs. This period augers well for certain parts of the country, but California appears to be waning in this regard. Those who are astute real estate investors have an unique opportunity in time to look at distressed properties as a perfect springboard to ride this cycle with positive cash flow combined with the added bonus of future appreciation. The next segment discusses what factors to consider in understanding cyclic behavior in order to take advantages of investment opportunities as they present themselves. The prudent investor who understands cycles is armed with a distinct advantage.

REAL ESTATE CYCLES

Real estate cycles, to a certain extent, are sensitive to interest rate activity. This sensitivity is even more acute in the area of commercial/industrial real estate investment than in the residential area. As a rule of thumb, once the interest rate on single family homes reaches the low 'teens, the demand factor diminishes rapidly on the part of the consumer. In the case of an income property investor, interest in the market place ebbs at a lower figure due to reduced cash flow and recent unfavorable tax legislation which discourages bracketed figures for tax reporting purposes. Since interest rates play such an important part in the demand factor for real estate consumption, considerable studies have been conducted in this area to derive what is referred to as "the 54 year interest rate cycle," which appears in three 18 year waves. Illustrative of these interest rate periods is the following:

	REAL ESTATE				INTEREST RATES
	LOW	HIGH	LOW	HIGH	
WAVE 1	1878	1888	1933	1946	LOW (1890s, 1940s)
WAVE 2	1898	1905	1952	1956	SMALL RISE
WAVE 3	1916	1925	1967	1988	RISING TO PEAK

Wave one begins just prior to a major interest rate low and generally runs about 10 to 12 years when the cycle peaks. Obviously major events, such as a war, could alter the pattern. Wave two following the low point, such as 1952 where permanent fixed rate real estate loans were running in the 4 to 5% range, are usually excellent times for real estate investment, since values tend to outstrip inflation factors, since interest rates do not rise as rapidly as the general real estate market. In wave three when the cycle is still relatively low, such as in 1967, again real estate will tend to outperform inflation and intense demand will be created at the end of the period due to the inability of consumers to invest. At the end of this period when rates fall those who have taken advantage of the lower rates at the beginning of the period are in an advantageous position for profit taking. The cycle points out three related factors which must be factored into any investment decision:

- An ideal time to purchase real estate is at the end of a recession.
- War affects demand for real estate.
- Changes in population growth affect demand.

In the next section, basic economic indicators which tend to impact decisions regarding real estate investments are examined in detail.

BE YOUR OWN ECONOMIC FORECASTER

An astute investor becomes an economic pundit by default. One must see how the forces of supply and demand interact in the market place in the decision macang process of whether to invest or pass. **Supply side** factors to consider are:

- Production is a function of the **availability of money and credit**. Strangely enough, in 1992 there was a lot of money and credit available, but not a lot of takers. The reason - lack of demand and a very soft market, particularly in retail, office and industrial space production. Potential investors must note at this time that there is a profusion of absentee management of **REO** (Real Estate Owned) properties which tend to actually expand vacancies in these properties above normal levels in a given area. The key to structures that are underutilized due to vacancy factors is to purchase at a price that will even be profitable at the existing vacancy level.

- **Return on Investment** - With the impact on real estate investing of our various tax laws, such as the Tax Reform Act of 1986, the need to examine projects with **positive cash flow** has never been more apparent. In recent years existing construction has more appeal than new construction due to the hidden costs added by government reducing land available for development, funding of

infrastructure on a "pay as you go" basis, extraction of numerous
fees and charges for processing permit applications as a means of
circumventing legislative edicts reducing the availability of monies
from property taxes and the like. Existing properties have a
greater degree of predictability relative to return on investment as
long as no structural modifications are required in the process. In
the urban areas of California, apartment development seldom will
generate an adequate return for the risk involved due to escalating
land costs. A typical apartment analysis is shown as Illustration
2-6. This clearly indicates why many developers have opted for
condominium projects in lieu of apartments in those areas.
**Return on investment is the highest when the terms of
purchase weighed with appropriate leverage are maximized.**
The positioning of the Resolution Trust Corporation and the
regulatory pressure on financial institutions has made the early
1990s an opportune time to maximize return on investment in the
long run.

- **Affordability** plays a large part in decisions for real estate
  purchase and/or rental. Some time investors will pay outlandish
  prices for a so-called "prestige" office building with a reward of
  low single digit returns. There are more customers at the low end
  of the market than there are at the apex of the pyramid where the
  number of players can turn out to be an endangered species.

- **Inflation** usually has a negative effect on cost of money and credit,
  but serves as a stimulus for active participation by investors in the
  market place in **anticipation of higher profits**. The wise investor
  anticipates the anticipation by buying during relatively low levels
  of inflationary activity taking advantage of reasonable interest rate
  levels, preferably in the single digit area.

- **Economic Climate** - If one were testing the economic climate
  during late 1992 after the presidential election, it would register a
  reading of **hope and optimism**. This reading would not play well
  with the General Motors employees in New Jersey and New York
  who learned at year end that their plants were being closed in a
  massive consolidation effort. Notwithstanding, with these fair
  weather indicators in mind, investors are faced with the fact that
  the trough presently experienced during that period may be on the
  wane with recovery a matter of months away. Critical decisions
  on the part of government combined with a positive response from
  the business sector may tend to accelerate growth.

Illustration 2-6

Land Cost @$50,000 per unit	=	$600,000
Improvements cost 12,000 square feet @$55.00 p.s.f.	=	$660,000
Total Project Cost	=	$1,260,000

Cost is now compared with the economic prospects of the project, examining whether rentals in the marketplace can support the cost. Suppose the project consists of 4 three bedroom, 2 1/2 bath units plus 8 three bedroom, two bath units. Comparable rents on the two bedroom units are $800 per month and the three bedrooms can be rented for $950 per month. This results in the following *economic analysis* of the building:

4 Units at $950 x 12	=	$45,600
8 Units at $800 x 12	=	$76,800
Total scheduled annual rent	=	$122,400
Vacancy and maintenance	=	– $6,120
Stabilized rent	=	$116,280
Expenses - 32%	=	– $37,210
Net income before debt service	=	$79,070

Considering an adequate return on risk to be 9 1/2%, the net income figure would be divided by .095 to derive an economic value based upon these income figures. The result is $832,316 as compared to the $1,260,000 it costs to produce the building. This example clearly illustrates one reason for the trend to condominiums and away from apartments. Unless the developer can acquire land at a reasonable price, apartments cannot be profitably developed.

Demand factors, too many times ignored, really serve as a true test for one's ability to predict the future. One's innate ability to predict demand **and the specific areas where such demand would be expected to reach its highest levels** puts the predictor in a unique position to posture sound investments in real estate for the long term. Some of these factors are:

- **Relocation of Major Industries** - The 1990s have already presented a variety of examples in this area including General Motors starting an entirely new line of automobiles, the Saturn, in Tennessee. Aerospace in California is going through a transitional process which will relocate and/or terminate employees located in that state in favor of Arizona, Missouri, Georgia, Texas and other areas where personnel costs, housing, rental levels and the like serve to dramatically reduce overhead. The entertainment industry has made a major moves to such places as Orlando, Florida and Branson, Missouri. But don't give up on California, however. This state serves as the gateway to the Pacific Rim with four major ports, two within the Los Angeles metropolitan area that funnel cargo from exotic locations to storekeeper's windows. This mecca of shipping can only get larger over time. Astute predictors will gather as much information on the utilization of our port facilities as possible trending the future outlook.

- **Other Shifts in Population** - At the present there seems to be a trend toward export of our highly trained and well paid professionals to be transferred out of state. These are the ones who contribute the most to the state's tax base. In return, the new arrivals tend to be younger or senior citizens who usually use more tax dollars than they provide. By studying the **demographics**, population statistics take on a new meaning. In Illustration 2-7, 1990 census data provides current numbers as well as historical population figures during this century. Illustration 2-8 provides some interesting insights on age distribution of our population together with trendings concerning our senior citizen population. Illustration 2-9 examines our major cities and their ethnic makeup. Within the city components lie economic opportunities for the 1990s which will be explored in depth in Chapter Four. Illustration 2-10 gives a further examination of racial components of population within major metropolitan areas with particular emphasis on the hispanic influence previously mentioned. Of particular interest to economic sages is the prediction of population size based on certain criteria of various areas of the country. Illustration 2-11 sheds considerable light as to what will be happening to the age and ethnic distribution of our population by the year 2000. Category A represents White; category B represents Black; category C represents Native Americans and category D represents Pacific Rim projections. Each of these tables is a valuable tool in one's ability to project the future through the use of population demographics.

* **Household Composition** - This, again, is a key demand factor that weighs heavily on business decision making concerning location of new retail outlets, officing, plant sites and the like. The traditional approach of locating a factory near a major metropolitan center may not be the wave of the future if current trends are any indication. Announcements of corporate relocations should be watched carefully in the media in order to be able to react to their significance.

* **Pricing** - The market place in the early 1990s represents a variety of market place opportunities for real estate investment based upon the excesses of the 1980s. The only question relative to the price is the factor of location and return on investment. Location is a function of **future potential**, while the latter's performance is coincidental with the former's ability to produce the expected results from the selected site.

* **General Prosperity** - The 1992 presidential election results were a clear indication that the then administration was not responding to the needs of more than 60% of the electorate. That sent a clear message to the White House that the American public was not in a very prosperous mood, particularly the legions of people that became jobless through layoffs being announced through the media on a daily basis. The time for the astute investor to enter the market place is when there is a more than adequate supply available, thus giving one with cash the ability to negotiate rock bottom prices and **a cash flow** from the investment.

* **Financing** - During difficult economic times, financing terms available from institutions anxious to remove foreclosed real estate from their books can meet or exceed attractive terms available in the market place. Where variable rate financing on residences was available at an entry level interest in the mid-5's and fixed rate financing was available in the low 8's, **loans to facilitate** have no restrictions as to their structure. Through astute negotiation purchasers may actually defer interest until certain occupancy

Illustration 2-7

Population

Figure 1.1
Percent Change in State Population: 1980 to 1990

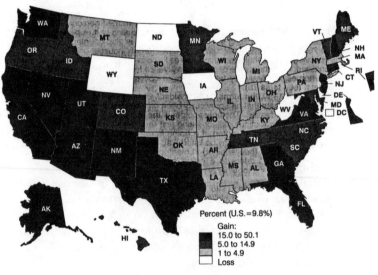

Source: Chart prepared by U.S. Bureau of the Census. For data, see table 26.

Figure 1.2
Distribution of Households, by Type: 1970 to 1990

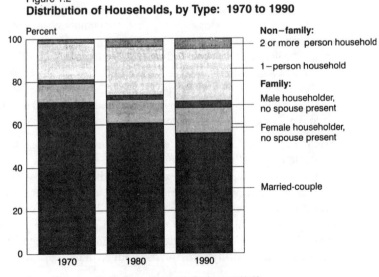

Source: Chart prepared by U.S. Bureau of the Census. For data, see table 56.

Illustration 2-7 (cont.)

Population and Area

No. 1. Population and Area: 1790 to 1990

[Area figures represent area on indicated date including in some cases considerable areas not then organized or settled, and not covered by the census. Total area figures for 1790-1970 have been recalculated on the basis of the remeasurement of States and counties for the 1980 census. The land and water area figures for past censuses have not been adjusted and are not strictly comparable with the total area data for comparable dates because the land areas were derived from different base data, and these values are known to have changed with the construction of reservoirs, draining of lakes, etc. Density figures are based on land area measurements as reported in earlier censuses]

CENSUS DATE	RESIDENT POPULATION					AREA (square miles)		
	Number	Per square mile of land area	Increase over preceding census			Gross	Land	Water
			Number	Percent				
CONTERMINOUS U.S.[1]								
1790 (Aug. 2)	3,929,214	4.5	(X)	(X)		891,364	864,746	24,065
1800 (Aug. 4)	5,308,483	6.1	1,379,269	35.1		891,364	864,746	24,065
1810 (Aug. 6)	7,239,881	4.3	1,931,398	36.4		1,722,685	1,681,828	34,175
1820 (Aug. 7)	9,638,453	5.5	2,398,572	33.1		1,792,552	1,749,462	38,544
1830 (June 1)	12,866,020	7.4	3,227,567	33.5		1,792,552	1,749,462	38,544
1840 (June 1)	17,069,453	9.8	4,203,433	32.7		1,792,552	1,749,462	38,544
1850 (June 1)	23,191,876	7.9	6,122,423	35.9		2,991,655	2,940,042	52,705
1860 (June 1)	31,443,321	10.6	8,251,445	35.6		3,021,295	2,969,640	52,747
1870 (June 1)	[2]39,818,449	[2]13.4	8,375,128	26.6		3,021,295	2,969,640	52,747
1880 (June 1)	50,155,783	16.9	10,337,334	26.0		3,021,295	2,969,640	52,747
1890 (June 1)	62,947,714	21.2	12,791,931	25.5		3,021,295	2,969,640	52,747
1900 (June 1)	75,994,575	25.6	13,046,861	20.7		3,021,295	2,969,834	52,553
1910 (Apr. 15)	91,972,266	31.0	15,977,691	21.0		3,021,295	2,969,565	52,822
1920 (Jan. 1)	105,710,620	35.6	13,738,354	14.9		3,021,295	2,969,451	52,936
1930 (Apr. 1)	122,775,046	41.2	17,064,426	16.1		3,021,295	2,977,128	45,259
1940 (Apr. 1)	131,669,275	44.2	8,894,229	7.2		3,021,295	2,977,128	45,259
1950 (Apr. 1)	150,697,361	50.7	19,028,086	14.5		3,021,295	2,974,726	47,661
1960 (Apr. 1)	178,464,236	60.1	27,766,875	18.4		3,021,295	2,968,054	54,207
UNITED STATES								
1950 (Apr. 1)	151,325,798	42.6	19,161,229	14.5		3,618,770	3,552,206	63,005
1960 (Apr. 1)	179,323,175	50.6	27,997,377	18.5		3,618,770	3,540,911	74,212
1970 (Apr. 1)	[3]203,302,031	[3]57.4	23,978,856	13.4		3,618,770	[3]3,540,023	[3]78,444
1980 (Apr. 1)	226,545,805	64.0	23,243,774	11.4		3,618,770	3,539,289	79,481
1990 (Apr. 1)	248,709,873	70.3	22,164,068	9.8		3,787,425	3,536,342	[4]251,083

X Not applicable.   [1] Excludes Alaska and Hawaii.   [2] Revised to include adjustments for underenumeration in southern States; unrevised number is 38,558,371 (13.0 per square mile).   [3] Figures corrected after 1970 final reports were issued.   [4] Comprises inland, coastal, Great Lakes, and territorial water. Data for prior years cover inland water only. For further explanation, see table 347.

Source: U.S. Bureau of the Census, *U.S. Census of Population: 1920* to *1980*, vol. I; and other reports and unpublished data. See also *Areas of the United States, 1940*, and *Area Measurement Reports, 1960*, series GE-20. No. 1.

No. 2. Population: 1900 to 1990

[In thousands, except percent. Estimates as of July 1. Prior to 1940, excludes Alaska and Hawaii. Total population includes Armed Forces abroad; civilian population excludes Armed Forces. For basis of estimates, see text, section 1. See also *Historical Statistics, Colonial Times to 1970*, series A 6-8]

YEAR	Resident population	YEAR	TOTAL		Resident population	Civilian population	YEAR	TOTAL		Resident population	Civilian population
			Population	Percent change				Population	Percent change		
1900. . . .	76,094	1951 . . .	154,878	1.71	153,982	151,599	1971 . . .	207,661	1.27	206,827	204,866
1905. . . .	83,822	1952 . . .	157,553	1.73	156,393	153,892	1972 . . .	209,896	1.08	209,284	207,511
1910. . . .	92,407	1953 . . .	160,184	1.67	158,956	156,595	1973 . . .	211,909	0.96	211,357	209,600
1915. . . .	100,546	1954 . . .	163,026	1.77	161,884	159,695	1974 . . .	213,854	0.92	213,342	211,636
1920. . . .	106,461	1955 . . .	165,931	1.78	165,069	162,967	1975 . . .	215,973	0.99	215,465	213,789
1925. . . .	115,829	1956 . . .	168,903	1.79	168,088	166,055	1976 . . .	218,035	0.95	217,563	215,894
1930. . . .	123,077	1957 . . .	171,984	1.82	171,187	169,110	1977 . . .	220,239	1.01	219,760	218,106
1935. . . .	127,250	1958 . . .	174,882	1.68	174,149	172,226	1978 . . .	222,585	1.06	222,095	220,467
1940. . . .	132,457	1959 . . .	177,830	1.69	177,135	175,277	1979 . . .	225,055	1.11	224,567	222,969
1941. . . .	133,669	1960 . . .	180,671	1.60	179,979	178,140	1980 [1] . . .	227,719	1.18	227,217	225,613
1942. . . .	134,617	1961 . . .	183,691	1.67	182,992	181,143	1981 [1] . . .	229,945	0.98	229,444	227,796
1943. . . .	135,107	1962 . . .	186,538	1.55	185,771	183,677	1982 [1] . . .	232,171	0.97	231,648	229,979
1944. . . .	133,915	1963 . . .	189,242	1.45	188,483	186,493	1983 [1] . . .	234,296	0.92	233,781	232,086
1945. . . .	133,434	1964 . . .	191,889	1.40	191,141	189,141	1984 [1] . . .	236,343	0.87	235,820	234,104
1946. . . .	140,686	1965 . . .	194,303	1.26	193,526	191,605	1985 [1] . . .	238,466	0.90	237,924	236,219
1947. . . .	144,083	1966 . . .	196,560	1.16	195,576	193,420	1986 [1] . . .	240,658	0.92	240,140	238,419
1948. . . .	146,730	1967 . . .	198,712	1.09	197,457	195,264	1987 [1] . . .	242,820	0.90	242,305	240,566
1949. . . .	149,304	1968 . . .	200,706	1.00	199,399	197,113	1988 [1] . . .	245,051	0.92	244,529	242,847
1950. . . .	152,271	1969 . . .	202,677	0.98	201,385	199,145	1989 [1] . . .	247,350	0.94	246,828	245,140
		1970 . . .	205,052	1.17	203,984	201,895	1990 [1] . . .	249,975	1.06	249,466	247,826

[1] Estimates reflect the census of April 1, 1990 and are subject to change.

Source: U.S. Bureau of the Census, *Current Population Reports*, series P-25, Nos. 311, 1045, and 1069.

1990 CENSUS NOTE: The population counts set forth herein are subject to possible correction for undercount or overcount. The United States Department of Commerce is considering whether to correct these and will publish corrected counts.

Illustration 2-8

Population 65 Years Old and Over

No. 41. Population 65 Years Old and Over, by Age Group and Sex, 1960 to 1989, and Projections, 2000

[As of July 1. Includes Armed Forces overseas. Projections are for middle series (series 14); for assumptions, see table 16. These projections were prepared prior to the release of 1990 census results and are therefore not based on 1990 census data. For explanation of methodology, see text, section 1]

AGE GROUP AND SEX	NUMBER (1,000)					PERCENT DISTRIBUTION				
	1960	1970	1980	1989	2000, proj.	1960	1970	1980	1989	2000, proj.
Persons 65 yrs. and over..	16,675	20,107	25,704	30,984	34,882	100.0	100.0	100.0	100.0	100.0
65-69 years old	6,280	7,026	8,812	10,170	9,491	37.7	34.9	34.3	32.8	27.2
70-74 years old	4,773	5,467	6,841	8,012	8,752	28.6	27.2	26.6	25.9	25.1
75-79 years old	3,080	3,871	4,828	6,033	7,282	18.5	19.3	18.8	19.5	20.9
80-84 years old	1,601	2,312	2,954	3,728	4,735	9.6	11.5	11.5	12.0	13.6
85 years old and over	940	1,430	2,269	3,042	4,622	5.6	7.1	8.8	9.8	13.2
Males, 65 yrs. and over.	7,542	8,413	10,366	12,636	14,273	100.0	100.0	100.0	100.0	100.0
65-69 years old.	2,936	3,139	3,919	4,631	4,382	38.9	37.3	37.8	36.7	30.7
70-74 years old.	2,197	2,322	2,873	3,464	3,860	29.1	27.6	27.7	27.4	27.0
75-79 years old.	1,370	1,573	1,862	2,385	2,971	18.2	18.7	18.0	18.9	20.8
80-84 years old.	673	883	1,026	1,306	1,739	8.9	10.5	9.9	10.3	12.2
85 years old and over	366	496	688	850	1,322	4.9	5.9	6.6	6.7	9.3
Females, 65 yrs. and over	9,133	11,693	15,338	18,348	20,608	100.0	100.0	100.0	100.0	100.0
65-69 years old.	3,344	3,887	4,894	5,538	5,109	36.6	33.2	31.9	30.2	24.8
70-74 years old.	2,577	3,145	3,968	4,549	4,892	28.2	26.9	25.9	24.8	23.7
75-79 years old.	1,711	2,298	2,966	3,648	4,311	18.7	19.7	19.3	19.9	20.9
80-84 years old.	928	1,429	1,928	2,422	2,996	10.2	12.2	12.6	13.2	14.5
85 years old and over	574	934	1,582	2,192	3,300	6.3	8.0	10.3	11.9	16.0

Source: U.S. Bureau of the Census, *Current Population Reports*, series P-25, Nos. 519, 917, 1018, and 1057.

No. 42. Persons 65 Years Old and Over—Characteristics, by Sex: 1970 to 1989

[As of March, except as noted. Covers civilian noninstitutional population, except 1970 includes institutional population. See headnote, table 43]

CHARACTERISTIC	TOTAL				MALE				FEMALE			
	1970	1980	1985	1989	1970	1980	1985	1989	1970	1980	1985	1989
Total [1] (million). . . . .:	19.9	24.2	26.8	29.0	8.3	9.9	11.0	12.1	11.5	14.2	15.8	16.9
White (million)	18.2	21.9	24.2	26.0	7.6	9.0	9.9	10.8	10.6	12.9	14.3	15.2
Black (million)	1.5	2.0	2.2	2.4	0.7	0.8	0.9	1.0	0.9	1.2	1.3	1.5
Percent below poverty level: [2]												
Family households [3] . . . .:	17.6	9.1	7.3	6.6	16.6	8.4	6.0	5.4	23.5	13.0	13.0	13.9
Unrelated individuals	47.3	29.3	24.2	24.1	40.0	25.3	20.8	19.5	49.9	30.5	25.9	25.5
PERCENT DISTRIBUTION												
Marital status:												
Single	7.6	5.5	5.2	4.9	7.5	4.9	5.3	4.7	7.7	5.9	5.1	5.0
Married	51.3	55.4	55.2	56.4	73.1	78.0	77.2	77.0	35.6	39.5	39.9	41.7
Spouse present	49.0	53.6	53.4	54.3	69.9	76.1	75.0	74.3	33.9	37.9	38.3	40.1
Spouse absent	2.3	1.8	1.8	2.1	3.2	1.9	2.2	2.7	1.7	1.7	-1.6	1.6
Widowed	38.8	35.7	35.6	34.3	17.1	13.5	13.8	14.0	54.4	51.2	50.7	48.7
Divorced	2.3	3.5	4.0	4.4	2.3	3.6	3.7	4.3	2.3	3.4	4.3	4.5
Family status:												
In families [4]	67.1	67.6	67.3	67.4	79.2	83.0	82.4	82.0	58.5	56.8	56.7	57.0
Nonfamily householders	26.6	31.2	31.1	31.3	14.9	15.7	15.4	16.6	35.2	42.0	42.1	41.8
Secondary individuals.	2.1	1.2	1.6	1.3	2.4	1.3	2.2	1.4	1.9	1.1	1.1	1.2
Residents of institutions	4.1	(NA)	(NA)	(NA)	3.6	(NA)	(NA)	(NA)	4.4	(NA)	(NA)	(NA)
Living arrangements:												
Living in household . . . . : . .	95.2	99.8	99.6	99.7	95.5	99.9	99.5	99.7	95.0	99.7	99.6	99.6
Living alone.	25.5	30.3	30.2	30.5	14.1	14.9	14.7	15.9	33.8	41.0	41.1	40.9
Spouse present	49.0	53.6	53.4	54.3	69.9	76.1	75.0	74.3	33.9	37.9	38.3	40.1
Living with someone else.	20.7	15.9	15.9	14.8	11.5	8.9	9.8	9.5	27.4	20.8	20.2	18.6
Not in household [5]	4.8	0.2	0.4	0.3	4.5	0.1	0.5	0.3	5.0	0.3	0.4	0.4
Years of school completed:												
8 years or less	58.3	43.1	35.4	[6]30.5	61.5	45.3	37.2	[6]31.7	56.1	41.6	34.1	[6]29.7
1-3 years of high school	13.4	16.2	16.5	[6]15.7	12.6	15.5	15.7	[6]15.6	13.9	16.7	17.0	[6]15.8
4 years of high school	15.7	24.0	29.0	[6]33.0	12.5	21.4	26.4	[6]29.4	18.1	25.8	30.7	[6]35.5
1-3 years of college.	6.2	8.2	9.8	[6]10.2	5.6	7.5	9.1	[6]9.8	6.7	8.6	10.3	[6]10.5
4 years or more of college	6.3	8.6	9.4	[6]10.6	7.9	10.3	11.5	[6]13.5	5.2	7.4	8.0	[6]8.5
Labor force participation: [7]												
Employed	16.4	12.2	10.4	11.5	25.9	18.4	15.3	16.2	9.4	7.8	7.0	8.1
Unemployed.	0.5	0.4	0.4	0.4	0.9	0.6	0.5	0.4	0.3	0.3	0.2	0.2
Not in labor force	83.0	87.5	89.2	88.2	73.2	81.0	84.2	83.4	90.3	91.9	92.7	91.6

NA Not available. [1] Includes other races, not shown separately. [2] Poverty status based on income in preceding year. [3] "Male" refers to married couples plus other families with a male householder. "Female" refers to female householder, no spouse present. [4] Beginning 1980, excludes those living in unrelated subfamilies. [5] In institutions (1970) and other group quarters. [6] Data for 1988. [7] Annual averages of monthly figures. Source: U.S. Bureau of Labor Statistics, *Employment and Earnings*,

Illustration 2-8 (cont.)

Population

No. 40. Cities With 105,000 Inhabitants or More in 1990—Population, 1970 to 1990, and Land Area, 1990—Continued

[See headnote, p.34]

CITY	1970, total[1] (1,000)	1980, total[1] (1,000)	POPULATION 1990 Total (1,000)	Rank	Percent change, 1980-1990	Percent— Black	Percent— American Indian, Eskimo, Aleut	Percent— Asian, Pacific Islander	Percent— Hispanic[2]	Per square mile	Land area 1990 (Square Miles)
Orange, CA	77	91	111	169	21.0	1.4	0.5	7.9	22.8	4,741	23
Orlando, FL	99	128	165	105	28.4	26.9	0.3	1.6	8.7	2,448	67
Overland Park, KS	78	82	112	165	36.7	1.8	0.3	1.9	2.0	2,007	55
Oxnard, CA	71	108	142	123	31.4	5.2	0.8	8.6	54.4	5,819	24
Paradise, NV [5]	24	85	125	150	47.0	4.9	0.6	4.0	10.5	2,616	47
Pasadena, CA	113	118	132	139	11.4	19.0	0.4	8.1	27.3	5,724	23
Pasadena, TX	90	113	119	154	6.0	1.0	0.5	1.6	28.8	2,727	43
Paterson, NJ	145	138	141	126	2.1	36.0	0.3	1.4	41.0	16,693	8
Peoria, IL	127	124	114	161	-8.6	20.9	0.2	1.7	1.6	2,776	40
Philadelphia, PA	1,949	1,688	1,586	5	-6.1	39.9	0.2	2.7	5.6	11,734	135
Phoenix, AZ	584	790	983	9	24.5	5.2	1.9	1.7	20.0	2,342	419
Pittsburgh, PA	520	424	370	40	-12.8	25.8	0.2	1.6	0.9	6,649	55
Plano, TX	18	72	129	142	77.9	4.1	0.3	4.0	6.2	1,943	66
Pomona, CA	87	93	132	138	42.0	14.4	0.6	6.7	51.3	5,770	22
Portland, OR	380	368	437	30	18.8	7.7	1.2	5.3	3.2	3,508	124
Providence, RI	179	157	161	108	2.5	14.8	0.9	5.9	15.5	8,707	18
Raleigh, NC	123	150	208	75	38.4	27.6	0.3	2.5	1.4	2,360	88
Reno, NV	73	101	134	134	32.8	2.9	1.4	4.9	11.1	2,328	57
Richmond, VA	249	219	203	76	-7.4	55.2	0.2	0.9	0.9	3,377	60
Riverside, CA	140	171	227	68	32.8	7.4	0.8	5.2	26.0	2,916	77
Rochester, NY	295	242	232	66	-4.2	31.5	0.5	1.8	8.7	6,474	35
Rockford, IL	147	140	139	130	-0.2	15.0	0.3	1.5	4.2	3,100	45
Sacramento, CA	257	276	369	41	34.0	15.3	1.2	15.0	16.2	3,836	96
St. Louis, MO	622	453	397	34	-12.4	47.5	0.2	0.9	1.3	6,405	61
St. Paul, MN	310	270	272	57	0.7	7.4	1.4	7.1	4.2	5,157	52
St. Petersburg, FL	216	239	239	65	0.0	19.6	0.2	1.7	2.6	4,032	59
Salem, OR	69	89	108	182	21.0	1.5	1.6	2.4	6.1	2,595	41
Salinas, CA	59	80	109	177	35.2	3.0	0.9	8.1	50.6	5,839	18
Salt Lake City, UT	176	163	160	109	-1.9	1.7	1.6	4.7	9.7	1,467	109
San Antonio, TX	654	786	936	10	19.1	7.0	0.4	1.1	55.6	2,810	333
San Bernardino, CA	107	119	164	106	38.2	16.0	1.0	4.0	34.6	2,980	55
San Diego, CA	697	876	1,111	6	26.8	9.4	0.6	11.8	20.7	3,428	324
San Francisco, CA	716	679	724	14	6.6	10.9	0.5	29.1	13.9	15,502	46
San Jose, CA	460	629	782	11	24.3	4.7	0.7	19.5	26.6	4,568	171
Santa Ana, CA	156	204	294	52	44.0	2.6	0.5	9.7	65.2	10,843	27
Santa Clarita, CA	(*)	(*)	111	170	(X)	1.5	0.6	4.2	13.4	2,733	40
Santa Rosa, CA	50	83	113	162	37.1	1.8	1.2	3.4	9.5	3,362	33
Savannah, GA	118	142	138	131	-2.9	51.3	0.2	1.1	1.4	2,198	62
Scottsdale, AZ	68	89	130	141	46.8	0.8	0.6	1.2	4.8	706	184
Seattle, WA	531	494	516	21	4.5	10.1	1.4	11.8	3.6	6,154	83
Shreveport, LA	182	206	199	77	-4.1	44.8	0.2	0.5	1.1	2,013	98
South Bend, IN	126	110	106	187	-3.8	20.9	0.4	0.9	3.4	2,897	36
Spokane, WA	171	171	177	94	3.4	1.9	2.0	2.1	2.1	3,169	55
Springfield, IL	92	100	105	188	5.2	13.0	0.2	1.0	0.8	2,474	42
Springfield, MA	164	152	157	112	3.1	19.2	0.2	1.0	16.9	4,890	32
Springfield, MO	120	133	140	128	5.5	2.5	0.7	0.9	1.0	2,068	68
Stamford, CT	109	102	108	181	5.5	17.8	0.1	2.6	9.8	2,865	37
Sterling Heights, MI	61	109	118	156	8.1	0.4	0.2	2.9	1.1	3,215	36
Stockton, CA	110	150	211	74	42.3	9.6	1.0	22.8	25.0	4,013	52
Sunnyvale, CA	96	107	117	157	10.0	3.4	0.5	19.3	13.2	5,353	21
Syracuse, NY	197	170	164	107	-3.7	20.3	1.3	2.2	2.9	6,528	25
Tacoma, WA	154	159	177	95	11.5	11.4	2.0	6.9	3.8	3,677	48
Tallahassee, FL	73	82	125	149	53.0	29.1	0.2	1.8	3.0	1,972	63
Tampa, FL	278	272	280	55	3.1	25.0	0.3	1.4	15.0	2,577	108
Tempe, AZ	64	107	142	124	32.7	3.2	1.3	4.1	10.9	3,590	39
Toledo, OH	383	355	333	49	-6.1	19.7	0.3	1.0	4.0	4,132	80
Topeka, KS	125	119	120	153	1.0	10.6	1.3	0.8	5.8	2,173	55
Torrance, CA	135	130	133	137	2.5	1.5	0.4	21.9	10.1	6,487	20
Tucson, AZ	263	331	405	33	22.6	4.3	1.6	2.2	29.3	2,594	156
Tulsa, OK	330	361	367	43	1.8	13.6	4.7	1.4	2.6	2,001	183
Vallejo, CA	72	80	109	175	36.0	21.2	0.7	23.0	10.8	3,613	30
Virginia Beach, VA	172	262	393	37	49.9	13.9	0.4	4.3	3.1	1,583	248
Warren, MI	179	161	145	120	-10.1	0.7	0.5	1.3	1.1	4,226	34
Washington, DC	757	638	607	19	-4.9	65.8	0.2	1.8	5.4	9,883	61
Waterbury, CT	108	103	109	176	5.5	13.0	0.3	0.7	13.4	3,815	28
Wichita, KS	277	280	304	51	8.6	11.3	1.2	2.6	5.0	2,640	115
Winston-Salem, NC	134	132	143	121	8.8	39.3	0.2	0.8	0.9	2,018	71
Worcester, MA	177	162	170	102	4.9	4.5	0.3	2.8	9.6	4,520	37
Yonkers, NY	204	195	188	84	-3.7	14.1	0.2	3.0	16.7	10,403	18

1990 Census Note: The population counts set forth herein are subject to possible correction for undercount or overcount. The United States Department of Commerce is considering whether to correct these counts and will publish corrected counts, if any, not later than July 15, 1991.

X Not applicable.   Z Less than .05 percent.   [1] Population totals include corrections made after tabulations were completed.   [2] Hispanic persons may be of any race.   [3] As of January 1.   [4] Anchorage city consolidated with Anchorage Borough September 15, 1975.   [5] Data represent the census designated place as delineated by State and local authorities.   [6] Not incorporated

Illustration 2-9

Population

No. 39. Cities, by Population Size: 1960 to 1988

POPULATION SIZE	NUMBER OF CITIES				POPULATION (mil.)				PERCENT OF TOTAL			
	1960	1970	1980	1988	1960	1970	1980	1988	1960	1970	1980	198
Total	18,088	18,666	19,097	19,252	115.9	140.3	152.2	100.0	100.0	100.0	100.0	100
1,000,000 or more	5	6	6	7	17.5	18.8	17.5	19.1	15.1	14.2	12.5	12.6
500,000-1,000,000	16	20	16	17	11.1	13.0	10.9	11.5	9.6	9.8	7.8	7.6
250,000-500,000	30	30	33	37	10.8	10.5	11.8	13.2	9.3	7.9	8.4	8.7
100,000-250,000	79	97	114	125	11.4	13.9	16.6	18.4	9.8	10.5	11.8	12.2
50,000-100,000	180	232	250	300	12.5	16.2	17.6	20.6	10.8	12.2	12.3	13.6
25,000-50,000	366	455	526	575	12.7	15.7	18.4	19.9	11.0	11.9	13.1	13.1
10,000-25,000	978	1,127	1,260	1,323	15.1	17.6	19.8	20.7	13.1	13.3	14.1	13.6
Under 10,000	16,434	16,699	16,892	16,868	24.9	26.4	28.0	28.7	21.5	20.0	20.0	18.5

Source: U.S. Bureau of the Census, *Census of Population: 1970* and *1980*, vol. I; and *Current Population Reports*, series P-3 No. 88-(five regional reports: NE, ENC, WNC, S, and W)-SC.

No. 40. Cities With 105,000 Inhabitants or More in 1990—Population, 1970 to 1990, and Land Area, 1990

[Population: As of April 1. Data refer to municipal limits as of January 1. Minus sign (-) indicates decrease]

CITY	POPULATION										Land area3 1990 (square miles)
	1970 total [1] (1,000)	1980 total [1] (1,000)	1990								
			Total (1,000)	Rank	Per-cent change, 1980-1990	Percent—				Per square mile	
						Black	Amer-ican Indian, Eskimo, Aleut	Asian, Pacific Islander	His-panic [2]		
Abilene, TX	90	98	107	184	8.5	7.0	0.4	1.3	15.5	1,035	103
Akron, OH.	275	237	223	71	-6.0	24.5	0.3	1.2	0.7	3,586	62
Albuquerque, NM	245	332	385	38	15.6	3.0	3.0	1.7	34.5	2,910	132
Alexandria, VA	111	103	111	168	7.7	21.9	0.3	4.2	9.7	7,281	15
Allentown, PA	110	104	105	189	1.3	5.0	0.2	1.3	11.7	5,934	17
Amarillo, TX	127	149	158	111	5.6	6.0	0.8	1.9	14.7	1,793	87
Anaheim, CA	166	219	266	59	21.4	2.5	0.5	9.4	31.4	6,016	44
Anchorage, AK [4]	48	174	226	69	29.8	6.4	6.4	4.8	4.1	133	1697
Ann Arbor, MI	100	108	110	174	1.5	9.0	0.4	7.7	2.6	4,231	25
Arlington, VA [5]	174	153	171	100	12.0	10.5	0.3	6.8	13.5	6,605	25
Arlington, TX	90	160	262	61	63.5	8.4	0.5	3.9	8.9	2,814	93
Atlanta, GA	495	425	394	36	-7.3	67.1	0.1	0.9	1.9	2,990	131
Aurora, CO	75	159	222	72	40.1	11.4	0.6	3.8	6.6	1,676	132
Austin, TX.	254	346	466	27	34.6	12.4	0.4	3.0	23.0	2,138	217
Bakersfield, CA	70	106	175	97	65.5	9.4	1.1	3.6	20.5	1,904	91
Baltimore, MD	905	787	736	12	-6.4	59.2	0.3	1.1	1.0	9,108	80
Baton Rouge, LA	166	220	220	73	-0.4	43.9	0.1	1.7	1.6	2,969	74
Beaumont, TX	118	118	114	159	-3.2	41.3	0.2	1.7	4.3	1,428	80
Birmingham, AL	301	284	266	60	-6.5	63.3	0.1	0.6	(Z)	1,791	148
Boise City, ID	75	102	126	148	23.0	0.6	0.6	1.6	2.7	2,726	46
Boston, MA.	641	563	574	20	2.0	25.6	0.3	5.3	10.8	11,860	48
Bridgeport, CT	157	143	142	125	-0.6	26.6	0.3	2.3	26.5	8,855	16
Buffalo, NY	463	358	328	50	-8.3	30.7	0.8	1.0	4.9	8,080	40
Cedar Rapids, IA	111	110	109	178	-1.4	2.9	0.2	1.0	1.1	2,034	53
Charlotte, NC	241	315	396	35	25.5	31.8	0.4	1.8	1.4	2,272	174
Chattanooga, TN	120	170	152	114	-10.1	33.7	0.2	1.0	0.6	1,287	118
Chesapeake, VA	90	114	152	115	32.7	27.4	0.3	1.2	1.3	446	340
Chicago, IL	3,369	3,005	2,784	3	-7.4	39.1	0.3	3.7	19.6	12,251	227
Chula Vista, CA	68	84	135	133	61.0	4.6	0.6	8.9	37.3	4,662	29
Cincinnati, OH	454	385	364	45	-5.5	37.9	0.2	1.1	0.7	4,714	77
Citrus Heights, CA [5] . . .	22	86	107	183	21.5	2.3	1.1	3.3	6.9	5,513	19
Cleveland, OH	751	574	506	23	-11.9	46.6	0.3	1.0	4.6	6,565	77
Colorado Springs, CO . . .	136	215	281	54	30.7	7.0	0.8	2.4	9.1	1,535	183
Columbus, GA	155	169	179	93	5.5	38.1	0.3	1.4	3.0	827	216
Columbus, OH	540	565	633	16	12.0	22.6	0.2	2.4	1.1	3,315	190
Concord, CA	85	104	111	167	7.3	2.4	0.7	8.7	11.5	3,778	29
Corpus Christi, TX	205	232	257	64	10.9	4.8	0.4	0.9	50.4	1,907	135
Dallas, TX.	844	905	1,007	8	11.3	29.5	0.5	2.2	20.9	2,941	342
Dayton, OH	243	194	182	89	-5.9	40.4	0.2	0.6	0.7	3,310	55
Denver, CO.	515	493	468	26	-5.1	12.8	1.2	2.4	23.0	3,051	153
Des Moines, IA	201	191	193	80	1.1	7.1	0.4	2.4	2.4	2,567	75
Detroit, MI.	1,514	1,203	1,028	7	-14.6	75.7	0.4	0.8	2.8	7,410	138
Durham, NC	95	101	137	132	35.1	45.7	0.2	2.0	1.2	1,972	69
East Los Angeles, CA . . .	105	110	126	146	14.9	1.4	0.4	1.3	94.7	16,828	7
Elizabeth, NJ	113	106	110	172	3.6	19.8	0.3	2.7	39.1	8,929	12
El Monte, CA.	70	79	106	186	33.6	1.0	0.6	11.8	72.5	11,180	9
El Paso, TX.	322	425	515	22	21.2	3.4	0.4	1.2	69.0	2,100	245
Erie, PA	129	119	109	179	-8.7	12.0	0.2	0.5	2.4	4,944	22
Escondido, CA	37	64	109	180	68.8	1.5	0.8	3.7	23.4	3,048	35
Eugene, OR	79	106	113	163	6.6	1.3	0.9	3.5	2.7	2,962	38
Evansville, IN	139	130	126	147	-3.2	9.5	0.2	0.6	0.6	3,102	40
Flint, MI	193	160	141	127	-11.8	47.9	0.7	0.5	2.9	4,161	33
Fort Lauderdale, FL	140	153	149	118	-2.5	28.1	0.2	0.9	7.2	4,763	31

1990 CENSUS NOTE: The population counts set forth herein are subject to possible correction for undercount or overcount. The United States Department of Commerce is considering whether to correct these and will publish corrected counts.

Illustration 2-9 (cont.)

Principal Cities

No. 40. Cities With 105,000 Inhabitants or More in 1990—Population, 1970 to 1990, and Land Area, 1990—Continued

[See headnote, p. 34]

CITY	1970 total [1] (1,000)	1980 total [1] (1,000)	Total (1,000)	Rank	Per-cent change, 1980–1990	Black	American Indian, Eskimo, Aleut	Asian, Pacific Islander	His-panic [2]	Per square mile	Land area [3] 1990 (square miles)
Fort Wayne, IN	178	172	173	99	0.4	16.7	0.3	1.0	2.7	2,762	62.7
Fort Worth, TX	393	385	448	28	16.2	22.0	0.4	2.0	19.5	1,592	281.1
Fremont, CA	101	132	173	98	31.4	3.8	0.7	19.4	13.3	2,250	77.0
Fresno, CA	166	217	354	47	62.9	8.3	1.1	12.5	29.9	3,573	99.1
Fullerton, CA	86	102	114	160	11.6	2.2	0.5	12.2	21.3	5,160	22.1
Garden Grove, CA	121	123	143	122	16.0	1.5	0.6	20.5	23.5	7,974	17.9
Garland, TX	81	139	181	91	30.1	8.9	0.5	4.5	11.6	3,150	57.4
Gary, IN	175	152	117	158	-23.2	80.6	0.2	0.2	5.7	2,322	50.2
Glendale, AZ	36	97	148	119	52.4	3.0	0.9	2.1	15.5	2,837	52.2
Glendale, CA	133	139	180	92	29.5	1.3	0.3	14.1	21.0	5,882	30.6
Grand Rapids, MI	198	182	189	83	4.0	18.5	0.8	1.1	5.0	4,273	44.3
Greensboro, NC	144	156	184	88	17.9	33.9	0.5	1.4	1.0	2,300	79.8
Hampton, VA	121	123	134	135	9.1	38.9	0.3	1.7	2.0	2,582	51.8
Hartford, CT	158	136	140	129	2.5	38.9	0.3	1.4	31.6	8,077	17.3
Hayward, CA	93	94	111	166	19.1	9.8	1.0	15.5	23.9	2,566	43.5
Hialeah, FL	102	145	188	85	29.4	1.9	0.1	0.5	87.6	9,772	19.2
Hollywood, FL	107	121	122	152	0.3	8.5	0.2	1.3	11.9	4,464	27.3
Honolulu, HI [5]	325	365	365	44	0.1	1.3	0.3	70.5	4.6	4,410	82.8
Houston, TX	1,234	1,595	1,631	4	2.2	28.1	0.3	4.1	27.6	3,020	539.9
Huntington Beach, CA	116	171	182	90	6.5	0.9	0.6	8.3	11.2	6,871	26.4
Huntsville, AL	139	143	160	110	12.1	24.4	0.5	2.1	1.2	972	164.4
Independence, MO	112	112	112	164	0.5	1.4	0.6	1.0	2.0	1,436	78.2
Indianapolis, IN	737	701	731	13	4.3	22.6	0.2	0.9	1.1	2,022	361.7
Inglewood, CA	90	94	110	173	16.4	51.9	0.4	2.5	38.5	11,552	9.2
Irvine, CA	(5)	62	110	171	77.6	1.8	0.2	18.1	6.3	2,607	42.3
Irving, TX	97	110	155	113	41.0	7.5	0.6	4.6	16.3	2,293	67.6
Jackson, MS	154	203	197	78	-3.1	55.7	0.1	0.5	0.4	1,804	109.0
Jacksonville, FL	504	541	635	15	17.9	25.2	0.3	1.9	2.6	837	758.7
Jersey City, NJ	260	224	229	67	2.2	29.7	0.3	11.4	24.2	15,359	14.9
Kansas City, KS	168	161	150	116	-7.1	29.3	0.7	1.2	7.1	1,389	107.8
Kansas City, MO	507	448	435	31	-2.9	29.6	0.5	1.2	3.9	1,397	311.5
Knoxville, TN	175	175	165	103	-5.7	15.8	0.2	1.0	0.7	2,137	77.3
Lakewood, CO	93	114	126	145	11.1	1.0	0.7	1.9	9.1	3,100	40.8
Lansing, MI	131	130	127	144	-2.4	18.6	1.0	1.8	7.9	3,755	33.9
Laredo, TX	69	91	123	151	34.4	0.1	0.2	0.4	93.9	3,739	32.9
Las Vegas, NV	126	165	258	63	56.9	11.4	0.9	3.6	12.5	3,101	83.3
Lexington-Fayette, KY [7]	108	204	225	70	10.4	13.4	0.2	1.6	1.1	792	284.5
Lincoln, NE	150	172	192	81	11.7	2.4	0.6	1.7	2.0	3,033	63.3
Little Rock, AR	132	159	176	96	10.5	34.0	0.3	0.9	0.8	1,709	102.9
Long Beach, CA	359	361	429	32	18.8	13.7	0.6	13.6	23.6	8,585	50.0
Los Angeles, CA	2,812	2,969	3,485	2	17.4	14.0	0.5	9.8	39.9	7,426	469.3
Louisville, KY	362	299	269	58	-9.9	29.7	0.2	0.7	0.7	4,332	62.1
Lubbock, TX	149	174	186	87	6.8	8.6	0.3	1.4	22.5	1,789	104.1
Macon, GA	122	117	107	185	-8.8	52.2	0.1	0.4	0.6	2,227	47.9
Madison, WI	172	171	191	82	12.1	4.2	0.4	3.9	2.0	3,311	57.8
Memphis, TN	624	646	610	18	-5.5	54.8	0.2	0.8	0.7	2,384	256.0
Mesa, AZ	63	152	288	53	89.0	1.9	1.0	1.5	10.9	2,653	108.6
Metairie, LA [5]	136	164	149	117	-9.0	4.9	0.2	1.8	6.2	6,424	23.3
Miami, FL	335	347	359	46	3.4	27.4	0.2	0.6	62.5	10,080	35.6
Milwaukee, WI	717	636	628	17	-1.3	30.5	0.9	1.9	6.3	6,537	96.1
Minneapolis, MN	434	371	368	42	-0.7	13.0	3.3	4.3	2.1	6,706	54.9
Mobile, AL	190	200	196	79	-2.1	38.9	0.2	1.0	1.0	1,663	118.0
Modesto, CA	62	107	165	104	54.0	2.7	1.0	7.9	16.3	5,458	30.2
Montgomery, AL	133	178	187	86	5.2	42.3	0.2	0.7	0.8	1,386	135.0
Moreno Valley, CA	(5)	(5)	119	155	(X)	13.8	0.7	6.6	22.9	2,418	49.1
Nashville-Davidson, TN	426	456	488	25	6.9	24.3	0.2	1.4	0.9	1,032	473.3
Newark, NJ	382	329	275	56	-16.4	58.5	0.2	1.2	26.1	11,554	23.8
New Haven, CT	138	126	130	140	3.5	36.1	0.3	2.4	13.2	6,922	18.9
New Orleans, LA	593	558	497	24	-10.9	61.9	0.2	1.9	3.5	2,751	180.7
Newport News, VA	138	145	170	101	17.4	33.6	0.3	2.3	2.8	2,488	68.3
New York, NY	7,896	7,072	7,323	1	3.5	28.7	0.4	7.0	24.4	23,701	309.0
Bronx Borough	1,472	1,169	1,204	(X)	(X)	37.3	0.5	3.0	43.5	28,641	42.0
Brooklyn Borough	2,602	2,231	2,301	(X)	(X)	37.9	0.3	4.8	20.1	32,620	70.5
Manhattan Borough	1,539	1,428	1,488	(X)	(X)	22.0	0.4	7.4	26.0	52,415	28.4
Queens Borough	1,987	1,891	1,952	(X)	(X)	21.7	0.4	12.2	19.5	17,839	109.4
Staten Island Borough	295	352	379	(X)	(X)	8.1	0.2	4.5	8.0	6,466	58.6
Norfolk, VA	308	267	261	62	-2.2	39.1	0.4	2.6	2.9	4,859	53.8
Oakland, CA	362	339	372	39	9.7	43.9	0.6	14.8	13.9	6,640	56.1
Oceanside, CA	40	77	128	143	67.4	7.9	0.7	6.1	22.6	3,157	40.7
Oklahoma City, OK	368	404	445	29	10.1	16.0	4.2	2.4	5.0	731	608.2
Omaha, NE	347	314	336	48	7.0	13.1	0.7	1.0	3.1	3,336	100.7
Ontario, CA	64	89	133	136	49.9	7.3	0.7	3.9	41.7	3,624	36.8
Orange, CA	77	91	111	169	21.0	1.4	0.5	7.9	22.8	4,741	23.3

1990 Census Note: The population counts set forth herein are subject to possible correction for undercount or overcount

One Up On Trump

Illustration 2-10

Racial and Hispanic Populations in Metropolitan Areas

No. 38. 70 Largest Metropolitan Areas—Racial and Hispanic Origin Populations: 1990
[As of April 1. Areas as defined by U.S. Office of Management and Budget, June 30, 1990. For definitions, see Appendix II]

METROPOLITAN AREA [1]	Total population (1,000)	PERCENT OF TOTAL METROPOLITAN POPULATION			
		Black	American Indian, Eskimo, Aleut	Asian and Pacific Islander	Hispanic origin [2]
New York-Northern New Jersey-Long Island, NY-NJ-CT CMSA ..	18,087	18.2	0.3	4.8	15.4
Los Angeles-Anaheim-Riverside, CA CMSA	14,532	8.5	0.6	9.2	32.9
Chicago-Gary-Lake County (IL), IL-IN-WI CMSA.	8,066	19.2	0.2	3.2	11.1
San Francisco-Oakland-San Jose, CA CMSA	6,253	8.6	0.7	14.8	15.5
Philadelphia-Wilmington-Trenton, PA-NJ-DE-MD CMSA.	5,899	18.7	0.2	2.1	3.8
Detroit-Ann Arbor, MI CMSA	4,665	20.9	0.4	1.5	1.9
Boston-Lawrence-Salem, MA-NH CMSA.	4,172	5.7	0.2	2.9	4.6
Washington, DC-MD-VA MSA.	3,924	26.6	0.3	5.2	5.7
Dallas-Fort Worth, TX CMSA	3,885	14.3	0.5	2.5	13.4
Houston-Galveston-Brazoria, TX CMSA	3,711	17.9	0.3	3.6	20.8
Miami-Fort Lauderdale, FL CMSA	3,193	18.5	0.2	1.4	33.3
Atlanta, GA MSA	2,834	26.0	0.2	1.8	2.0
Cleveland-Akron-Lorain, OH CMSA	2,760	16.0	0.2	1.0	1.9
Seattle-Tacoma, WA CMSA	2,559	4.8	1.3	6.4	3.0
San Diego, CA MSA	2,498	6.4	0.8	7.9	20.4
Minneapolis-St. Paul, MN-WI MSA.	2,464	3.6	1.0	2.6	1.5
St. Louis, MO-IL MSA	2,444	17.3	0.2	1.0	1.1
Baltimore, MD MSA	2,382	25.9	0.3	1.8	1.3
Pittsburgh-Beaver Valley, PA CMSA	2,243	8.0	0.1	0.7	0.6
Phoenix, AZ MSA.	2,122	3.5	1.8	1.7	16.3
Tampa-St. Petersburg-Clearwater, FL MSA	2,068	9.0	0.3	1.1	6.7
Denver-Boulder, CO CMSA	1,848	5.3	0.8	2.3	12.2
Cincinnati-Hamilton, OH-KY-IN CMSA	1,744	11.7	0.1	0.8	0.5
Milwaukee-Racine, WI CMSA	1,607	13.3	0.5	1.2	3.8
Kansas City, MO-KS MSA	1,566	12.8	0.5	1.1	2.9
Sacramento, CA MSA.	1,481	6.9	1.1	7.7	11.6
Portland-Vancouver, OR-WA CMSA.	1,478	2.8	0.9	3.5	3.4
Norfolk-Virginia Beach-Newport News, VA MSA.	1,396	28.5	0.3	2.5	2.3
Columbus, OH MSA	1,377	12.0	0.2	1.5	0.8
San Antonio, TX MSA.	1,302	6.8	0.4	1.2	47.6
Indianapolis, IN MSA	1,250	13.8	0.2	0.8	0.9
New Orleans, LA MSA	1,239	34.7	0.3	1.7	4.3
Buffalo-Niagara Falls, NY CMSA.	1,189	10.3	0.6	0.9	2.0
Charlotte-Gastonia-Rock Hill, NC-SC MSA	1,162	19.9	0.4	1.0	0.9
Providence-Pawtucket-Fall River, RI-MA CMSA	1,142	3.3	0.3	1.8	4.2
Hartford-New Britain-Middletown, CT CMSA	1,086	8.7	0.2	1.5	7.0
Orlando, FL MSA	1,073	12.4	0.3	1.9	9.0
Salt Lake City-Ogden, UT MSA.	1,072	1.0	0.8	2.4	5.8
Rochester, NY MSA.	1,002	9.4	0.3	1.4	3.1
Nashville, TN MSA	985	15.5	0.2	1.0	0.8
Memphis, TN-AR-MS MSA.	982	40.6	0.2	0.8	0.8
Oklahoma City, OK MSA.	959	10.5	4.8	1.9	3.6
Louisville, KY-IN MSA.	953	13.1	0.2	0.6	0.6
Dayton-Springfield, OH MSA	951	13.3	0.2	1.0	0.8
Greensboro—Winston-Salem—High Point, NC MSA.	942	19.3	0.3	0.7	0.8
Birmingham, AL MSA	908	27.1	0.2	0.4	0.4
Jacksonville, FL MSA	907	20.0	0.3	1.7	2.5
Albany-Schenectady-Troy, NY MSA.	874	4.7	0.2	1.2	1.8
Richmond-Petersburg, VA MSA.	866	29.2	0.3	1.4	1.1
West Palm Beach-Boca Raton-Delray Beach, FL MSA	864	12.5	0.1	1.0	7.7
Honolulu, HI MSA.	836	3.1	0.4	63.0	6.8
Austin, TX MSA	782	9.2	0.4	2.4	20.5
Las Vegas, NV MSA	741	9.5	0.9	3.5	11.2
Raleigh-Durham, NC MSA	735	24.9	0.3	1.9	1.2
Scranton—Wilkes-Barre, PA MSA.	734	1.0	0.1	0.5	0.8
Tulsa, OK MSA	709	8.2	6.8	0.9	2.1
Grand Rapids, MI MSA	688	6.0	0.5	1.1	3.3
Allentown-Bethlehem, PA-NJ MSA	687	2.0	0.1	1.1	4.2
Fresno, CA MSA	667	5.0	1.1	8.6	35.5
Tucson, AZ MSA	667	3.1	3.0	1.8	24.5
Syracuse, NY MSA.	660	5.9	0.6	1.2	1.4
Greenville-Spartanburg, SC MSA.	641	17.4	0.1	0.7	0.8
Omaha, NE-IA MSA	618	8.3	0.5	1.0	2.6
Toledo, OH MSA	614	11.4	0.2	1.0	3.3
Knoxville, TN MSA.	605	6.0	0.2	0.8	0.5
El Paso, TX MSA	592	3.7	0.4	1.1	69.6
Harrisburg-Lebanon-Carlisle, PA MSA	588	6.7	0.1	1.1	1.7
Bakersfield, CA MSA	543	5.5	1.3	3.0	28.0
New Haven-Meriden, CT MSA	530	12.1	0.2	1.6	6.2
Springfield, MA MSA.	530	6.6	0.2	1.0	9.0

1990 Census Note: The population counts set forth herein are subject to possible correction for undercount or overcount. The United States Department of Commerce is considering whether to correct these counts and will publish corrected counts, if any, not later than July 15, 1991.

[1] Metropolitan areas are shown in rank order of total population of consolidated metropolitan statistical areas (CMSA) and metropolitan statistical areas (MSA).   [2] Persons of Hispanic origin may be of any race.

Source: U.S. Bureau of the Census, press release CB91-66 and unpublished data.

Illustration 2-10 (cont.)

Population

No. 37. Metropolitan Areas with Large Numbers of Selected Racial Groups and of Hispanic Origin Population: 1990

[As of April 1. For Black, Hispanic origin, and Asian and Pacific Islander populations, areas selected had 100,000 or more of specified group; for American Indian, Eskimo, and Aleut population, areas selected are ten areas with largest number of that group. CMSA=consolidated metropolitan statistical area. MSA=metropolitan statistical area. For definitions and components of all metropolitan statistical areas, see Appendix II]

METROPOLITAN AREA	Number of specified group (1,000)	Percent of total metro.	METROPOLITAN AREA	Number of specified group (1,000)	Percent of total metro.
BLACK			**HISPANIC ORIGIN** [1]		
New York-Northern New Jersey-Long Island, NY-NJ-CT CMSA	3,289	18.2	Los Angeles-Anaheim-Riverside, CA CMSA	4,779	32.9
Chicago-Gary-Lake County (IL), IL-IN-WI CMSA	1,548	19.2	New York-Northern New Jersey-Long Island, NY-NJ-CT CMSA	2,778	15.4
Los Angeles-Anaheim-Riverside, CA CMSA	1,230	8.5	Miami-Fort Lauderdale, FL CMSA	1,062	33.3
Philadelphia-Wilmington-Trenton, PA-NJ-DE-MD CMSA	1,100	18.7	San Francisco-Oakland-San Jose, CA CMSA	970	15.5
Washington, DC-MD-VA MSA	1,042	26.6	Chicago-Gary-Lake County (IL), IL-IN-WI CMSA	893	11.1
Detroit-Ann Arbor, MI CMSA	975	20.9	Houston-Galveston-Brazoria, TX CMSA	772	20.8
Atlanta, GA MSA	736	26.0	San Antonio, TX MSA	620	47.6
Houston-Galveston-Brazoria, TX CMSA	665	17.9	Dallas-Fort Worth, TX CMSA	519	13.4
Baltimore, MD MSA	616	25.9	San Diego, CA MSA	511	20.4
Miami-Fort Lauderdale, FL CMSA	591	18.5	El Paso, TX MSA	412	69.6
Dallas-Fort Worth, TX CMSA	555	14.3	Phoenix, AZ MSA	345	16.3
San Francisco-Oakland-San Jose, CA CMSA	538	8.6	McAllen-Edinburg-Mission, TX MSA	327	85.2
Cleveland-Akron-Lorain, OH CMSA	442	16.0	Fresno, CA MSA	237	35.5
New Orleans, LA MSA	430	34.7	Denver-Boulder, CO CMSA	226	12.2
St. Louis, MO-IL MSA	423	17.3	Philadelphia-Wilmington-Trenton, PA-NJ-DE-MD CMSA	226	3.8
Memphis, TN-AR-MS MSA	399	40.6	Washington, DC-MD-VA MSA	225	5.7
Norfolk-Virginia Beach-Newport News, VA MSA	398	28.5	Brownsville-Harlingen, TX MSA	213	81.9
Richmond-Petersburg, VA MSA	252	29.2	Boston-Lawrence-Salem, MA-NH CMSA	193	4.6
Birmingham, AL MSA	246	27.1	Corpus Christi, TX MSA	182	52.0
Boston-Lawrence-Salem, MA-NH CMSA	239	5.7	Albuquerque, NM MSA	178	37.1
Charlotte-Gastonia-Rock Hill, NC-SC MSA	232	19.9	Sacramento, CA MSA	172	11.6
Milwaukee-Racine, WI CMSA	214	13.3	Tucson, AZ MSA	163	24.5
Cincinnati-Hamilton, OH-KY-IN CMSA	204	11.7	Austin, TX MSA	160	20.5
Kansas City, MO-KS MSA	201	12.8	Bakersfield, CA MSA	152	28.0
Tampa-St. Petersburg-Clearwater, FL MSA	186	9.0	Tampa-St. Petersburg-Clearwater, FL MSA	139	6.7
Raleigh-Durham, NC MSA	183	24.9	Laredo, TX MSA	125	93.9
Greensboro—Winston-Salem—High Point, NC MSA	182	19.3	Visalia-Tulare-Porterville, CA MSA	121	38.8
Jacksonville, FL MSA	181	20.0	Salinas-Seaside-Monterey, CA MSA	120	33.6
Pittsburgh-Beaver Valley, PA CMSA	179	8.0	Stockton, CA MSA	113	23.4
Indianapolis, IN MSA	172	13.8	**ASIAN AND PACIFIC ISLANDER**		
Jackson, MS MSA	168	42.5	Los Angeles-Anaheim-Riverside, CA CMSA	1,339	9.2
Columbus, OH MSA	165	12.0	San Francisco-Oakland-San Jose, CA CMSA	927	14.8
San Diego, CA MSA	159	6.4	New York-Northern New Jersey-Long Island, NY-NJ-CT CMSA	873	4.8
Baton Rouge, LA MSA	157	29.6	Honolulu, HI MSA	526	63.0
Charleston, SC MSA	153	30.2	Chicago-Gary-Lake County (IL), IL-IN-WI CMSA	256	3.2
Nashville, TN MSA	152	15.5	Washington, DC-MD-VA MSA	202	5.2
Columbia, SC MSA	138	30.4	San Diego, CA MSA	198	7.9
Orlando, FL MSA	133	12.4	Seattle-Tacoma, WA CMSA	164	6.4
Mobile, AL MSA	131	27.4	Houston-Galveston-Brazoria, TX CMSA	132	3.6
Dayton-Springfield, OH MSA	126	13.3	Philadelphia-Wilmington-Trenton, PA-NJ-DE-MD CMSA	123	2.1
Louisville, KY-IN MSA	125	13.1	Boston-Lawrence-Salem, MA-NH CMSA	121	2.9
Augusta, GA-SC MSA	123	31.1	Sacramento, CA MSA	115	7.7
Seattle-Tacoma, WA MSA	123	4.8	**AMERICAN INDIAN, ESKIMO, ALEUT**		
Buffalo-Niagara Falls, NY CMSA	122	10.3	Los Angeles-Anaheim-Riverside, CA CMSA	87	0.6
Shreveport, LA MSA	117	35.0	Tulsa, OK MSA	48	6.8
Greenville-Spartanburg, SC MSA	111	17.4	New York-Northern New Jersey-Long Island, NY-NJ-CT CMSA	46	0.3
West Palm Beach-Boca Raton-Delray Beach, FL MSA	108	12.5	Oklahoma City, OK MSA	46	4.8
Montgomery, AL MSA	105	36.0	San Francisco-Oakland-San Jose, CA CMSA	41	0.7
Sacramento, CA MSA	102	6.9	Phoenix, AZ MSA	38	1.8
Little Rock-North Little Rock, AR MSA	102	19.9	Seattle-Tacoma, WA CMSA	32	1.3
Oklahoma City, OK MSA	101	10.5	Minneapolis-St. Paul, MN-WI CMSA	24	1.0
			Tucson, AZ MSA	20	3.0
			San Diego, CA MSA	20	0.8

1990 Census Note: The population counts set forth herein are subject to possible correction for undercount or overcount. The United States Department of Commerce is considering whether to correct these counts and will publish corrected counts, if any, not later than July 15, 1991.

[1] Persons of Hispanic origin may be of any race.

Source: U.S. Bureau of the Census, unpublished data.

Illustration 2-11

Population

No. 29. State Population Projections: 1995 and 2000

[In thousands. As of July 1. These projections were prepared prior to the release of 1990 census results and are therefore not based on 1990 census data. For explanation of methodology, see text, section 1]

REGION, DIVISION, AND STATE	1995				2000			
	Series A	Series B	Series C	Series D	Series A	Series B	Series C	Series D
U.S.	259,620	259,620	259,620	259,620	267,748	267,748	267,748	267,748
Northeast	51,665	50,976	51,357	52,553	52,419	51,005	51,662	53,583
N.E.	13,575	13,320	13,498	13,427	14,002	13,486	13,788	13,647
ME	1,295	1,275	1,301	1,243	1,344	1,313	1,359	1,262
NH	1,276	1,196	1,270	1,128	1,410	1,255	1,373	1,148
VT.	597	582	597	582	619	594	619	593
MA	6,032	5,913	5,939	6,096	6,159	5,909	5,959	6,190
RI	1,021	1,005	1,027	1,030	1,048	1,010	1,046	1,049
CT.	3,354	3,349	3,363	3,348	3,422	3,405	3,432	3,405
M.A	38,090	37,656	37,859	39,126	38,417	37,519	37,874	39,936
NY.	17,909	17,724	17,727	18,857	17,966	17,548	17,563	19,412
NJ.	8,100	7,991	8,062	8,050	8,382	8,119	8,238	8,229
PA.	12,080	11,942	12,070	12,219	12,069	11,852	12,073	12,295
Midwest.	60,712	60,914	61,213	62,665	60,528	61,342	61,815	64,231
E.N.C	42,678	42,631	43,066	44,079	42,557	42,779	43,499	45,176
OH	10,958	10,889	11,027	11,237	10,930	10,869	11,096	11,436
IN	5,688	5,656	5,738	5,785	5,696	5,697	5,831	5,910
IL	11,759	11,795	11,814	12,337	11,722	11,856	11,887	12,765
MI	9,364	9,317	9,534	9,653	9,365	9,331	9,692	9,879
WI	4,908	4,974	4,954	5,067	4,844	5,027	4,993	5,186
W.N.C	18,035	18,283	18,146	18,586	17,971	18,563	18,316	19,055
MN	4,501	4,481	4,513	4,542	4,566	4,568	4,615	4,672
IA	2,703	2,825	2,741	2,949	2,549	2,808	2,671	3,013
MO	5,353	5,320	5,369	5,331	5,473	5,425	5,495	5,434
ND	631	687	635	705	596	698	615	728
SD.	719	733	720	751	715	746	723	775
NE.	1,582	1,641	1,595	1,682	1,539	1,660	1,583	1,730
KS.	2,546	2,597	2,574	2,626	2,534	2,658	2,613	2,703
South	91,227	91,317	90,781	89,132	95,575	95,382	94,483	91,750
S.A.	47,859	45,767	47,034	44,106	51,930	47,770	49,843	44,966
DE.	739	690	723	690	802	706	760	704
MD	5,180	4,908	5,090	4,830	5,608	5,073	5,370	4,936
DC.	592	593	590	645	595	588	586	660
VA.	6,758	6,475	6,676	6,320	7,275	6,741	7,066	6,482
WV	1,749	1,883	1,779	1,929	1,651	1,882	1,717	1,958
NC	7,197	6,943	7,102	6,702	7,717	7,226	7,492	6,803
SC.	3,772	3,733	3,769	3,645	3,962	3,894	3,956	3,743
GA	7,288	6,949	7,196	6,682	8,005	7,329	7,733	6,882
FL.	14,583	13,593	14,110	12,663	16,315	14,330	15,162	12,798
E.S.C	15,978	16,125	16,146	16,020	16,242	16,603	16,636	16,419
KY.	3,740	3,832	3,785	3,886	3,689	3,887	3,813	3,978
TN.	5,239	5,199	5,288	5,068	5,424	5,386	5,533	5,156
AL.	4,282	4,331	4,345	4,279	4,358	4,474	4,498	4,383
MS	2,717	2,764	2,727	2,787	2,772	2,856	2,791	2,902
W.S.C	27,390	29,425	27,602	29,006	27,402	31,009	28,004	30,365
AR.	2,473	2,528	2,501	2,486	2,509	2,615	2,562	2,544
LA.	4,274	4,690	4,316	4,725	4,141	4,868	4,258	4,927
OK	3,072	3,466	3,105	3,389	2,924	3,624	3,042	3,481
TX.	17,572	18,741	17,680	18,406	17,828	19,903	18,142	19,413
West	56,015	56,412	56,269	55,271	59,226	60,019	59,788	58,186
Mt	14,515	14,940	14,581	14,381	15,207	15,922	15,326	15,048
MT	774	861	780	839	744	897	766	858
ID	1,018	1,126	1,036	1,093	1,008	1,202	1,056	1,156
WY	439	546	446	523	409	582	430	550
CO	3,407	3,656	3,460	3,525	3,424	3,861	3,548	3,649
NM	1,639	1,697	1,642	1,624	1,735	1,818	1,727	1,701
AZ	4,149	3,899	4,097	3,692	4,633	4,149	4,457	3,809
UT.	1,807	1,930	1,841	1,963	1,845	2,082	1,929	2,166
NV.	1,283	1,225	1,279	1,122	1,409	1,331	1,414	1,159
Pac	41,500	41,473	41,688	40,890	44,019	44,097	44,462	43,138
WA	5,052	5,185	5,157	4,919	5,191	5,535	5,477	5,076
OR	2,887	3,032	2,960	2,906	2,903	3,206	3,086	2,986
CA.	31,749	31,390	31,780	31,307	33,963	33,328	33,981	33,218
AK.	560	609	538	578	599	655	550	614
HI	1,253	1,256	1,253	1,180	1,362	1,373	1,368	1,244

Source: U.S. Bureau of the Census, *Current Population Reports*, series P-25, No. 1053.

Illustration 2-11 (cont.)

Population Projections

No. 30. Population Projections, by Age—States: 2000

[As of July 1. These projections were prepared prior to the release of 1990 census results and are therefore not based on 1990 census data. For explanation of methodology, see text, section 1]

REGION, DIVISION, AND STATE	UNDER 18 YEARS				18-64 YEARS				65 YEARS AND OVER			
	Series A	Series B	Series C	Series D	Series A	Series B	Series C	Series D	Series A	Series B	Series C	Series D
U.S.	65,713	65,715	65,716	65,714	167,156	167,147	167,152	167,149	34,884	34,884	34,876	34,880
Northeast	12,229	11,787	12,006	12,148	32,841	31,892	32,329	33,617	7,351	7,323	7,328	7,817
N.E.	3,249	3,082	3,181	3,044	8,869	8,516	8,720	8,652	1,885	1,886	1,888	1,950
ME	333	319	335	296	834	817	845	789	176	178	179	176
NH	351	303	339	268	906	804	881	736	153	148	153	143
VT.	156	147	155	143	391	375	392	379	72	71	72	72
MA	1,393	1,317	1,336	1,360	3,913	3,738	3,775	3,935	854	853	849	895
RI	236	224	235	232	660	633	657	660	152	152	153	157
CT.	780	772	781	745	2,165	2,149	2,170	2,153	478	484	482	507
M.A	8,980	8,705	8,825	9,104	23,972	23,376	23,609	24,965	5,466	5,437	5,440	5,867
NY.	4,200	4,085	4,091	4,496	11,307	11,024	11,040	12,178	2,459	2,439	2,431	2,738
NJ.	2,003	1,922	1,961	1,868	5,228	5,053	5,131	5,161	1,152	1,143	1,146	1,200
PA.	2,777	2,698	2,773	2,740	7,437	7,299	7,438	7,626	1,855	1,855	1,863	1,929
Midwest.	15,138	15,393	15,553	15,755	37,375	37,865	38,171	39,934	8,012	8,086	8,089	8,541
E.N.C	10,682	10,731	10,975	11,037	26,398	26,527	26,981	28,224	5,478	5,520	5,542	5,913
OH	2,694	2,671	2,746	2,741	6,766	6,723	6,867	7,131	1,469	1,475	1,483	1,563
IN	1,427	1,424	1,469	1,428	3,542	3,538	3,624	3,713	727	734	738	769
IL	2,981	3,016	3,031	3,210	7,265	7,355	7,355	7,927	1,477	1,485	1,484	1,628
MI	2,365	2,350	2,468	2,386	5,860	5,832	6,061	6,237	1,140	1,148	1,163	1,255
WI	1,215	1,270	1,261	1,272	2,965	3,079	3,057	3,216	665	678	674	698
W.N.C.	4,456	4,662	4,578	4,718	10,977	11,340	11,190	11,710	2,534	2,566	2,547	2,628
MN	1,148	1,146	1,164	1,150	2,834	2,835	2,864	2,916	584	588	587	606
IA	608	692	650	727	1,536	1,700	1,613	1,848	404	416	408	438
MO	1,352	1,335	1,358	1,327	3,351	3,320	3,366	3,336	769	771	771	771
ND	145	183	153	189	366	427	377	445	85	88	85	94
SD.	190	202	194	208	421	439	427	459	103	105	103	109
NE.	385	430	402	438	925	998	951	1,053	228	233	229	238
KS.	628	674	657	679	1,544	1,621	1,592	1,653	361	365	364	372
South	23,259	23,271	22,936	22,756	59,581	59,452	58,900	57,113	12,735	12,660	12,649	11,881
S.A.	12,190	10,891	11,543	10,406	32,445	29,816	31,135	28,154	7,294	7,063	7,167	6,405
DE.	199	169	186	170	501	440	475	439	101	98	100	94
MD	1,373	1,207	1,299	1,119	3,613	3,266	3,459	3,194	622	600	612	624
DC.	106	102	102	148	409	407	405	427	80	79	79	85
VA.	1,734	1,554	1,660	1,457	4,734	4,394	4,603	4,233	807	793	803	791
WV	375	446	397	453	1,025	1,171	1,067	1,229	251	264	254	276
NC	1,809	1,641	1,729	1,525	4,910	4,601	4,769	4,353	997	984	994	924
SC.	987	960	982	929	2,505	2,465	2,504	2,369	469	469	470	446
GA	2,087	1,861	1,995	1,741	5,094	4,661	4,919	4,365	825	808	820	776
FL.	3,520	2,951	3,193	2,864	9,654	8,411	8,934	7,545	3,142	2,968	3,035	2,389
E.S.C	3,992	4,091	4,109	4,055	10,116	10,306	10,371	10,242	2,135	2,163	2,156	2,122
KY.	887	948	926	967	2,312	2,437	2,390	2,504	491	501	496	507
TN.	1,256	1,233	1,283	1,184	3,453	3,436	3,529	3,275	714	717	721	698
AL.	1,093	1,130	1,140	1,090	2,687	2,757	2,774	2,722	578	587	585	571
MS	756	780	760	814	1,664	1,719	1,678	1,741	352	358	354	346
W.S.C.	7,077	8,289	7,284	8,295	17,020	19,287	17,394	18,717	3,306	3,434	3,326	3,354
AR.	618	647	633	639	1,512	1,577	1,545	1,540	379	391	384	365
LA.	1,105	1,356	1,147	1,381	2,991	3,491	2,608	3,015	501	521	504	531
OK	683	919	724	861	1,818	2,253	1,890	2,173	423	452	427	448
TX.	4,671	5,367	4,780	5,414	11,154	12,466	11,351	11,989	2,003	2,070	2,011	2,010
West.	15,087	15,264	15,221	15,055	37,359	37,938	37,752	36,485	6,786	6,815	6,810	6,641
Mt	4,025	4,268	4,065	4,118	9,410	9,865	9,485	9,245	1,776	1,788	1,772	1,680
MT	179	231	187	212	465	561	478	537	100	105	100	110
ID	276	347	294	334	614	728	641	697	118	127	120	124
WY	109	169	116	152	263	372	276	352	38	41	38	46
CO	813	940	849	882	2,242	2,534	2,325	2,376	370	386	373	390
NM	485	513	483	474	1,057	1,105	1,051	1,032	193	200	193	194
AZ.	1,188	1,031	1,131	996	2,796	2,502	2,688	2,297	649	616	638	514
UT.	651	743	683	789	1,036	1,172	1,084	1,213	159	167	161	163
NV.	324	294	322	279	937	891	942	741	149	146	149	139
Pac	11,062	10,996	11,156	10,937	27,949	28,073	28,267	27,240	5,010	5,027	5,038	4,961
WA	1,225	1,333	1,316	1,192	3,364	3,584	3,547	3,281	602	618	613	602
OR	689	781	745	704	1,839	2,033	1,955	1,901	375	393	385	381
CA.	8,664	8,379	8,626	8,601	21,471	21,135	21,516	20,847	3,829	3,813	3,838	3,770
AK.	174	191	158	176	397	437	367	398	29	27	26	40
HI	310	312	311	264	878	884	882	813	175	176	176	168

Source: U.S. Bureau of the Census, Current Population Reports, series P-25, No. 1053.

levels are met, pay interest only, or in other fashions restructure the debt in order to create a proper return on equity. Leverage may be as high as 100% of the purchase price, in some instances. Such terms are not available during times of prosperity where the leverage remains in the hands of the seller.

- **Taste and Fashion** - Trends in housing are much more effected than in the area of commercial and industrial properties in this area, other than where these properties may be impacted by environmental concerns, such as asbestos, unreinforced brick buildings, methane gas emissions, lead exposure, toxic chemicals and the like. This will be covered in Chapter seven.

- **Public Confidence** - During the early 1990s, public confidence had been eroded to shocking levels. It is difficult to determine whether it is a product of the media through constant negative reports concerning economic matters or whether this represents the **true** public attitude. Nonetheless, the results are the same. The public serves as a major barometer in economic weather forecasting. If the public decides that big ticket items are not on their purchasing agenda for a particular time, big ticket sales will suffer dramatically. Conversely, if the attitude changes, big ticket sales will soar, prices will rise due to a shortage of supplies and the factors of supply and demand affecting price will be in place. A quick study of the media will give one a fairly good impression of the level of public confidence. Lack of confidence is a killer to sales of tangibles and intangibles.

- **Taxes** - A definite concern to all real estate investors is the attitude of our government concerning the tax advantages of real estate ownership. Chapter nine will have an in-depth discussion of these implications. For prediction purposes, investors should follow the major business publications who tend to take the pulse of government concerning attitudes towards capital gains, allowable deductions, tax deferred exchanges, tax shelters and the like.

Real estate investors should be **anticipatory** and not **reactionary**. The rational mind will end up the winner in the investment race. By looking at some of the early warning signs, and there were many during the early 1990s, astute investors can anticipate entry of attractive real estate investments at reasonable levels of return to be introduced to the market place. Cooling economies occur once inflation levels have discouraged major ticket purchasers and buyers withdraw from the market place. Employment, due to reduction in demand, ebbs. Population outflow from one area can be a boon to another. The classic example is the relocation of east coast residents to the sun belt states. Funds availability for financing is also a key factor. This is closely related to savings levels. In the United States, a consumer based economy, our savings rate has been at a tepid three to five percent of our incomes for the past several years, while Japan, a large investor in our government obligations, has a savings rate exceeding 20 percent! Financing rates for real estate remained at highly attractive levels during 1992 due to **lack of demand**, not through increased supplies of funds for that purpose. This implies that investors have a unique window of opportunity to maximize yield on real estate acquisitions during a unique period such as this.

HOW TO SELECT THE PROPER TIME TO INVEST WITHIN THE CYCLE

The best approach in analyzing a cycle for advantageous real estate investing is to carefully study the various cyclical supply/demand components and track their activity. There are several useful sources to aid you in this quest. **Economic Indicators** is a monthly publication available from the U.S. Government Printing office in Washington, D.C. The data contained therein is probably the most recent available for determining economic trending. Each of the Federal Reserve Banks offers publications of economic interest to subscribers examining various segments of the economy including the real estate arena. **The Statistical Abstract of The United States** is a Department of Commerce publication with extremely valuable economic information that is published on an annual basis. For those individuals that are interesting in investment in a particular state, there are usually in state publications, such as the **California Almanac**, which provides information on a regional basis. For those who want to pinpoint a particular area of study, local chambers of commerce, media sources and local libraries provide a wealth of information from an historical and economic standpoint about the area.

As the introduction to this chapter indicated, the timing of an investment in real estate is critical. Those who invest right at the peak of economic expansion are usually the big losers in the market place. Just as in any supply/demand situation, the greatest advantage comes to the buyer who enters the market place with an overabundance of supply and relatively little demand to drive up prices. During a market of this nature the best buys are available. The question of **what** to buy and **how** to buy become critical components of the investment decision. The unique situation developed in the early 1990s with Federal Deposit Insurance

Corporation and the Resolution Trust Corporation turning into mass liquidators in the market place contributes to a burgeoning supply that seems to be limitless in its scope. Probably one of the areas hardest hit by this abundance is office buildings, retail and industrial properties. The raw land categories represent the highest investment risk due to the "as is" label placed on this property by the regulators. In one instance the RTC has an "environmental" package which is the ultimate oxymoron. This so-called "package" represents properties with various ecological problems ranging from toxic waste to other types of environmental clean up needs that can inflate acquisition costs to the point of obscurity.

As the new administration takes office in 1993, real estate investors have several areas of the country which offer unique opportunities for the astute. Taking advantage of these opportunities requires evaluation of one's entire portfolio to determine if a real estate investment will provide the proper balance in the process of estate planning and future growth of capital.

Carl Sandburg said:

> "Lay me on an anvil, O God.
> Beat me and hammer me into a crowbar.
> Let me pry loose old walls.
> Leave me lift and loosen old foundations."

Never was there a greater need for flexibility in the world of investment. Real estate is but one possibility. The following chapter will explore the competition and show how real estate can compatibly serve to compliment a diverse portfolio.

3
ATTAINING BALANCE IN YOUR INVESTMENT PORTFOLIO

INVESTMENT ALTERNATIVES

In John Maynard Keynes **A Treatise on Money**, published in 1930 he noted:
> "The engine that drives Enterprise is **not** Thrift, but **Profit.**"

These sage words are as applicable today as they were some six decades ago. The only possible modification of Lord Keynes' observation would be that investors characteristically should have some liquidity back up for unforseen events.

In any case, when establishing any investment strategy, individual investors must pose some pertinent questions:

- How much capital is to be devoted to investment?
- What are the basic investment objectives?
- Is the investment compatible with tax and estate planning?
- What type of investment portfolio meets the criteria after the first three questions have been answered?

With respect to the first query, the amount of capital available may serve as a limitation of investment alternatives. One who allocates $10,000 to invest does not have the same type of investment products available as others with several million to dicker in the market place. To those with limited capital, its preservation is of prime concern. More affluent investors may be more willing to take the entrepreneurial approach of risk taking in certain areas. Also flexibility in the components of investment portfolios is readily available to those who have adequate capital to pursue alternative profit centers to channel their savings dollar.

In the case of one with lesser amounts available, some form of savings plan in a F.D.I.C. insured account or possibly a treasury bill investment would minimize the incidence of capital loss.

As far as those with a six or seven figure portfolio potential, it is important to explore the wide variety of investment products and their features.

Creation of any assets marshalling plan involves the establishment of suitable criteria to meet specific guidelines. A basic foundation of goals and objectives serves this purpose. For example, if a certain amount of monies is required to be devoted to the providing future college tuition for minor children, deferred annuities might be an appropriate investment to assure availability of tuition monies at the time the children reach college age. Conversely, if short-term liquidity is an objective, bond investments would not normally be pursued due to their extended maturity. On the other hand, if long-term growth was in the investment plan, stocks and real estate might be considered. Many seniors who have limited income may opt for investments that supplant social security payments while protecting capital adequacy. In each specific instance decision making evolves around the amount of risk willing to be assumed by the investing party.

Within the investment matrix, tax and estate planning play a key role. Prudent portfolio formation can mitigate the effect of both income and estate taxes. If the estate is sizeable, professional advice may be required to properly assess investment alternatives. This phase will be discussed in more detail in Chapter nine.

Portfolio composition is a function of analyzing investment alternatives, tax-wise and otherwise; weighing their consequences; and providing a balancing strategy that will mitigate the risk of loss in the long run. The market place provides a wide variety of products to lure capricious dollars from the investment community. Illustration 3-1 shows some of the investment instruments that are generated by the nation's banking system. Financial intermediaries provide various types of demand deposit (checking) and savings account products such as the following:

- **Checking Accounts** - These type of accounts are normally used by individuals and business to handle payments relative to household obligations or the daily operations of the firm. In certain cases, these accounts may pay nominal interest on the average collected balances. Bank charges for servicing these accounts may be waived dependent upon the average collected monthly balance or the customer's age. Many financial institutions waive charges for seniors as well as establish senior clubs to encourage their deposits which tend to be larger in size than their more youthful counterparts.

- **Insured Money Market Accounts** - When capital is not immediately needed for current operations, these demand deposit (checking) accounts serve as a backup to up to regular checking accounts. Check writing is limited to three checks or a combination of six transactions, when over the counter (at the branch location where the account is housed) withdrawals are involved. If withdrawal activity in the form of checks or withdrawals exceeds the limitation, the customer is penalized by service charge. If the activity of this nature is repetitive in nature, the account may be closed. The reason for this is the fact that the objective of the account is to house funds that will remain over an extended period in exchange for an interest return in excess of normal term savings rate, but somewhat less than rates available on certificates of deposit.

- **Savings Accounts** - The regular savings account does not have the popularity that it enjoyed during Regulation Q days where there were no alternative investment products available. Today the list of alternatives is endless. The advantage of a regular savings account is the fact that unlimited withdrawals are available on an as-needed basis. What many clients do not realize when they sign their signature cards with a financial institution is the fact that the institution has the option to defer a withdrawal request for 30 days from the date of the request. From a practical standpoint financial institutions do not enforce this provision, but it serves as a grim lesson learned from the "bank holidays" of the 1930s which saw runs on even the most stable institutions of the day.

- **Certificates of Deposit** - These savings instruments may range in maturity from seven days to several years, at the option of the depositor. Larger deposits (those over $100,000 and $1,000,000, respectively) can usually command a higher rate structure. The Wall Street Journal regularly publishes average rates on these instruments on a daily basis allowing customers to judge how the rate offered by their bank or thrift measures to the market place. This area served to create the demise of many financial institutions during the 1980s, as they were forced to pay premium rates for broker-controlled deposits in order to prop up essentially non-performing loan portfolios. One of the factors that actually increased the cost of the thrift crisis was the continuing of this activity by the regulators after takeover, but prior to closure of the institution which added considerably to the cost of liquidation.

Everyone is relatively familiar with the various accounts available through banks and thrifts. Due to the fact that these institutions are financial intermediaries (i.e., they take depositors cash which serves as their liabilities to convert assets in the form of loans and investments) they serve as a conduit for depositor's monies to create higher yielding assets than most of the depositors could on a direct basis. For example, how many account holders have the ability to fully fund a $100,000 real estate loan which is effected in multiples by the institution where they bank? If the institution is a mutual one, the depositors are also the owners and share in the institution's successes and failures.

Individual Retirement Accounts (IRAs) have allowed banks and thrifts to attract longer term deposits with tax deferred advantages to the depositor by deferring tax impact until withdrawal from these accounts between the ages of 59 and one half and 70 and one half. Due to the fact that returns from this source vary with the fluctuations in the money market a conscious decision must be made to commit these monies for a longer time period in a certificate of deposit account, rather than money market accommodations in order to freeze in higher rates when they are available. Many IRA account holders opt for self-managed accounts in order to increase yields in anticipation of building a more substantial capital base for retirement years. Some have sought real estate investment as one means of fulfilling the objective to outperform the money market in their investment activities.

The advantages of financial intermediaries sometimes also represent drawbacks in this form of investment vehicle, since returns are limited in the form of interest or dividends and, after a minimal tax credit, are subject to income tax on both the state and federal levels.

In recent years through holding company devices and other arrangements, banks and thrifts have entered into a variety of investment activities beyond merely offering accounts to customers. Competition has forced them into this aggressive posture as a means of preserving their depository customers. The prohibition of stock brokerage activities under the Glass-Steagall Act has pretty well been circumvented and now many banks have investment departments that handle financial products in a similar fashion to stock brokerage operations in these subsidiary activities.

Some of the investment vehicles available through the stock brokerage community are the following:

Illustration 3-1

COMPONENTS OF MONEY STOCK AND LIQUID ASSETS

[Averages of daily figures; billions of dollars, seasonally adjusted, except as noted by NSA]

Period	Currency	Demand deposits	Other checkable deposits its (OCDs)	Overnight repurchase agreements (RPs), net, plus overnight Eurodollars [1]	Money market mutual fund balances [2] General purpose and broker/dealer	Institution only	Savings deposits, including money market deposit accounts (MMDAs)	Small denomination time deposits [3]	Large denomination time deposits [3]	Term repurchase agreements (RPs)	Term Eurodollars (net)	Savings bonds	Shortterm Treasury securities	Bankers' acceptances	Commercial paper
				NSA							NSA	NSA			
1982: Dec	132.5	234.0	103.7	39.9	184.5	51.1	398.5	847.2	323.3	33.4	81.7	68.0	183.6	44.5	113.7
1983: Dec	146.2	238.5	131.8	55.6	138.3	42.7	684.0	780.8	324.8	49.9	91.5	71.1	211.9	45.0	133.2
1984: Dec	156.1	243.9	147.2	60.6	167.1	63.7	704.2	884.9	415.6	57.6	82.9	74.2	260.9	45.4	160.8
1985: Dec	167.9	266.7	179.7	73.5	176.1	65.8	814.4	881.7	436.1	62.4	76.5	79.5	298.2	42.0	207.5
1986: Dec	180.8	302.0	235.3	82.3	208.0	86.1	940.1	854.8	439.5	80.6	83.8	91.8	ʳ279.8	37.1	231.2
1987: Dec	197.0	286.8	259.3	84.1	221.7	92.1	937.0	917.5	489.1	106.0	91.0	100.6	ʳ252.8	44.3	260.5
1988: Dec	212.3	286.5	280.6	83.2	241.9	91.0	926.2	1,032.9	541.2	121.8	105.7	109.4	ʳ268.8	39.8	336.1
1989: Dec	222.6	279.0	285.1	77.6	316.3	107.2	891.2	1,148.5	559.3	99.1	79.5	117.5	ʳ324.4	40.1	348.6
1990: Dec	246.8	277.1	293.9	74.7	348.9	133.7	920.7	1,168.7	494.9	89.6	68.7	126.0	ʳ331.3	34.0	359.3
1991: Dec	267.3	289.5	333.2	76.3	360.5	179.1	1,042.6	1,063.0	437.1	70.4	57.2	137.9	ʳ316.2	23.3	339.7
1991: Aug	261.3	280.1	317.3	67.6	362.4	158.6	994.1	1,120.8	465.5	78.2	63.6	134.4	ʳ328.9	27.2	336.3
Sept	262.9	280.6	320.6	66.9	359.9	162.6	1,002.4	1,111.0	458.5	76.5	61.5	135.2	ʳ321.2	25.8	337.7
Oct	264.8	283.8	324.5	70.1	359.3	168.2	1,015.0	1,095.2	450.0	75.2	62.8	136.1	ʳ319.7	25.3	336.2
Nov	266.0	287.6	329.7	73.8	359.5	173.6	1,028.7	1,079.2	442.3	73.3	61.5	137.1	ʳ322.9	24.5	337.9
Dec	267.3	289.5	333.2	76.3	360.5	179.1	1,042.6	1,063.0	437.1	70.4	57.2	137.9	ʳ316.2	23.3	339.7
1992: Jan	269.4	293.9	339.0	77.8	ʳ358.6	182.4	1,061.2	1,042.9	427.9	70.3	55.3	138.9	ʳ310.0	23.2	334.8
Feb	271.6	305.1	346.3	77.8	ʳ361.7	188.2	1,083.9	1,019.8	420.7	71.5	55.9	140.1	ʳ320.0	22.9	327.5
Mar	271.8	309.6	349.5	74.8	ʳ358.3	185.3	1,098.0	1,002.8	413.0	73.0	57.9	141.2	ʳ327.8	22.2	337.0
Apr	273.6	311.2	350.0	72.8	ʳ355.3	189.2	1,111.2	985.3	405.7	72.2	55.0	142.4	ʳ327.7	21.6	341.7
May	274.7	315.1	356.4	69.4	ʳ356.1	194.8	1,122.4	968.7	400.9	73.0	ʳ52.8	143.5	ʳ329.0	22.0	329.4
June	276.2	311.0	356.7	72.3	ʳ354.2	199.7	1,127.0	956.2	395.3	73.0	ʳ52.3	144.6	ʳ333.5	22.0	347.1
July	ʳ278.9	315.6	ʳ358.4	72.8	ʳ350.8	207.7	1,134.3	941.7	388.5	71.6	ʳ51.7	145.9	ʳ325.5	21.7	ʳ350.3
Aug ʳ	282.3	320.7	362.7	76.1	349.1	217.2	1,145.5	925.9	384.6	71.9	50.6	ᴾ147.5	ᴾ329.3	ᴾ21.0	ᴾ352.4
Sept	286.4	327.8	366.9	74.3	344.1	217.2	1,159.4	912.2	379.9	73.2	47.8				

[1] Includes continuing contract RPs.
[2] Data prior to 1983 are not seasonally adjusted.
[3] Small denomination and large denomination deposits are those issued in amounts of less than $100,000 and more than $100,000, respectively.

NOTE.—Travelers checks of nonbank issuers are a component of money stock but are not shown here.

Source: Board of Governors of the Federal Reserve System.

Common and Preferred Stocks - Through listing on a variety of exchanges and, in some cases, unlisted variety, corporate America spreads its ownership among the investment community. The key to astute stock investment lies not only in the analysis of the basic value of the company stock, but the workings of the exchange where it is traded. Understanding the nuances of management changes, balance sheet and profit and loss analysis together with the myriad analytical pronunciations that are constantly cranked out by financial public relations pundits, it is difficult to separate the real from the fictional when it comes to stock investments. One of the areas that gets a lot of play from the stock brokers is a new stock issue. What they don't tell you is that if the stock issue is designed to provide new capital for the corporation only about 80 cents of the corporate dollar ever reaches the corporate coffers. Another ploy sometimes used is that large equity holders (usually part of the company top management) may cut a deal on a leveraged buy out to end up with cash for their position while the balance of the shareholders obtain stock in the leveraged survivor considerably diluted from their former equity ownership position. Stock holdings of **any** size require constant investor attention with possibilities of loss of capital and/or dividend income in hard times. When entering into stock investments one must separate the objectives of earnings versus long term growth, since there are few stocks which would satisfy both objectives. Either one chooses a stock for its earnings record or for the possibility of long term growth. Real estate investments may follow a similar pattern, depending upon the type of investment chosen.

Bonds represent obligations of the issuer which are secured in some fashion. This market is the one which is generally in direct competition for institutional funds with real estate loans. When one follows the yield pattern of the corporate bond market, long term trends in yields on real estate loans can be determined from this source. Since servicing real estate loans is somewhat more burdensome than bonds, there will be a rate differential of 50 to 100 basis points (a basis point is one hundredth of one percent), generally, between the two markets in the long run. The bellwether rate in the bond market is the 30 year treasury bond. This rate is one that is followed closely by the investment community. Other government obligations, such as tax-free municipal bonds, GNMAs, treasury notes, and the like serve as a smorgasbord of eclectic investment devices for investors who have the understanding and savvy to cope with this sophisticated market. The possibilities of capital loss are considerable in this market if liquidation of investment is required prior to the maturity of the basic investment instrument. In certain cases complete or partial exemption from income taxes on interest income may be available. Investment usually requires increments in multiples of $10,000.

Debentures or Commercial Paper also serve as another form of investment vehicle. Subordinated debentures (unsecured corporate obligations, in other words, a note) that were convertible to stock were a popular high yield investment vehicle offered by some of the highly leveraged real estate investment trusts of the early 1970s. In many cases it was an unfortunate, albeit costly, experiment. In the case of commercial paper, these are unsecured IOU's of commercial finance companies such as CIT (Ford's vehicle and equipment financing subsidiary), GMAC (General Motors Acceptance Corporation), Chrysler Financial and the like who turn to the money market financing their lending operations on the basis of these short term notes sold to investors based upon competitive market rates. Normally the rate paid on this paper is below New York prime. Interest on these obligations is taxable.

Mutual Funds use the basic investment philosophy of diversification as their base. A wide variety of these products are available to meet varying investment objectives. Usually a mutual fund is designed with a certain investment objective in mind. There are funds that concentrate on earnings, others on growth, still others on tax-exempt portfolios, and the list goes on. Careful study should be undertaken by the investor by reading the fund's prospectus as well as obtaining independent information concerning the fund's performance over time with other funds with the same objective. Heavy concentrations of a fund in one particular issue could be a sign of potential future weakness. How would an investor feel about a mutual fund that concentrated in asbestos related stocks, such as Manville, when the carcinogenic nature of the product was revealed to the public and the lawsuits started? Even with some diversity, the fund's performance could be eroded considerably by this event. With the exception of certain tax exempt funds, all income derived from this source is taxable.

Securitization Products are relatively new in the market place with real estate loans serving as the cutting edge of this new market device. Mortgage-backed securities are now openly accepted and freely traded in the market place. Joining this list of loan products that are securitized are auto paper, installment loan paper, credit card paper and other credit products created by the financial community. Latest to join the securitization parade is commercial real estate where securities are being offered underwritten by NYSE member companies for projects in excess of $10 million in size. This new device is to supplant the void created by insurance company's reluctance to take an aggressive stance in the commercial/industrial market while they are licking their wounds from the portfolio beatings endured in the late 1980s. Other securitization of real estate is accomplished through the sale of limited partnership interests by brokerages based upon the prospectus. This will be covered in detail in Chapters eight and nine. Certain partnership investments dealing with affordable housing have certain tax advantages. Generally the income derived from these investments is taxable.

Money Market Products offering varying yields are also offered by brokerages as a means of diverting these deposits which would normally go to the banking community allowing their customers easy access to transfer quickly into a hopefully attractive investment opportunity that might be afforded by the market. Again, interest on these products is generally taxable.

Retirement Products, whether they be of the 401K, Keogh or IRA variety are vigorously sought by the bankers and brokerage houses, since these funds represent long-term investment holdings. The law relative to suitable investment vehicles for retirement plans is somewhat complex. On an individual basis, IRA holders have the ability to self-direct their investments to see if they can outperform the market place. The down side to this activity is the possibility that the investment may not perform as well or become a total loss. Provision for the retirement years is an integral part of the financial planning process. Failure to prepare for this eventuality has caused considerable discomfort when retirement rolls around and there isn't sufficient income to live in the manner accustomed by the retiree.

The brokerage community deals with both debt and equity instruments offering a wide variety of products for the investor to choose. In order to gain any degree of sophistication in this type of investment activity requires considerable study and in-depth knowledge of the market place. Dealing with the customer's men in this business can be a harrowing experience. If your broker calls you on the phone to tout a stock, it may be to get rid of a large position in the company that has been acquired by his employer. They may have advanced knowledge of bad news about the company and want to unload it. This is not an isolated example, it happens. If one is fortunate enough to obtain a knowledgeable, astute and **honest** broker, hold on to this person for dear life. You can make a lot of money in any venture if you are positioned right. Now we come to the field of **real estate**. Again, the guidance of experts in this complex maze of product availability offers substantial rewards for **informed** investors.

Residential Property can be classified as **single family** and **multi-family**. Single family is defined as one to four residential units with multi-family being classified as five or more residential units. From an economic standpoint, residential investments do not usually offer the rewards that are available through investment in distressed commercial and industrial projects. Usually the return on investment is minimal or negative on single family properties and multi-family properties in urban areas lack the yields attendant to the risk of a substantial down payment required to acquire them. Additionally, long term appreciation has been tempered by the deterioration of the marketplace caused by the glut of properties, both distressed and otherwise, into the market place with lack of adequate buyer support to buoy prices. The no-qualifier single family loans of the late 1980s have come back to haunt real estate lenders who naively took the borrower's word for income levels with no verification. It now turns out that much of the income represented was created with a magic slate - totally fallacious. Particularly vulnerable, in California at least, are those homes in the $200,000 to $800,000 range which have gone begging during the lackluster sale days of the early 1990s. Affordability is the key issue as we enter the 21st century. Median incomes in California will probably be lower in the next decade after adjustment for inflation. The reason for this is the fact that our structural unemployment will find many job seekers accepting positions several pegs, money wise, below their previous positions. The 10.1% unemployment figure published for California in December, 1992 is probably closer to 15% due to the fact that unemployment is based on those who are still **receiving** or have **applied for** unemployment benefits. It fails completely to measure those who no longer collect or are totally discouraged from seeking employment that should also be counted as part of the work force but unable to find work. This high degree of unemployment also discourages investment in multi-family projects because of the increased management problems generated from high vacancy levels, collection and eviction problems that are attendant to an economy of this nature.

Commercial Property investments consist of office and retail space, which can range from a multi-story class A (steel and concrete) office to a lowly corner mini-mall. Each type of property displays its own unique form of management challenges. In Southern California, for example, there is a profusion of excess office space, yet they still have millions of feet planned for downtown Los Angeles in the future. It is the same with retail space which is suffering from the throes of a sharply battered economic climate. California investors, however, should not be disheartened by the current conditions, since there are business investment opportunities not only within the Golden State for commercial property investment, but windows of opportunity opening up throughout the country, many at California's expense. Chapter six will go into detail as to how under performing properties, when bought right and properly managed, can still offer attractive returns to the real estate investor.

Industrial Property runs the gamut from special purpose facilities like oil refineries to the massive warehouses of industrial cities like Commerce, Santa Fe Springs, Industry and La Puente. The pulse of America can be felt by the heartbeat of the machinery creating the goods out of raw materials carved from meadow, mine and forest distributed to the consumer by the avalanche. America invented the expression "shop 'til you drop" and it takes its mission very seriously. Our penchant for consumption also prevents our savings account from getting too fat along the way creating capital shortages. Illustration 3-2 provides an example of how industry fits into our economic turntable.

Trust Deeds, especially junior liens have always been popular with real estate professionals since their yields usually outperform other instruments in the market place. There is a reason for that because the risk of this investment is higher. If one takes on a junior lien, reserves of six months payments on senior obligations must be maintained in order to protect the junior position. When liens are held on properties in a declining market place, sometimes what appeared to be an adequate equity erodes to the point that foreclosure of a superior encumbrance will not be defended by the junior lienholder due to a lack of equity.

Real Estate Securities may be comprised of collateralized pools of notes, limited partnership interests, stock interests in real estate related activities or a variety of products that are real estate related. These types of investments require inquiring minds with an entrepreneurial flair. Those who enter into this investment kingdom must wear the crown of **knowledge**. Failure to be properly prepared and informed when dealing in this area does not afford the investor with the wide range of opportunities that buying with knowledge can afford. Chapter six will analyze opportunities to illustrate how properly prepared investors can maximize their hard earned dollars. It should be noted that much of real estate investing can be advantageous from a tax standpoint. The nature and extent of the investment has a direct bearing on the tax advantages available.

Heed well the words of Sinclair Lewis in **Babbitt** noting;

> "His name was George F. Babbitt, and he was nimble in the calling of selling houses for more than people could afford to pay."

Real estate investors should take the words of Lewis to heart. William Zeckendorf, Donald Trump and other major players in this country have felt the sting of overextension of their means. Invest wisely, but well, as we will see areas of opportunity present themselves all over this great country of ours in the next chapter.

Illustration 3-2

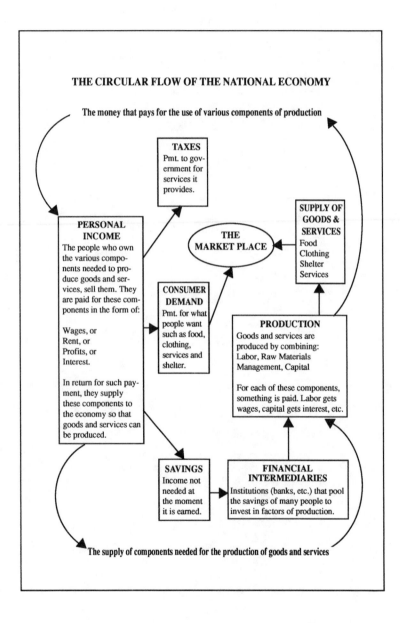

THE CIRCULAR FLOW OF THE NATIONAL ECONOMY

The money that pays for the use of various components of production

TAXES
Pmt. to government for services it provides.

SUPPLY OF GOODS & SERVICES
Food
Clothing
Shelter
Services

PERSONAL INCOME
The people who own the various components needed to produce goods and services, sell them. They are paid for these components in the form of:

Wages, or
Rent, or
Profits, or
Interest.

In return for such payment, they supply these components to the economy so that goods and services can be produced.

THE MARKET PLACE

CONSUMER DEMAND
Pmt. for what people want such as food, clothing, services and shelter.

PRODUCTION
Goods and services are produced by combining:
Labor, Raw Materials
Management, Capital

For each of these components, something is paid. Labor gets wages, capital gets interest, etc.

SAVINGS
Income not needed at the moment it is earned.

FINANCIAL INTERMEDIARIES
Institutions (banks, etc.) that pool the savings of many people to invest in factors of production.

The supply of components needed for the production of goods and services

4

HOW TO KNOW WHERE TO INVEST YOUR REAL ESTATE DOLLAR

NATIONAL TRENDS

Wendell Lewis Wilkie led a formidable presidential campaign in 1940 and in the process provided forward thinking concepts to be adopted by our Country in future years. The creed by which this man lived is inscribed on his grave in Rushville, Indiana:

> "I believe in America because in it we are free -
> free to choose our government, to speak our minds,
> to observe our different religions
> Because we are generous with our freedom we share
> our rights with those who disagree with us.
> Because we hate no people and covet no people's lands.
> Because we are blessed with a natural and varied abundance.
> Because we have great dreams and because we have the
> **opportunity** to make these dreams come true."

Arkansas has as its creed "The Land of Opportunity." For those visionaries pockets of twinkling stars of economic advantage can lie interspersed in a universe plagued with despair. Such is true in the harsh economic realities of the early 1990s. Opportunity lies far beyond the boundaries of Arkansas in one's quest for an appropriate real estate investment. With the January, 1993 inauguration of Bill Clinton as president, obviously there will be some Arkansas fall out that will benefit the new president's home state. What the investment community must consider is how the next four years of the presidential administration and its thrust will confer economic opportunities throughout our land.

Economics involves tracing the interaction involved in the production, exchange, consumption and distribution of goods and services within a given study area whether it be a hamlet, city, county, state, country or the international scene. The key to economic success in any given area is when production exceeds consumption leading to a "trade surplus," so to speak, in that given area of influence. Even with the devastating effect of the erosion of aerospace companies, the flight of motion pictures and television locales, weakness in tourism and the like, the sixty mile circle spreading out from Los Angeles City Hall is still one of the most powerful economies in the world. More will be addressed on this subject later in the chapter.

When one ponders the circular flow of our economy, as shown in Illustration 3-2, the interdependence of all of the elements shown above becomes crystal clear. The so-called lubricant that makes it work is **capital - our capital** which serves as the lubricant to make the whole economic system work through the conversion of **savings** into **investment vehicles.** Such conversion should only be accomplished on the basis of accumulation of the data necessary to make and **informed** decision.

National trends have significance on local activity. One clear national trend is emanating from executive suites throughout the country. Businesses that are personnel intensive, such as manufacturing and service industries are seeking methods of reducing staff, expanding the span of control and still being able to "deliver the goods" to the customer. Because of the escalating cost of benefits, full time help is being supplanted by part timers who receive no benefits. Those who can still avail themselves of benefits find themselves being exposed to "cafeteria plans" where they can select from an array of benefits that have a cost cap on them. This cost-effective approach which has almost reached paranoid levels, in certain cases, has filtered down to the consumer. No longer are many consumers satisfied with paying the higher costs of department stores and have opted for shopping at freeway-oriented "factory stores" or the so-called "power centers" where retail giants like Wal Mart, K-Mart, Marshalls, Ross, Circuit City, Home Base, Pace and Price Club ply their wares.

In the area of office space, different types of office layouts are emerging avoiding the paneled offices for partitioning. The era of electronics is causing a revolution in the manner that users are addressing officing in general. At the present time in this country there are in excess of five million people who conduct their office work at home. Through the means of computers, FAX machines, modems and the like, many workers avoid the daily commute and perform their tasks at home. **This trend will not abate, but only grow larger!** This does not mean that office space users will abandon space in droves. This just means that a different type of occupant will take their place. Many still feel the need for a business address. The Fegin suite concept first started out a few years ago geared to the legal profession where whole floors in office buildings were master leased and then sub-let to attorneys who would office there taking advantage of a community conference room, stenographic and answering service capabilities. This not only reduced personnel and rent costs, it was a very efficient mode of operation. Since the inception of this concept, many other users of smaller spaces have seen the advantages of this pooled arrangement and sought to sub-let spaces in this type of an arrangement.

The trends nationally in available office, retail and industrial space in the early 1990s are definitely tenant oriented in nature, since vacancy levels are in a state of imbalance leaning toward users and not landlords. This does not mean that there are not areas where acquisition of office space allowing proper cash flow does not hold opportunities through proper management allowing considerable potential for appreciation. Some specific areas of advantage will be covered later in this chapter.

Trends nationally evolve around people, their mobility, their job status and the buying power that they bring to the market place. Not only is population important, but the **composition** of the population in a given area as seen in some of the illustrations in Chapter two. The early 1990s show a fluidity in movement in our work force as companies are relocating to areas that allow them to reduce operating expenses and operate more efficiently. In some cases, such as Los Angeles, this represents moving from high cost housing areas where workers require higher compensation, to areas where the cost of living is at a more acceptable level. There is also some consideration relative to climate which gives a certain edge to the sun belt states. In a November 2, 1992 issue of Fortune Magazine, six of the top ten best cities cited for business opportunities were located in sun belt states. Eight of the ten are major transportation hubs. **All** have a receptive attitude toward the business community. The net exports of goods and services from each of them is **positive**.

At the subcutaneous level of these top ten cities are areas which are impacted by the **maquiladora** industry in Mexico. American investors who have sought commercial real estate investments in the principal zones of Tijuana, Cuidad Juarez and Matamoros which serve as principal maquiladora (or free enterprise) zones have the potential of low double digit returns on investment. Some of the benefits of maquiladora ownership include low cost labor and utilities; favorable duty treatment; 100% ownership of subsidiary company for U.S. owners; proximity to this country and its support with reciprocal free trade zones; and ease of access to the Mexican market.

Equity partners are sought by small to mid-sized companies in this market place due to the fact that restrictions on U.S. banking activity preclude loan availability and Mexican bank rates are steep. Most construction is performed on a cash basis, thus the need for equity partners who can obtain significantly higher returns than available domestically. The advantage of return can be seen in the chart below, since lease rates are roughly equivalent, but costs of land and improvements, on average, are much lower.

Chart 4-1

CONSTRUCTION COSTS		
	U. S.	MEXICO
Finished Land	$6-12	$ 3-4
Construction	$25-28	$15-18
RENTAL LEVELS		
	U. S.	MEXICO
NNN Lease	$0.35-0.45	$0.30-0.35

When entering into one of these **maquila** lease partnerships a specific tenant on a long term lease will have the lease guaranteed by a credit worthy United States or Foreign corporation. This reduces the investment risk involved for the capital providers in dealing with projects in a foreign country.

Those who wish to profit **domestically** with the maquiladora investment should look to the United States counterparts of these Mexican zones, namely, San Diego, California; El Paso and Brownsville, Texas. These locales will be domestic beneficiaries of this foreign activity with goods and services freely flowing between the United States and their Mexican counterparts. Investment in Mexico by United States companies will continue to expand due to the vast and inexpensive labor base. Although this activity may detract from the locales where these companies have departed to the less expensive operational locations, there still exists opportunities for those areas which interface with the maquiladora activities. There are different laws affecting land ownership in Mexico. Before one undertakes investments of this nature, a thorough understanding of the mechanics of land ownership and the rights acquired through these investments should be acquired.

IMPACT OF NATIONAL TRENDS ON SPECIFIC AREAS

In any form of economic trends there are beneficiaries and losers. The story of the early 1990s finds the Los Angeles area in Southern California as a major loser of jobs to other segments of the country. Some of the beneficiaries of these activities have been the midwest, eastern and sun belt states. Within these locales, with the notable exception of San Francisco, will be found nine of the ten cities Fortune cites as the best cities for business.

As the United States accommodates to conversion from a defensive and offensive weapons producer to domestic applications for our vast aerospace industry, a certain degree of molting is taking place. Conversion from a continuous array of armaments to the need for immediate attention to decaying infrastructure is a painful process calling for job displacements, retraining and replacement in new activities for much of the nations's work force. Aerospace companies now find themselves bidding for contracts on high speed rail transportation systems and other forms of infrastructure applications which require adaptability, changes in marketing techniques, and a new technological mind set. Within this eclectic arrangement, relocation of key facilities and major worker movement is inevitable. Knowing the business stars that will shine in the economic universe leads real estate investors to proper areas of concentrating their capital infusion for projects worthy of attention.

Investors may spend wearing hours collecting reams of data on specific locations or invest in projects where others have performed the research. In the case of Fortune Magazine, considerable study had been exerted before the first word of their article went to print. For this reason, coverage will be given to the top ten cities in their survey and some selected remarks about some of the cities that did not make the top ten, but still offer special opportunities for the investor.

WINDOWS OF OPPORTUNITY IN A DEPRESSED ECONOMY

The apex of Fortune's top ten business cities is **Seattle, Washington**. Not only is the city a vast distribution point for raw materials and finished goods, its remarkable diversification of industrial base insulates it from some of the economic woes that have beset the rest of the country. The vastness of airframe giant Boeing permeates the economy from the lowly fisherman to the corner grocer. The vast panorama and breathtaking beauty of its natural surroundings make it a virtual sportsman's and environmentalist's paradise. As gateway to Alaska and sporting some of the finest educational systems in the country, the quality of life in the area makes it ideal for raising families in an atmosphere of tranquility devoid of the usual violence and gangs attributed to life in the big city. Business doesn't stop at Boeing, however. Nintendo, computerized game giant; Immunex, capstone of 50 companies in the biotech pyramid; and import/export companies abound in profusion. This international city is a business hub beyond comparison. Real estate investment within this environment will probably not bring the desired results of other areas outlined below, since supply/demand dynamics would indicate that prices favor sellers, thus lowering expected rates of return on investment in this area. Water view oriented property is offered at totally prohibitive prices.

At number two on this power list, **Houston, Texas** has the unusual feature of lack of any zoning ordinances to hamper the developer with high rises dotting the urban skyline like toads perched on lily pads. The city displayed remarkable resilience from the oil glut years of 1982 to 1987 with 221,000 jobs being lost from energy related areas including the largest employer, Texaco, Inc. The substance of Houston's recovery has been its devotion to infrastructure with $7 billion being devoted to that effort since 1985. This specific area, nationally, is expected to add significantly to the country's labor force during the Clinton administration. A concerted effort has been generated by the city to attract aerospace, biotechnical and manufacturing jobs to supplant those lost during the energy crunch. This effort was designed to accommodate to the talents of the displaced workers and their talents avoiding their downgrading in life style caused by conversion to service jobs. Transportation is a key to Houston's success, as it is the main port for goods bound for Mexico. It handles more goods destifed for south of the border than all of the Mexican ports combined. Just as other cities that have a proximity to Mexico, Houston will be a major beneficiary of the North American Free Trade Agreement. The foreign influence continues with one of the largest firms attracted being a joint venture between Mitsubishi Heavy Industries and Caterpillar in the manufacture of fork lift trucks. Of the 900,000 jobs that have left California between May, 1990 and the end of 1992, many have found their way to Houston's open arms where there employer has either relocated or has a division there. This is an area where real estate investment opportunities abound for knowledgeable investors. Doing real estate business in Texas is complex with lease terms differing slightly on income producing properties in

California. The need for dealing with persons knowledgeable in that area is extremely important.

Rounding out the top three is **San Francisco** who turns out to be one of the major beneficiaries of Los Angeles' economic woes. Los Angeles' financial clout was tempered considerably with the mega-merger of Los Angeles based Security Pacific National Bank with San Francisco behemoth, Bank of America. San Francisco actually represents a string of cities that rim the bay area. Due to its importance as an international port combined with a certain degree of cosmopolitan sophistication usually reserved for New Yorkers, "Baghdad by the Bay" has always attracted the interest of Pacific Rim business and serves as a mecca for import/export activities. Japan based Hoya Crystal and Hyundai have recently relocated in the Bay area. Large stock brokerage firms have relocated staff in the area to take advantages of the shift in financial power that has taken place. The former bright star in the Bay area's crown, silicon valley has taken some economic hits, particularly due to Japanese competition in the computer chip business. The main attractions for this area in general are geographic location, climactic conditions, educational level of the inhabitants and cultural opportunities that abound. Drawbacks for the real estate investor consist of the highest median housing costs in the state which convert to similar high costs of acquiring income producing properties, much of what can be attributable to land. The best investment opportunities exist in the outlying areas in the path of progress rather than in the city itself.

The almost 3 million inhabitants of **Atlanta, Georgia** find themselves in fourth position. Although lacking the port capabilities of the top three, Atlanta serves as a transportation mecca for domestic air transportation for both passenger and freight. It serves as the operations hub for giant Federal Express. Coca Cola dominates the scene with its international headquarters located there. As we mentioned before there are economic events that are periodic, but predictable. Such an event is scheduled for the Atlanta area in 1996 creating an Olympic boom town during the games which are scheduled for that location. This will be a one-time $1.4 billion dollar economic surge for the business community. Although the quality of labor force does not meet the standards of the top three cities, Atlanta offers the advantages of more stability in real estate values than the upper troika. Its business doors remain open for one and all who want to establish a business there and provide jobs for the locals. The international flavor and sophistication of the other metropolitan areas is also surprisingly lacking in the Atlanta area. From a real estate investment standpoint this Georgia location provides the possibility of a steady and stable income stream sans the fluctuations of areas that concentrate on attracting high tech industries.

Ranking fifth, but never far out of the hunt, is **New York**. Gotham's appeal, even with city taxes, seems never really to go out of style. Harry Helmsley, one of New York's shrewdest players, having the Empire State Building in one of his syndicates, once noted to a reporter "...Real estate is the best game around...and when you're ahead in a game you like to keep on playing." The Helmsley philosophy was to continue to plow back real estate profits to acquire other properties. Here is a man who is so shrewd that his spouse is now serving time for tax evasion and he was not charged. Now that's chutzpa! The advantages of The Big Apple are legend with more than adequate public transportation, financial hub of the country, cultural blockbuster, retail maven, port of entry, all describe this legendary town.   Social ills, crime, pestilence, poverty, increasing budgetary problems and the like preclude New York from attaining its customary number one status.   A glut of office vacancies create unique investment opportunities for the astute where contrived financial pyramids are formed through sophisticated arrangements combining master leases with leverage into high yielding investment vehicles. Investing in New York is not for the faint at heart. It takes industrial strength money to keep in the hunt. For those who have the courage to play, there are rewards available at the end of the investment rainbow.

High tech and the cutting edge of automation serve to forge sixth ranked **Raleigh and Durham, North Carolina** as a major business player. The economic glue bonding these two cities together is Research Triangle Business Park. Included within this facility are IBM's PC facility combined with 60 research and development facilities including Galxo and Reichold Chemical as tenants. The combined metropolitan areas also house three major universities and serves as a secondary airport hub for the southeastern area of the United States. Its strong points are a highly educated labor force with cultural advantages of the area. Again, it offers the same investment opportunities as Atlanta with a higher educational level of the residents not characteristic of the Georgia city. Again, one looking for stable values combined with adequate returns might be attracted to investment opportunities in this area.

Number seven, **Denver,** is the quintessential representation of the Timex aphorism "takes a licking and keeps on ticking."   After the disastrous effects of the over building of the 1980s created from the dissipation of energy related activity, depressed real estate values and severe blows to its banking industry, Denver picked itself up, dusted itself off and is trying to do it all over again.   A major contributor to its resurgence, economically is the vast regional airport located there that employs some 7500 workers.   Other contributors to the resuscitated economic base are agricultural interests, stock brokerage, cable television and telecommunications interests that have help fill the void of lost employment in the past few years. Add to this formula the vast array of high tech manufacturing in neighboring areas of Fort Collins to Colorado Springs with a sprinkling of influence from the Adolph Coors Brewery located in Golden, and the ingredients for a rapidly recovering economy are in place. Especially interesting from an investor standpoint is the potential for office building investment at attractive prices which can still generate cash flow sufficient to maintain profitability. In an area which has experienced a glut of office vacancies in recent years, it takes expertise to identify the proper investment vehicle.

> "Hog butcher for the world,
> Tool maker, stacker of wheat,
> Player with railroads and the nation's
>   food handler;
> Stormy, husky, brawling,
> City of big shoulders"

These poignant words penned by Carl Sandburg give a pretty good economic picture of the **Chicago** of 1916, our eighth town friendly to business in the Fortune series. The description hasn't changed much from this depiction of some eight decades ago. Food processing and the like still play a role in Chicago's make up. Additionally the town has taken on some financial muscle and headquarters some major players in the economic arena the likes of R.R. Donnelly Company, one of the nation's largest printing firms; Navistar; Quaker Oats; and Sara Lee, among others. The already abundant recreational and cultural opportunities will be buoyed with plans for a theme park in the area. As a major airline and railroad transportation hub, the shores of Lake Michigan also provide water transportation facilities as well. Chicago also suffers from inner city malaise in the form of crime and gang activities within its urban environs. From an investment standpoint, areas to the northeast and south of the city itself offer the best opportunities for serious consideration. No matter what the contemplated investment may be, transportation corridors to major employment centers should be considered before any dedication of capital to a particular piece of real estate.

Second only to the Raleigh/Durham area in its inventory of skilled workers, **Boston** offers economic opportunities for the business entrepreneur especially those devoted to high-tech applications in the market place. Research and design together with access to some of the finest institutions of higher learning are a driving force in this historical harbor town. Potential for future growth attracting new businesses to the area is a devotion of billions of dollars to the creation of an infrastructure to deal with the challenge of the 21st century. The downside of the area is the cost of doing business combined with high tax rates (similar to California's problems) that sent most of the mills that were previously located there to southern locations where costs were less.

Since Boston is basically a mixture of older properties in its environs with newer facilities in its suburbs of Haverill and the like, careful study must be made of ecological matters that might influence any real estate investment in commercial or industrial properties in the area, particularly in older properties.

Although tenth on the list, the best has been saved for last. **Orlando, Florida** has served as a magnet attracting a diverse economic base. To give a potential investor the economic magnitude of its phenomenal growth, chart 4-2 provides a vivid example:

Chart 4-2

SELECTED ORLANDO ECONOMIC DATA — AN AVERAGE WEEK IN METRO ORLANDO

1,117 New adult residents
246,692 visitors
351 births
252 marriages
571 new jobs
353,804 air travelers
357 residential building permits
190 million dollars in retail sales
294 million dollars in buying income*

Orlando provides an impressive economic profile positioned for serious consideration as a real estate investment vehicle. Chart 4-3 provides a divergent array of data derived from a variety of reliable sources including the U. S. Bureau of Census, Sales and Marketing Management; major air carriers; Amtrak; Florida's Bureaus of Labor and Employment Security, Division of Driver's Licenses, Film Bureau, Division of Tourism; Woods and Poole Economics; The Scarborough Report on the Orlando MSA; and Chicago Title Insurance Company; together with an array of professional association and agency statistics provided from similar reliable sources.

Chart 4-3

PERTINENT ECONOMIC DATA EMPHASIZING THE GREATER ORLANDO STANDARD METROPOLITAN STATISTICAL AREA

POPULATION STATISTICS

STATE OF FLORIDA
1. The state ranks fourth in the Country with a population of 13,219,000 in 1991.
2. With a 35.6% population increase in the past decade, it ranks number one in growth in the United States.

METROPOLITAN ORLANDO AREA
1. Among the top 50 consolidated metropolitan areas Orlando ranks 14th in total population gain growing from 700,055 in 1980 to 1,104,800 in 1991 - a whopping 57.8% increase!
2. Between the years 1990 and 2000, Orlando population is projected to increase an impressive 39.6% to rank 31st in the entire country.

DEMOGRAPHICS OF GREATER ORLANDO

AVERAGE HOUSEHOLD SIZE   2.67
MEDIAN INCOME $28,067
MEDIAN AGE   32.3

POPULATION BY AGE GROUP*

0-34	35-64	65+
55%	34%	11%

*This population surge of new residents represents the relocation of young affluent adults from the number one relocation source of New York state to the tenth ranked state of Illinois. Fourth in relocation ranking is the state of California which has sacrificed a variety of positions in the entertainment industry to the Sunshine State.

Chart 4-3 (cont.)

ETHNICITY

White	Black	Asian	American	Hispanic	Indian Others
82.9%	12.4%	1.9%	0.3%	9.0%	2.5%*

*percentages exceed 100% due to rounding

EDUCATION LEVELS

Local colleges report a total enrollment of 96,210 students. 49% of all adults in the area have attended college, half of whom have attained a college degree.

GREATER ORLANDO ECONOMIC PROFILE

1. 24% of the capital investment by new industry in the state of Florida was devoted to the Greater Orlando area.
2. A preliminary study of industrial dispersion of employment in the Greater Orlando area in 1990 shows a wide diversity of industrial distribution as follows:

	1990 Annual Payroll	1990 Avg. Employment
Manufacturing	13%	10%
Construction	7%	6%
Transportation, Communications, & Utilities	7%	5%
Wholesale Trade	7%	6%
Retail Trade	12%	21%
Finance, Insurance & RE	7%	6%
Services	33%	33%
Government	13%	11%
Other	1%	2%

Chart 4-3 (cont.)

FILM MAKING - State of Florida

Within this diverse industrial category, the entertainment industry, with film making in particular, has made a dramatic impact on the Florida economy, ranking third in importance behind only California and New York in this activity. In comparing 1980 activity to the current levels, the results are impressive.

FEATURE FILMS

Year	Number	Budget*	Employment
1980	19	$ 78,512	3,184
1990	55	$226,539	5,975

COMMERCIAL RECORDING

Year	Number	Budget*	Employment
1980	N/A	$ 50,000	2,000
1990	19,757	$ 71,674	18,521

TOTAL PRODUCTION

Year	Number	Budget*	Employment
1980	N/A	$128,512	5,184
1990	19,812	$298,213	24.496

FINANCIAL INSTITUTIONS

There are 86 thrifts with $2.8 billion in deposits as of the end of 1991 in the Greater Orlando area. Additionally there are 245 banks with a total deposit base of $7.9 billion as of the same date. The customer base of these institutions avail themselves of a wide variety of financial services that are offered.

*Total budget spent in Florida in thousands.

Chart 4-3 (cont.)

EMPLOYMENT

Principal employers are Walt Disney World Co., Martin Marietta,
American Telephone and Telegraph Company, Naval Training
Center Orlando (aviation), and General Mills Restaurant Group
with a total labor force of 630,000 enjoying a relatively low
unemployment level of 4.9% at the end of 1991. Employment is
projected to increase 35.8% between the years 1990 and 2000 in the
Greater Orlando area following a healthy 83.4% increase in the
previous decade. Manufacturing jobs during the previous period
increased 65.7%. All industrial classifications experienced similar
significant increases in employment levels.

TOURISM

Orlando hosted 13 million visitors, three times their 1980 figures
in 1990, representing 28.3% of the 46 million that visit Florida
annually. The recent addition of new entertainment facilities in the
area assure these figures being sustained or exceeded in the last
decade of the 20th century. These visitors spend some $5 billion
on local goods and services. 20% of that amount, or $1 billion is
spent by the 1.4 million conventioneers that visited during that same
period. Greater Orlando boasts 81,000 hotel rooms, a 125%
increase over their 1980 numbers, to accommodate the flood of
visitors to the area's attractions.

TRANSPORTATION

Orlando's airport has doubled its passenger volume to 18.4 million
travelers annually ranking 18th in the Country and **first** in the state
of Florida. With a whopping 47.2% growth mode, Orlando ranks
third in the United States behind Phoenix and Las Vegas in that
category. Amtrak's ridership increase by 36,799 passengers to
109,528 for a 33.6% increase between 1985 and 1990.

Chart 4-3 (cont.)

REAL ESTATE DATA

Greater Orlando has averaged 20,000 new homes annually since 1982. The mid-1980s found a doubling of office, retail and industrial space. A snap shot of this activity is as follows:

SQUARE FEET IN THOUSANDS

	1980	1991
Industrial	26,052	61,654
Retail	12,775	33,012
Office	8,735	22,478

As noted above, the tremendous surge in office and industrial space has created a unique investment opportunity while inventories are being absorbed for selected buys with excellent future potential. There are presently $15 billion in construction projects either underway or on the drawing board in this dynamic economic microcosm.

In reviewing the data displayed by this vast data bank, it paints a clear picture of an area poised for upward mobility, economy-wise. Smart buys of real estate owned from institutional lenders in the area can provide not only a current positive cash flow, but excellent future cash flow through aggressive knowledgeable management of the property.

Within the remaining sixty locations surveyed by Fortune, some locations stand out among the others. Two areas that consider attention are poles apart, climate-wise, and they are **Grand Rapids, Michigan** and **Greensboro, North Carolina**. The former shares its strength in labor relations with its southern neighbor, while continuing its specialization in furniture making. Greensboro relies on tobacco and textiles with finance and electronics gaining strong footholds in the area. These are still areas of low housing costs that could provide unique real property investment opportunities.

Kansas City, Missouri and its neighboring **Independence** not only serve as a major transportation link, but house the headquarters of Sprint and Hallmark Cards. Some 115 foreign firms are housed there with local firms selling $6.7 billion in imports in 1991. The area also serves as a religious "gathering place" for those affiliated with the Reorganized version of the Latter Day Saints and Mormons as well with many churches affiliated with the two religions located there. Independence serves as world headquarters for the Reorganized church with a newly constructed facility designed to seat some 6,000 people. Real estate prices in this midwest location are still reasonable allowing good return for the investment dollar.

Although beset by myriad problems, much dealing with too little money chasing too many needs, **Los Angeles** stands as a "sleeper" investment opportunity. Its 9 million inhabitants represent an eclectic display of divergent racial backgrounds melded into a melting pot of ethnicity to challenge local authorities. The sheer magnitude and force of the location preclude ignoring its potential which, in the future, lies in the area of interface with the Pacific Rim countries to pick up steam in the import/export arena.

Matching the phenomenal growth occurring in the Orlando area is the shifting sifting sands of **Las Vegas, Nevada**. Many disgruntled Californians have trudged over to this tourist mecca to find jobs and solace from the rat race of the big city. Due to the hopscotch method of development in the area, competitive sites abound and affect the investor's ability to insulate the affect of competitive sites in exercising due diligence.

Concentrating on the attraction of foreign business, **Norfolk, Virginia** has emerged as the highest percentage of manufacturing activities derived from the high-tech area. A major port and keystone of the U.S. Navy's Atlantic Fleet operations, it stands poised as a potential investment gem. Due to its heavy concentration in military operations, Department of Defense decisions relative to future operations in this area could be critical.

Although land locked, **Oklahoma City, Oklahoma** ranks in the top ten cities as far as labor-management relations and the quality of labor force is concerned. This is why the area is particularly attractive for hagh-tech industries allowing for more affluent citizens. This area provides considerable investment potential for future study.

Another port heard from is **Philadelphia** with a higher ranked educational system than New York City, a tad lower in the cosmopolitan ranks, but home to information technology, communications, telecommunications, pharmaceuticals and biotech firms. Henry Louis Mencken once described Philadelphia as "...the most pecksniffian of

American cities, and thus probably leads the world. Don't let Mencken's tribute to insincerity count Philadelphia out on a potential real estate investment list.

The hidden nugget with its 2.621 million inhabitants in the 60 business stars is the city of **San Diego**. As was previously noted in this chapter, the **maquiladora** industry combined with the free trade zones being created in the Southern California area make it an ideal investment candidate. 21% of the goods manufactured in the area are exported. Its manufacturing base is growing at a faster rate than the average U.S. major metropolitan statistical area. Investment in warehouse/office facilities appears to be a bright spot on the real estate horizon. The major drawback is the area's attitude toward business and its lack of adequate vocational training. With its strategic location vis-a-vis Mexico combined with port facilities, the economic future of the area has a bright halo around it.

Even more sequestered than the investment opportunity mentioned above is the connecting link between **Los Angeles** and **San Diego** counties, **Orange County, California**. Although overlooked by the Fortune survey, with a 36% increase in population between the years 1970 to 1990, Orange County ranks seventh in the nation in population growth recognizing the dynamism of enterprise conducted in that area. The Santa Ana/Anaheim metropolitan statistical area is projected to increase from its 1990 census population figure of 2,411,000 to close to 3 million citizens by the year 2000. Participating in this growth will be the city of Westminter where American Capital Investments, Inc. has recently purchased a four building office complex contiguous to the West Orange County Civic Center which houses various city and county government offices. In this ideal location various law firms and other service oriented companies who do business with the various government entities are strategically located to conduct their business in a more efficient manner. Office building locations are principally in the area immediately surrounding the civic center, such as subject complex typically of the garden office variety from one to three stories in height. Typical of the types of purchases in syndication today, this project even at 71% occupancy will show a positive cash flow of in excess of $100,000 based upon a $4 million purchase price with $800,000 down predicated upon only moderately active marketing effort. Already a marketing plan is underway to further enhance the value of this 19 year old, 80,395 square foot brick and stucco complex on 5.64 acres of land to increase earnings to their maximum potential to yield and economic value to $7,750,000, some 93.75% above the current purchase price. Value enhancement and attractive purchase terms serve as the basis of all syndication investment decisions in dealing with real estate owned properties such as the one described above.

Carl Lotus Becker is quoted as saying:

"Economic distress will teach men, if anything can, that realities are less dangerous than fancies, that fact-finding is more effective than fault finding."

In the next chapter a scenario will be provided indicating how opportunities for purchase of commercial and industrial properties can be effected at very attractive terms. It will also indicate the motivation behind the sellers' eagerness to dispose of these properties under such attractive circumstances.

5
WHY DISTRESSED PROPERTIES?

In his work **Progress and Power**, Carl Becker noted:

". . . Economic distress will teach men, if anything can, that realities are less dangerous than fancies, that fact-finding is more effective than fault-finding..."

In the roller coaster realities of the 1980s, many financial institutions found that seemingly rational decisions to grant credit on commercial and industrial real estate loans were far from that. Some of these decisions were prompted by ignorance (which was characteristic of the thrifts who were granted this authority without sufficient expertise to wield it), improper valuations (a polite word for fraud), and the ever present motivation of greed (high interest and loan fees to take on unusual risks). The net result of these excesses has been the largest accumulation of real estate owned in our financial institutions and their regulator authorities since the great depression of the 1930s. This time there is no Reconstruction Finance Corporation to restructure flagging residential loans saving them for home owners. The new kid on the block, thanks to FIRREA, is the Resolution Trust Corporation to serve as a massive liquidator for a staggering inventory of real estate ranging from loans to actual property ownership in all categories ranging from residential to commercial/industrial in nature. This shock wave that has unsettled the financial community as well as the American public, since this massive delinquency clean up is being supported by tax dollars, has caused financial institutions to be subject to increased regulatory scrutiny.

REGULATORY POSTURE WITH FINANCIAL INSTITUTIONS

Each of the regulatory bodies that review financial institutions is concerned with the safety and soundness of the firm as well as its ability to continue to conduct business. The principal objective of any financial institution is to convert liabilities, in the form of deposits, into assets, in the form of loans and investments. Hopefully, the result of this activity will create a profit margin of the excess of the cost of servicing liabilities in the form of interest and dividends combined with personnel costs and the interest and dividend income derived from assets. If the lending side of the ledger shows signs of weakness in the form of non-performing loans, these items get special attention by the regulators. In order to get a better perspective, it might help to show some of the regulatory bodies that interface with the financial community:

INSTITUTION	POTENTIAL REGULATORS
Commercial Bank	Federal Deposit Insurance Corp.
	Federal Reserve (holding companies)
	State Banking Commissioner
	Comptroller of Currency (National Banks)
Thrifts	Federal Deposit Insurance Corp.
	Office of Thrift Supervision
	State S & L Commissioner
Finance Companies,	
Loan Brokers,	Corporations Commissioner
Thrift and Loans	
and Mortgage Bankers	Real Estate Commissioner

The financial community represents one of the most highly regulated industries in the country yet, with all of this oversight, there is no way to prevent unsafe and unsound lending practices. These regulators, who regularly examine the financial institutions under their aegis, are supplanted by internal auditors appointed by the institutions together with CPA firms who certify their financial statements. One would think that with all of this scrutiny something the scale of the well-publicized "savings and loan bailout" would not occur. If the regulators spotted shoddy lending practices, they would take steps to prevent further deterioration of the loan portfolio to reduce the possibility of further losses to the institution. It doesn't necessarily work that way. In the examination of banks, regulators have a very set regimen of verifying deposits, loan balances and the like. Much of these procedures are accounting oriented. When it comes to **really** understanding how well the loan portfolio is performing, that's another question all together. On the other side of the coin is the investment portfolio. Thanks to Mr. Milken, many of the thrifts were caught with a bundle of junk bonds that had to be written down or written off their books. In the case of Columbia Savings and Gibraltar Savings, it proved to be their death knell. Other savings institutions went far afield, thanks to the Garn-St. Germain Bill to invest in fast food franchises and joint ventures with disastrous results. The regulatory community was not necessarily equipped to properly assess some of these unusual assets and their impact on balance sheet performance. They were not aided in their examination process by the institutions themselves who used various methods to hide problem situations. A typical example was the old State Savings and Loan Association (now a much stronger American Savings under the Bass family) who would regularly roll over construction loans and the accumulated **unpaid** interest to builders on non-performing projects. Another ploy used by this institution which drained their cash flow in the early 1980s was their "silent second" program which, ostensibly, allowed home purchasers to enjoy a lower interest rate on their financing. The program worked like this:

Sale price of the property: $100,000
1st Trust Deed: $60,000 (15% - 30 year terms - amortized)
2nd Trust Deed: $30,000 (15% - 30 year amortization -
                                          5 year due date*)
Down Payment $10,000

*All principal and interest **accrues** for the five year period.

It doesn't take any brain surgeon to figure out that by the end of five years the homeowner's equity has disappeared, since the monthly payments **not made** were approximately $380, the majority of which went to interest. The original $30,000 borrowed now has an approximate $50,000 price tag to pay off in five years. The sales pitch for this silent second program was that the effective interest rate for the monies lent to the borrower was only 11%, some 400 basis points below the market rate. Wrong! The interest rate was 15% on everything, there was just a timed released howitzer in the form of a balloon bomb shell that didn't go off for five years. Due to this type of financing, State Savings was constantly having to pay premium rates on jumbo CDs ($100,000 and more) from brokers to prop up their loss in cash flow. On the financial statement there **accrued** income was marvelous while they bled to death on a cash basis. This was obviously exacerbated by their non-performing construction loans and joint venture projects. The latter didn't produce income until the project was sold. In some instances sales either flagged or didn't materialize at all.

SCHEDULED ITEMS GET EXTRA ATTENTION

If financial institutions accumulate non-performing assets or acquire real estate through the foreclosure process, regulators, outside and internal auditors pay special attention. If an examiner feels that there is high potential that an asset that is delinquent (the key number is 90 days or more) and there is a high degree of possibility that the borrower will be unable to perform, it becomes a scheduled item. As such the regulator has several choices as to how to deal with the item. If the item is collateralized, as real estate credits are, they have to determine whether the collateral has adequate value to make the institution whole after foreclosure. In the topsy turvy world of the early 1990s, that involves a **current** appraisal, since one even six months old might be suspect. If, upon appraisal, it is determined that there is not sufficient collateral to cover the debt, the institution will be required to write off that portion of the debt that is expected as a potential loss. Even if there is no expected potential loss, the item will be written up as a potential loss until such time as the loan is reinstated or foreclosed and liquidated. In the latter case, foreclosure reclassifies this asset from a loan to **real estate owned**. It is in this category that regulators exert pressure upon the financial institution to dispose of this property in an expeditious manner in order to either realize the loss or gain resulting from the sale. After the property has been foreclosed, the regulators may then require a new appraisal which may write down the asset even further. In any event, financial institutions are encouraged to dispose of real estate owned as rapidly as possible. One can see from the activities of Resolution Trust Corporation, Federal Deposit Insurance Corporation's (deposit insurer for both banks and thrifts) super liquidator, that they have resorted to the bulk sale method for massive property liquidation in the form of performing and non-performing trust deeds and real property formerly held by failed financial institutions.

One of the principal reasons for the massive merger between Bank of America and Security Pacific National Bank is the fact that there were a considerable amount of non-performing real estate credits in the latter bank's portfolio. One of the aspects of the merger that has not been well publicized is the fact that they resulting organization will be a combination of a "good bank" and a "bad bank." The former will contain the performing assets with the latter serving as a sort of informal RTC. In any event, this regulatory pressure serves to the advantage of investors, particularly in the commercial and industrial property areas where the greatest degree of pressure is being exerted by regulators for lenders to take their losses, lick their wounds and go on.

In the case of residential loans, lenders have been using unique approaches to avoid acquiring any more real estate owned. In areas where their are estate properties which have plummeted in value, lenders facilitate sales of these properties at lower than their loan balance, **fully leveraged**, and write off the difference rather than foreclose. Why this strange behavior in the market place? Why doesn't the lender foreclose, wait out the market until prices improve, and then sell the house? The answer to this question lies in the regulatory attitude toward institutions that fail to deal with scheduled items in an expeditious manner.

UNFAVORABLE PERFORMANCE RATINGS

In the case of California Banks, Charles Findley, banking consultant has a rating system for banks conferring titles such as "Super Performing Bank" and the like. Sometimes this conferring of titles has a way of acting in reverse. Many of these so-called super performing institutions have turned out to be performing "bombs" in later years. The FDIC ranks banks into five categories relative to safety and soundness with one being the highest and four and five being on shaky ground. It is called the CAMEL system. Even though this is an internal regulatory rating, bankers are familiar with the process. Most banks in California are in the two to three range with a few like the cash cow, Farmers and Merchants Bank of Long Beach, probably garnering a one rating. Where a bank or thrift ranks in the regulatory pecking order has a definite effect on the latitude of their activity. As one goes down on the rating scale, there may be harsh sanctions imposed on the institution requiring them to curtail or completely cease lending activity. If the latter occurs, this is just the first step toward closure of the institution in most cases.

LETTER AGREEMENTS REQUIRING ADDITIONAL CAPITAL OR REFRAIN FROM CERTAIN LENDING AND INVESTMENT PRACTICES

If, after examination of an institution, the regulator finds that there are unsafe or unsound lending practices evident, or that capital is inadequate to meet regulatory requirements, there will be a mandatory requirement that the institution enter into a letter agreement with the agency relative to performance. These letters range from a regulatory "slap on the wrist" to much more serious circumstances, such as the removal of key officers or directors, ceasing lending operations, curtailing deposit accumulation and the like. In late 1992 City National Bank of Beverly Hills announced that it had entered into a letter agreement with the regulators dealing with the fact that their real estate problems had allowed their capital to reach a level that no longer meant minimum capital requirements and that they were required to provide more capital. This is one of the more serious problems that face financial institutions, since small independent banks, not necessarily City National who has some influential and wealthy directors and shareholders, do not have the directorship support to handle capital inadequacy and would probably be liquidated by the regulators as a result. Due to the new capital requirements for financial institutions prompted by FIRREA, many institutions of long standing, such as Glendale Federal Savings, find themselves in a capital inadequacy situation. One of the ways that institutions alleviate a capital inadequacy situation is to sell assets, hopefully at a profit. Once an institution falls into categories four and five, the regulators increase the frequency of audits until they finally reach the point of permanent residency to prepare a bid package to offer the assets and liabilities of the institution to others who are financially sound.

BIDDING PROCEDURE PENDING CLOSURE

Once the bidding package is complete, the regulator, whether it be FDIC, Federal Reserve, state banking or savings and loan commissioners, etc. then contacts institutions who they feel would be a potential bidder for the institution or its customers. The contents of the bid package are a summary of the deposit liabilities and classification of the assets. The regulator allows the bidder to pick the assets that are to be retained, therefore the bidder is really acquiring a deposit and customer base in this process with the assets being a bonus. It is up to the bidder to decide what proportion of the deposits can be salvaged upon acquisition and whether the deposit base is adequate enough to warrant a bid. Sometimes the premium offered in the form of a bid is minimal if the deposit base, although attractive, does not seem that beneficial to the bidder.

If the bid is acceptable to the regulatory agency, the successful bidder and the agency then appear in superior court to formally declare the institution closed and transfer to the successful bidder. At that point in time, the transition process begins and the successful bidder assigns operations and lending personnel to effect the conversion. Lending personnel review the loan portfolio and have a time limitation, usually 30 to 60 days to sell loans back to the regulator. Many of these loans find their way into RTC's portfolio.

Unfortunately for landlords, the regulator has the authority to give landlords of the financial institutions 30 days notice of cancellation of **any** existing leases, regardless of length and to depart the premises. Many landlords have found this out the hard way. Typically an institution may be closed on Friday and reopen Monday with a new name as if nothing had happened. There are certain instances where financial institutions are closed and liquidated due to lack of bidders, as they were too far gone to have any value to their deposit base. At this point in time it is important to understand the functioning of FDIC insurance, since deposits are only insured up to $100,000. Depositors in failed institutions can only expect up to that amount. In the case of bidders taking over the operation, deposits in excess of $100,000 are salvaged. Bidders for institutions subject to closure have to be careful in the due diligence process. For example, if one is bidding on an institution that is owned more than 50% by minorities, a large percentage of this deposit base may be in the form of certificates of deposit from major corporations under a minority investment program. All of these deposits will be lost and cannot be counted in your calculations for bidding on the institution. When Wilshire State Bank acquired West Olympia Bank in the mid-1980s through the bidding process, they were the unhappy recipient of this fact. Wilshire State had a minority interest through shareholders in the 40% range, not enough to preserve the several million deposited by major corporations throughout the country in a bank formerly composed of a majority Koreans and black shareholders.

INTERNAL DECISION MAKING PROCESS BY FINANCIAL INSTITUTIONS

Boards of Directors when faced with the results of a regulatory examination have varied reactions. It is the job of the banker board members to point out the significance of the report. If the report notes that operationally and loan-wise that the bank is in good shape, that is one scenario. Usually this is not the case. Either one side or the other shows some form of weakness that needs attention. It may be that these items are minor, such as requiring riders to be added to financial statements by borrowers certifying to the bank under penalty of prosecution that the figures accurately reflect the financial condition of the firm, or more significant, like a lost note. In some cases, failure to provide adequate documentation to prove the evidence of the debt or the collateral position of the debt might lead to a charge-off of the asset. This is when directors become almost militant at time, since this may effect the value of their investment.

BOTTOM LINE CONSIDERATIONS

The proof of a bank's performance lies in the operating statement. How much income is left after taking into consideration expenses and income tax deductions? After the tidal wave of red ink produced by the financial community during the 1980s, the pressure for profits to recoup for the resounding losses was considerable during the latter part of that decade. Joint ventures, construction loans, consumer credit and the like with their high yielding potential led the parade to increase bottom line potential. In this insatiable quest for profits, commercial and industrial projects led the way in this wave of credit risk taking. As the real estate market waned in the very late 1980s and early 1990s, pressure to continue profitability remained. For this reason bankers scrambled every 90 days to extract the last dollar of profit they could for each quarter. Long range profit plans went out the window. Eventually this quest had the inevitable result of massive write-offs (Security Pacific Bank is a prime example) and stockholder unrest.

PRESSURE FROM STOCKHOLDERS AND DIRECTORS

As poor earnings performance exacerbates, financial institutions are forced to take measures to alleviate the situation concerning their non-performing assets and, in particular, their real estate owned. The real estate owned portfolio becomes the focal point of attention by this pincers movement of regulators combined with the group that represents the ownership of the institution. Each month bank officers have to present a report to the directors as to the status of the loan portfolio and, in certain instances, loans for their approval. In the case of credit arrangements for bank officers, there are specific regulatory requirements that must be met prior to granting such credit. In some of the larger banks, officer lending programs are managed by a special division of the bank where these credits are placed with competing institutions.

As the directors continue to see that certain real estate owned still remains on the banks books with the potential for even larger write-offs of value from the property's sale, directors aggressively encourage the bank's management to seek means of disposal. One of the methods used to effect disposal is by creating an attractive financial and purchase package that will attract potential purchasers of the property. Through the sale of such properties, even under very creative full leveraged financing terms, the lender can convert a non-performing asset into a **loan to facilitate** - which is a performing asset. The usual loan to value limitations do not apply to these loans to facilitate.

DIFFICULTIES OF PROPERTY MANAGEMENT AND DISPOSAL

The management and marketing aspects of lenders are not their strongest points even in the largest of financial institutions. If the lender is modest in size, reliance on outside vendors for management and property disposal is sought. This means that professional property managers will operate the property representing the lender/owner. These firms range in their degree of effectiveness. They are also motivated by the amount of fees that the financial institution is willing to pay for their services. If the institution haggles over fees, the quality of property management will suffer accordingly. Expected yields on income producing property are affected dramatically by the effectiveness of a property manager. In the case of property disposal, lenders may hire their residential broker to dispose of income producing property. This can only be advantageous to prospective buyers and not the seller, since residential brokers are not normally proficient in properly negotiating the sale of commercial or industrial properties. One should always deal with a broker who is associated with the Society of Industrial Realtors who specialize in this type of property. Lack of expertise in both the management and disposal of property by lenders always works to the investor's advantage, since one is dealing with absentee ownership in many cases.

F.D.I.C. AND RTC ATTITUDE TOWARDS PROPERTY DISPOSITION

FDIC, the principal deposit insurer, and RTC, its disposal arm have a mission to dispose of liquidated financial institutions' assets in an expeditious manner. This places tremendous downward pressure on **all** real estate values throughout the country where vast inventories of foreclosed, performing or non-performing assets exist, since the market place has to content with these factors. In the case of real estate owned, there is a bidding process. Most of the process is done on the basis of offering blocks of properties in the commercial/industrial arena, as opposed to real estate owned in financial institutions which is usually negotiated one property at a time. Real estate investors usually enjoy greater negotiation flexibility when able to deal on a one on one basis, rather than a package of projects. It allows the investor to focus upon the opportunity and have a clearer picture of its investment potential. For example, consider an office structure containing 100,000 square feet of leasable space that is 60% occupied. The data on the structure is as follows:

Monthly rents avg. $1.00/sq. ft/mnth, or $60,000—Annually　$720,000
　　Allowing for 7.5% vacancy contingency of　　　　　　<u>54,000</u>
　　Effective income is　　　　　　　　　　　　　　　　$666,000
　　Considering operating expenses of　　　　　　　　　<u>186,000</u>
　　Potential net operating income would be　　　　　　 $480,000

If one attaches a 10% risk of capital to this investment, the NOI is converted to a capitalized value of $4,800,000. If the lender would accept a 10% down payment of $480,000 and take back a loan to facilitate for $4,320,000 at 8% on a 30 year amortization, this would be the results for the investor:

　　　　　Purchase price　　　　　　　　　$4,800,000
　　　　　Down Payment　　　　　　　　　　480,000

Loan terms $4,430,000 at 8% payable in monthly P & I of $31,038 annualized to $372,460.

　　　　　Project NOI　　　　　　　　　　$ 480,000
　　　　　Less debt service　　　　　　　　<u>372,460</u>
　　　　　Cash flow **after** debt service　　$ 107,540

　　Percentage return on down payment

　　　　=　$107,540 divided by　$480,000

　　=　22.4% Return!

As tempting as this return may seem, there are many aspects to making the proper investment decision in dealing with commercial/industrial properties. The next chapter will cover the due diligence aspect in detail.

Cervantes, through his very perceptive character of Don Quixote, had his own observation of this aspect of decision making by noting:

"Diligence is the mother of good fortune."

This serves as the guideline for the information that follows.

6

MAKING THE PROPER INVESTMENT DECISION — WHICH TYPE OF PROPERTY?

RESIDENTIAL

In 1846, Punch magazine originated the quotable quote of:

"...You pays your money and you takes your choice..."

As a real estate investor this axiom continues to hold true on the threshold of the 21st century. There are a wide variety of choices in the type and style of improved property available for real estate investment today. One will note that there is one very notable exception to the array of choices noted in this chapter. This exclusion deals with undeveloped land. This requires a unique form of entrepreneur, the real estate developer - the true gamblers in the real estate fraternity. The reason land is omitted from the choices is quite simple. Land is cost intensive extracting capital without any return until the land is converted into some economic unit which will produce income in some form. In the interim, land owners may be snake bitten by a variety of unsavory factors:

- Inability to develop to its "highest and best use."

- Environmental hazards requiring capital exceeding the land's worth to clean up.

- Involvement with the governmental approval process creating expensive unforseen requirements for development, such as devotion of a certain segment for affordable housing, thus penalizing the balance of the proposed project in the way of higher prices to subsidize the low cost areas.

- Dedications of park sites, school sites, road widening areas and the like **without compensation** in order to develop the balance of the landholding, thus reducing or possibly eliminating projected profit levels.

- Downsizing ordinances passed by municipal or county bodies, thus reducing the expected densities contemplated at purchase.

All of these factors and more preclude other than the hardiest risk takers from speculating in land. Once the land has been developed and the permitting hurdle has been surmounted, that's a different story. Residential real estate is a comfort zone for many investors because it is a category with which they are the most familiar. They probably already live in a detached single family residence. They also know neighborhoods and their characteristics that appeal to residents. Some of the types of residential choices are outlined below.

HOUSES

For purposes of classification, single family residences are classified as one to four residential units by the lending fraternity. Thus one has to examine the detached single family residence as opposed to two to four unit properties which are "mom and pop" types of investments. One of the drawbacks of single family residences is the fact that land values, particularly in urban areas, may reduce the economic productivity of the rent levels that can be obtained to the point that it makes no sense, investment-wise. During times of economic hardship in the trough of cyclical activity, however, this area can prove to be economically productive. It is important at this point to elicit the factors of value that renters of residential property consider important when choosing a location. Some of the more important factors are:

- Location within a community which offers a safe and secure enclave for its residents. Thus, police and fire protection are considerations.

- Educational opportunities for growing children and the adult population. Grade schools within walking distance is a plus with schools of higher education within easy reach.

- Transportation or freeway access — Public transportation within walking distance and proximity to on-ramps to through roads or freeways.

- Community services — Shopping for groceries and services (cleaners, hairdressers, etc.) within a few blocks and major retail centers within a three mile radius. Entertainment opportunities (theaters, bowling, restaurants, etc.) in the immediate community. Houses of worship for the major religions should be located within the community where the property is located.

- Infrastructure — In addition to well maintained streets, adequate public sewers, gas, electricity, phone service, public water, street lights, garbage and trash removal are considerations in the choice of any real property investment.

- Economic climate — Is the economy of the location well diversified without reliance on one particular industry for its survival. For example, if you are thinking of Arcata, California to invest in property, you probably couldn't obtain a property, since it is a company town totally dependent upon the lumber industry for survival. Company towns, even though private property ownership may be available, offer the least attractive investment vehicle due to their vulnerability. Lindsay, California relied heavily on its namesake, Lindsay Olives. Guess what, Lindsay Olives abandoned the town in 1992, thus decimating the local economy in the process.

Once the factors of value have been established in the region, whatever the type of property may be, then it is time to select a site within the neighborhood of the community that has been chosen. In the era of economic uncertainty that surrounds the early 1990s, this choice largely evolves around unique buys that afford themselves. One of the best methods is to drive the neighborhood and observe the degree of maintenance which real estate sales people like to refer to as "pride of ownership" or "curb appeal" of the property. If the area, on the whole is well-maintained with the majority of the homes showing manicured lawns attractive landscaping, relatively new paint jobs, etc., this is a good indication. **Do not look for the top conditioned property in the area - look for the "runt in the litter," - that's the property worth further investigation.** When negotiating with the person who has the so-called "cherry" property, they will want a price that fits the condition. Even though real property, in itself, is heterogeneous, **homogeneity** of use is one of the hallmarks of maintaining stable values. In the case of that one property that lacks the tender loving care of its neighbors, there are usually reasons for this state of condition. They range from economic hardship to the fact that the owner has died and the property has not been properly maintained for these reasons. In these times it also may represent the fact that the property is real estate owned by a financial institution or the RTC. This last situation can create a negotiation opportunity favorable to the investor, particularly in the case of financial institutions who may also be willing to provide attractive leverage in a purchasing package. Even though the unkempt property may not have a sign on it, it still may be for sale. A check with the local title company concerning the name and location of the owner will enable an investor to determine its availability. The best areas of investment are usually satellite communities surrounding major urban areas, such as Los Angeles, San Diego or San Francisco, with particular emphasis on the last two cities who remain more economically viable during the trying 90s. Typical economic analysis of any area would also involve a rent survey to determine typical rent levels for single family residences of similar size. Those forward thifking investors who snapped up residences in the Encino Park area of San Fernando Valley shortly after its development in the late 1950s are clipping coupons from that initial step up the investment ladder today. The think about single family investment is the fact that it is a step up the escalator of estate building allowing appreciation, albeit small in the initial stages, to allow one to take the next step by converting equity into larger projects. In the case of residential investors they usually tend to graduate to apartments from houses, as they feel comfortable in that arena. As a matter of analysis, here is a typical purchase situation that might be available in Desert Hot Springs, the area where service workers in the Palm Springs area live:

Type of property:	3 bedroom 2 bath home on R-2 lot (expansion possibilities)
Sale Price:	$50,000 offered as a bank repossession
Potential financing:	90% loan at 7.5%, monthly payments of $314.65 on 30 year terms
Required down pmt:	$5,000 - seller to pay all closing costs.

Investment Analysis

Rental income:	$650.00 per month plus utilities except water –	
	annual	$7,800
Vacancy allowance	10%	780
Effective income		$7,020

Expenses:	
Taxes	$ 525
Insurance	150
Water (very modest rates)	150
Maint. & Repairs	500
Total	$1,325

Net operating income	$5,695
Annual debt service	3,776
Annual cash flow after debt service	$1,919

Investor's return on down payment =
1,919 divided by 4,500, or **42.6%**!

And this doesn't include tax benefits from depreciation. Allowing $15,000 for land value and giving the property a 31 and one half year life, annual depreciation on the improvements would be $1,111 reducing annual reported income to $808.

At all costs, avoid areas subject to rent control unless your property is exempt from its restrictions!

In the case of three to four unit investments, there are occasions where positive cash flow may be attained, again seeking those fringe areas around major metropolitan centers. In many cases these types of investments involve the owner/manager living on the premises using the rental income from the remaining units to contribute toward reduction of the owner's debt service and housing expense. A four unit property will be used as an example of this type of situation. The investment details are as follows:

Typical sales price @ $50,000 per unit	$200,000
Down payment required	40,000
Available financing (8.5%, 30 year terms)	160,000

Investor Profile

Rental from units other than owners @ $500 each – annualized	$18,000
Vacancy allowance 10%	1,800
Effective income	$16,200

```
        Expenses:
Taxes                                    $  2,200
Insurance                                    600
Utilities (incl. own.)                     3,800
Maintenance and Repair                     1,500
    Total                               $  8,100
Net income before debt service          $  8,100
Annual debt service = $1,230 x 12 =      $14,763
Negative cash flow from investment      ($  6,663)
```

Even though this example is negative in nature, there are real estate owned properties of this nature that will pencil out with positive cash flow.

CONDOMINIUMS

Condominium ownership is a bit trickier than the detached single family residence due to the fact that a homeowners association is involved who are charged with enforcement of a variety of restrictions that one doesn't necessarily confront with single family residences. In addition to the fact that there is usually an architectural committee which governs any contemplated improvements to your property, monthly maintenance fees are not necessarily within the individual owner's control. The reason for this anomaly is the fact that most homeowners groups have their own political structure. This means that if you have "big spenders," the monthly maintenance fees will be industrial strength. It is very difficult to pass on homeowners fee increases to tenants, thus reducing the investment return in the process. A similar profitability analysis would be performed in this type of property as was done with single family residences adding on the factor of homeowners dues with a realistic outlook as to potential increases in them. The best condominium rental levels are usually attainable in resort areas such, as mountains, ocean-oriented and desert communities during season.

APARTMENTS

Residential properties in excess of four units are classified as apartments. They come in all sizes and varieties, but enjoy distinct classifications:

- By services offered - apartments may range from no services offered to full hotel services including maid, laundry, valet parking and the like.

- By design - ranging from residences forming a row in a court, to garden apartments, to a class A high rise structure.

- By financing - FHA projects require considerable reporting requirements concerning tenant income, etc., since usually return on investment is limited to 6% of a fictional 11% equity investment. Conventionally financed projects require less paperwork, although effective management is essential in each category as a method of expense reduction and maintenance of higher occupancy levels.

There are many investors that feel perfectly comfortable with apartment investments and have made a conscious decision to remain in this area. The opportunities lie in **existing** buildings where economic circumstances due to over building have created investment opportunities. In most urban areas new apartment development has been discouraged, since the return on investment when land cost starts getting to $50,000 to $75,000 per unit no longer makes sense economically. For this reason, many developers in the apartment area have sought conversion to condominiums in order to make the project financially feasible. Usually a minimum optimum economic unit for investment in apartments is in the 16 unit range. A typical 16 unit building will be used as an investment vehicle example for this purpose. Apartment investors must be aware of the local requirements relative to resident managers, any taxes that may be imposed for business purposes on apartment owners and the like. Each added expense goes right back to reducing the return on investment.

Our 16 unit building is composed of 4 - 1's and 12 - 2's. The one bedrooms rent for $500 per month and the two's rent for $700 per month, which are considered competitive by a local rental survey. In surveying historical data, it has been determined that a normal vacancy allowance would be 5% and that expenses would be in the range of 35%. Based upon the data derived, the following income and expense analysis applies:

Investor Analysis

Monthly income $10,400 x 12 = annual rents of	$124,800
Vacancy allowance = 5%	6,240
Effective income	$118,560
Expenses = 35%	41,496
Net operating income =	$ 77,064

Net income capitalized at 9% = $855,000 (rounded)

Loan available under conventional terms would be 75% of value ($640,000), 8 1/2%, 30 year amortization fixed with a 7 year call. Monthly payments of $4,921 annualized are $59,053.

Subtracting from the net operating income of $77,064 the annual debt service of $59,053, leaves $18,011 available for return on the investor's down payment of $215,000. The return on income after debt service of 8.4% (rounded) is not too attractive to the average investor for the ownership risk involved, particularly in light of the litigious nature of our society combined with the management problems attached to residential property that require extensive personal contact on a regular basis. This example represents a normal financing situation. In the case where an apartment is in a real estate owned category there is usually a reduction in the quality of management which allows prospective purchasers more leverage in negotiating sale prices and loans to facilitate purchase terms that can double the return shown above.

There are special investment opportunities available for those familiar with FHA project financing in the various programs available which require specialized knowledge. In addition Section 8 leases negotiated on apartments with local housing authorities can provide assured income to apartment owners without the hassle of qualifying tenants.

COMMERCIAL

In this highly specialized area of investments American Capital Investments has found a unique investment window that has been opened by the vulnerability of financial institutions to regulatory criticism of real estate owned as well as the liquidated institutions representative, the Resolution Trust Corporation in their combined quest to clear this inventory of **unwanted** properties off of their books. In addition to the area amenities noted in the residential property categories, population density, buying power and the availability of qualified labor force drive the users of retail establishments and office structures to a particular specific location. Where the location that the area falls in an economic cycle is also of great importance. For example, you are not going to open a store that deals principally in ski rental and the sale of other winter related sports equipment in July. There wouldn't be much call for your wares. On the other hand, if you, as a retailer, diversified your product line to include, ski, camping and swimming gear, you're destined for a year round operation. Timing is extremely important in the opening of a retail business as the following might indicate.

SHOPPING CENTERS — RETAIL

Shopping activity has gravitated from the central districts of the past where strip shops predominated to the vast malls stretching the length of our land today. Probably the most successful shopping center developer of regional malls is California based Ernest W. Hahn, Inc. It seems as if the Hahn organization had an unlimited supply of major department store clients which served as the anchor catalyst creating a magnet to draw satellite stores to the anticipated honey of eager shoppers tramping the mall aisles. Sometimes one cannot discern the ugly specter of diminishing returns. There were imitators of the successful Hahn formula who tried with varying degrees of success to follow in Mr. Hahn's footsteps. Sometimes the path got a little rocky. A good example of this is the Old Town Mall located on Hawthorne Blvd. in Torrance, California. The developers of this mall tried the arty/crafty approach to vending wares in their over 200 shops by parasiting off a free standing K-mart store to the north and using a Mann Theaters multi-screen complex as their southern anchor. As a way of attracting families, they placed a merry-go-round in the center of the project and created a food court for a variety of fast food type operations. To this day the mall is still trying to understand its identity and obtain the proper tenancy to remain on a profitable basis. The shop owners, other than the fast food places and the merry-go-round found themselves with a bunch of lookie-loos who weren't willing to buy in sufficient quantity to warrant their continued existence.

In the case of larger retail operations, such as regional malls, establishment of identity and purpose is an important element in preservation of income stream in the long run. During the frantic 1980s, new retail space, particularly in the form of one to four acre mini-malls created the pock marked effect of total retail hysteria in the market place. Corner service stations (a current oxymoron) were supplanted by the La Manchas, Seven Elevens, Circle Ks, Windsors, Key Shopping Centers and their ilk with tiny shopping enclaves, usually terribly under parked, to serve the buying habits of a neighborhood with high density. The net result of this vast building spree of the '80s is a proliferation of vacancies to greet the '90s. This is true at **all** retail levels today reflective of the general economic atmosphere, particularly in California, vis-a-vis the balance of the nation. Typical economic analysis of the shopping center would be on the same basis as any other type of income producing property by using the economic analysis of the property. An additional wrinkle that this type of property adds to the analysis is not only the quantity of the income stream but the **quality** of the income stream. In this event, that means that leases that are negotiated on individual spaces have to be analyzed not only on the basis of the amount of income that is being derived, but the term of the lease and the innate ability of the tenant to service the lease. For example, Seven Eleven Markets and Chief Auto Parts are franchises of Dallas based Southland Corporation. From a financing standpoint, the individual franchisee stands little chance of obtaining real estate financing on their stores. This means that to obtain adequate financing, the Southland Corporation had to guarantee lease payment on many of their stores in order for their franchisees to obtain permanent financing. Under the accounting board rules, guaranteed lease payments are a **contingent liability** and, as such, erode the potential borrowing power of the guarantor. In the case of Southland Corporation in their quest for expansion, some of these lessee's operations failed and Southland had to take over the payments. This, along with other operating problems, caused Southland to seek Chapter 11 bankruptcy protection. In addition, they immediately ceased further store expansion in Southern California concurrent with their financial problems. This, theoretically, created and investment opportunity for Circle K Corporation, Southland's Arizona competition to move from the fringes of Los Angeles into the Los Angeles area in their store expansion program. Guess What? Circle K is entered into a similar Chapter 11 proceeding in the year 1992.

Successful retail operations today are leaning toward the discount mode. The introduction of the discounters into the mainstream through the use of "power centers" devoted strictly to the K-marts, Wal Marts, Ross, Home Base, Pace, Price Club and the like has changed the shopping habits of even the wealthy. It is not uncommon to see the pricey automobiles ensconced in a Wal Mart parking lot. Along with this phenomena is the factory stores which are usually freeway oriented in relatively remote locations like Cabazon, Lake Elsinore and Victorville, for example. This places some of the more posh areas as Rodeo Drive in Beverly Hills and El Paseo in Palm Desert in jeopardy. Retailers, such as Bullocks, Robinsons, I. Magnin, The Broadway, May Company and similar operations in a very precarious competitive situation. Their ability to subsist, in the long run, is subject to question. Stores like Sears, Penneys, Montgomery Ward and similar operations have had to completely change their philosophy just to keep up with this new discounting competitiveness. With a variety of retailers competing for the limited amount of retail dollars available, there's bound to be some fall out. Discounters the likes of Fed Mart; Federated's White Front

Stores; Lucky Stores Gemco Division (largely supplanted by Dayton-Hudson's Target Stores); Pay N Pak and others have been chopped down by the ax of competition.

Lease payment terms on retail operations will usually contain in addition to the basic rent, annual increases for increased cost based on the cost of living index and additional percentage rents over and above the basic rents when retail sales exceed a certain minimum. For example, if a 25,000 square foot retail store pays a $1.00 p.s.f. NNN (all expenses born by the tenant) rental, when sales exceed $2,500,000 the lease might provide for a 1% of gross above that amount as additional rent. Thus, if annual sales for the outlet were $3,000,000, the basic annual rent would be $300,000 plus 1% of $ $500,000, or $5,000. This may not be a typical example, but is illustrative of the concept involved. Retail represents the last area in a recovery stage to prosper from increased population buying power.

OFFICE BUILDINGS

One of the first stages to recover is the area of office space where corporate headquarters utilize these areas as a focal point of expansion.

Office space users are of the type that their needs vary dependent upon the vicissitudes of the economy. It can be likened to the expanding and contracting bellows of an accordion. Some of the advantages of office building ownership lie in areas where economic activity is projected to outperform the economy generally. Two such areas previously mentioned in Chapter four were Orlando, Florida and San Diego, California. In the case of the former, a broad economic base combined with excellent demographics has provided excellent investment potential for capital infusion into office building projects. Just, as in other areas, each of these locations has been suffering from higher vacancies, but the potential for future absorption is excellent. As with other property types, availability of local services and amenities is important. Similar to retail, office tenants need to have access to a qualified labor pool; a prestige address; adequate parking for employees and guests; competitive rent levels; competent and efficient property management; and access to clients, among other things. Demographics of Orlando fit into a typical office user's profile as an office location. Conversely, the surge of new space that was created in the late 1980s in the Orlando area has created uncomfortable situations for commercial lenders who have advanced monies on commercial properties with the expectation of 80% or higher occupancy levels only to be disappointed in this expectation. As it can be seen by the two opportunities created by American Capital Investments,

Inc. of office situations in the Orlando area the lender's **distress** can be converted into investor's **success.** Two outstanding examples of how investment in Orlando can keep pace with the individual real estate investor's goals for tax benefits and attractive return on investment lie in the analysis of the offerings on Grand National Plaza executive office park and Wilshire Plaza. These offerings were created as a result of extensive study of the Orlando area and its upside potential for the future. Pertinent data on Grand National are exhibited in Illustration 6-1.

It should be noted that the current financial institution owner, in this case, is taking a <u>minimum</u> write-down of $4,950,000 from their original loan amount! This is typical of the deals being negotiated by lenders on real estate owned as an effort to clean up their books succumbing to regulatory pressure along with their own Boards of Directors' needs to avoid sanctions by regulatory authorities for failure to act in a responsible manner.

A smaller project, but equally attractive is Wilshire Plaza where the bank owner is taking a minimum loss of $1,450,000 in order to dispose of the property. This project has retail and office prospects in its tenant mix where one use compliments the other. Financial details of this project are shown in Illustration 6-2.

Not to be outdone by the prospect of Orlando, the maquiladora influence in the San Diego area has generated considerable investment potential for office space in that location. American Capital Investments, Inc., through its REO negotiation capabilities has found another investment opportunity in the Sorrento Mesa area in North San Diego that warrants particular attention in their offering of Sorrento Reo Partners III. Some of the pertinent investment data is shown in Illustrations 6-3 and 6-4.

Again it should be noted that the current lender/owner is experiencing a considerable write-down of their investment as a means of disposing of the property and easing regulatory pressure for property disposal in the process.

These three examples are typical of commercial property investments available within areas which Fortune Magazine rates as tops for business. In order for office space to be utilized, interest in industrial space must also be fostered. In some cases, land use applications fuzzy up the investor's conception of the difference between office space and industrial space.

Illustration 6-1

GRAND NATIONAL PLAZA
7001-7111 GRAND NATIONAL DRIVE
ORLANDO, FLORIDA
8 Office Buildings
12.9 Acres of Land

Purchase Price	$ 3,050,000
Original Loan Balance	$ 8,000,000
Previous Appraisal (02/24/92)	$ 4,900,000
Current Loan Balance	$ 2,119,000
Terms of Loan	30 yr. amortization--due in 7 yrs.
	Mos. 1-6 @ 0%
	Mos. 7-12 @ 8.75%
	Mos. 13-84 @ 9.5%

Current Payment (Month 7)	$ 16,676
Square Footage	136,104
Price per Square Foot	$ 22.41
Age	8

FINANCIAL ANALYSIS (SUMMARY)

	CURRENT (50% Leased)	PROJECTED (75% Leased)
Income	$ 727,458	$ 1,032,000
Expenses	*$ 526,256	*$ 317,280
NOI	$ 201,202	$ 714,720
Debt Service	$ 200,112	$ 200,112
Cash Flow	$ 1,090	$ 274,608

Comments: Property had been bank-operated for 2 years and is in excellent condition. 12.9 acres of core office/industrial park in an area with little competition. Services tourist oriented and satellite offices. Good tenant mix. Very clean. Being absorbed rapidly. At this extremely low cost basis, no other center can compete. Expenses were cut $75,000 by eliminating bank's on-site administrative services.

*The current expenses reflect a one-time extraordinary building improvement expense of $240,000 paid in 1991. The expenses also reflect property taxes based on an inflated value resulting from the original $8,000,000 loan. Following close of escrow, the taxes were reduced by approximately $70,000 per year.

INDUSTRIAL

Industrial users have a varied agenda concerning their needs. Sometimes the owners of a firm will dictate the firm's location based upon desirability as a place to live, attractive climate, a pro-business attitude by the city fathers, tax incentives and the like. Over and above these obvious attractions, industries, whether they be extractive, assemblage, fabrication, or whatever have a few basic requirements that must be met in any location. Usually the greatest promoters and providers of industrial space for development are the nation's railroads who have a financial incentive to provide locations in an effort to attract more freightage.

The attractiveness of location as a desirable residential area has already been covered in the residential section of this chapter. In addition to these attributes, industry usually has some special needs:

- Adequate labor pool - in some cases labor must be imported from other areas, such as General Motors location of the Saturn assembly plant in Tennessee, a boon economically to the area.

- Transportation - rail, surface, air, car and sea - raw materials and finished products need a way of reaching the location and being shipped from there. This becomes a definite bottom line consideration in all industrial locations.

- A Building that will accommodate stacking heights - As one will note with warehouse facilities, such as the Price Club, Pace, Levitz Furniture, Home Base and similar operations, ceiling height for stacking of goods to maximize cubic footage available is essential to their operation.

- Dock high loading facilities - Those firms dealing with trucking as well as rail served need this type of accommodation.

- Adequate parking - sufficient to satisfy the needs of employees, vendors and clients.

- Accessibility to raw materials and customers - It's no surprise that Detroit's automotive muscle has some degree of proximity to Pittsburgh's steel mills. That is why fabrication of most autos is back east, while assembly of components shipped by rail may be done in other locations. The garment industry clusters in New

Illustration 6-2

WILSHIRE PLAZA
110-210 WILSHIRE BOULEVARD
CASSELBERRY, FLORIDA
ORLANDO, FLORIDA
2 Office Buildings
2 Acres of Land

Purchase Price	$ 2,650,000
Original Loan Balance	$ 4,100,000
Appraisal Value	$ 3,500,000
Current Loan Balance	$ 2,159,750
Terms of Loan	30 yr. amortization - due in 7 yrs.
	Mos. 1-6 @ 0%
	Mos. 7-12 @ 8.75%
	Mos. 13-84 @ 9.5%
Current Payment (Month 7)	$ 16,991.33
Square Footage	51,457
Price per Square Foot	$ 51.49
Age	6

FINANCIAL ANALYSIS (SUMMARY)

	CURRENT (56% Leased)	PROJECTED (75% Leased)
Income	$ 310,193	$ 551,667
Expenses	$ 51,240	$ 64,300
NOI	$ 258,953	$ 452,367
Debt Service	$ 203,895	$ 203,895
Cash Flow	$ 55,058	$ 248,472

Comments: Most leases are NNN so expenses are low. Great neighborhood center. Cash flows with 56% occupancy. Just taken back by bank -- in bankruptcy for 9 months. Had not been marketed for sale. Great upside!

Illustration 6-3

SORRENTO REO PARTNERS III
PROPERTY ANALYSIS

Mesa View Office Center
6725 Mesa Ridge Road
San Diego, CA 92121

Parcel size: 1.52 acres
Net Profitable Sq. Ft.: 32,549
Year Completed: 1986

ANNUAL INCOME AND EXPENSES

		CURRENT (78% OCCUPANCY)	PROJECTED (90% OCCUPANCY)
GROSS INCOME		$414,168.	$477,886.15
EXPENSES			
REAL ESTATE TAXES (1.067%)	($20,270.)		
INSURANCE	($4,321.)		
MANAGEMENT (4%)	($11,790.)		
UTILITIES	($19,770.)		
MAINTENANCE	($15,960.)		
JANITORIAL	($11,807.)		
		($83,918.)	($93,000.)
NET OPERATING INCOME		$330,250.	$384,886.
ANNUAL PRINCIPAL & INTEREST PAYMENT		($144,900.)	($144,900.)
ANNUAL PRETAX CASH FLOW		$185,350.	$239,986.

REO–ORIGINAL LOAN AMOUNT	$3,6000,000.
10% CAP	$3,302,500.
7/92 APPRAISAL	$3,300,000.
PARTNERSHIP COST	$2,273,153.
BUILT-IN-PROFIT	$1,026,847. = 45%

Illustration 6-4

SORRENTO REO PARTNERS III
ONE YEAR PROJECTED INVESTMENT RETURN

CAPITAL INVESTED	ANNUAL +16% INTEREST	MONTHLY CHECK	MINIMUM RETURN	*PLUS 45% BUILT-IN-PROFIT	TOTAL
$200,000.	$32,000.	($2,666.)	$232,000.	$90,000.	$322,000.
$150,000.	$24,000.	($2,000.)	$174,000.	$67,000.	$241,500.
$100,000.	$16,000.	($1,333.)	$116,000.	$45,000.	$161,000.
$50,000.	$8,000.	($666.)	$58,000.	$22,500.	$80,500.
$25,000.	$4,000.	($333.)	$29,000.	$11,200.	$40,200.

Plus 100% Profit Appreciation on a Pro-Rata Basis, of net Proceeds of Sale, above Partnership Cost Basis
* Built-in-Profit is realized when property is sold; Plus 100% of additional profit appreciation.

Note: 1. Cost basis of building to partnership/investors is   = $2,273,153.

2. Current appraisal is   = $3,300,000.

3. Built-in profit to Partnership is: $3,300,000.
   $2,273,153.
   $1,026,847. = 45%

York because clients nationwide have been attuned to visiting the Big Apple as the manufacturers show off their new fashions.

- Proper design to meet the tenant's needs - Some industrial applications, such as an oil refinery or coal mining operation, have special purpose applications that are not readily accommodated to other uses.

Weighing these factors of value noted above is the fact that in order for any industrial operation to be successful, competent management knowledgeable in the field is essential to the continued operation of the firm. In some cases, Boards of Directors will hire senior management in a manufacturing firm right out of Harvard, Stanford, Wharton or some other prestigious business school only to find out that theory alone won't cut the management mustard. Lenders not only look at financial statement performance, but the quality of management and provision for successor management when dealing with industrial firms.

PARKS

Today it is sometimes difficult to ascertain the difference between what is office, retail and industrial. A good example is the eclectic display of an industrial park. To some extent the description of Grand National Plaza in Orlando is an eclectic tenancy that represents this type of diversity. Obviously well located facilities such as this offer tremendous future potential if acquired at the proper phase of the real estate cycle in a positioning for growth.

LARGER INDUSTRIAL STRUCTURES

Larger structures (those above 100,000 square feet in size) are usually constructed with pre-cast walls in tilt-up construction with glu-laminated beam ceiling supports. Typically this office/warehouse type of building will have 10-15% air conditioned office space and sprinklered warehouse space with exposed beams. Many times this larger building is subdivided into 10,000 to 15,000 square foot sections for individual tenants.

These are the types of buildings in established industrial areas that attract life insurance company financing. Insurance companies generally prefer new construction and offer the most attractive terms for projects where the financing needs are minimally $2,000,000 or more. Some of the weakness of the commercial market has caused many of the players to back off of their aggressive lending attitudes toward this type of property during the slump of the early 1990s, especially in light of the problems experienced (very publicly) by New Jersey located Mutual Benefit Life Insurance Company. Due to the fact that insurance companies have timed released financial data, the picture as to how badly the insurance companies have been affected by their commercial/industrial portfolios is still a bit hazy. Suffice to say, there are also real estate owned opportunities that the knowledgeable investor can obtain from this source as well. The key in all REO situations is having enough capital accumulated to have the lenders take notice. Again financial analysis would follow the same pattern as shown in the office building section of this chapter. Finding the right location, analyzing the opportunities available and coming up with the appropriate recommendation is an extensive process. This is best fitted to the experts who have the ability to structure the investment to make it attractive for capital providers to join in this activity.

INCUBATOR BUILDINGS

In this world of risks and rewards, incubator buildings show that element of risk, but the rewards are substantial. These buildings, which are normally concrete block or brick in nature, are usually rented on the basis of small spaces, say 800 to 1,100 square feet, on short-term leases (allowing quick upward rent adjustments) to tenants who are not the General Electrics or American Telephone type credits. These buildings can be very profitable. Some variations of this type of theme are the auto bays which have become very popular due to the lack of service facilities at gas stations and mini-warehouses for the storage requirements for users needing excess storage capacity. Each of this modifications of smaller industrial facilities where properly located have shown steady growth in popularity. This type of investment is usually not of the size that would warrant syndication.

SPECIAL PURPOSE PROPERTIES

In the case of special purpose properties conduct of the business is key to continued operation. Lending in these areas is so specialized as to not be attractive to the investment community unless the individual investor has peculiar knowledge of the specific industry involved.

Some of the properties that are classified as special purpose include:

- Bowling alleys - Usually require a minimum of 32 lanes together with cocktail and eating facilities located near an industrial area, preferably with three shifts. The principal ingredient for satisfactory bottom line performance lies in the ability of the operator to attract leagues on a year round basis. Loans are usually limited to 50% of economic value with the lanes, usually provided by AMF or Brunswick being considered personal property. Some thought should be given to the convertability factor of the facility to other uses.

- Hotels/Motels - Panell, Kerr, Foerster, a national accounting firm is the one that provides most of the feasibility studies for this type of property. Most financing of the major chains and/or franchises is provided through commercial lines of credit secured by trust indentures on all property holdings of the operator. Successful operations maintain occupancy in the 60-70% range. Main asset of chains is the reservations network assuring them of some degree of occupancy from clients using a convenient 800 number with the exception of Motel 6 which operates under a number that clients have to pay the toll to make a reservation. The motivation in the latter is the savings on the daily rate by this national chain.

- Churches - Generally self-financed by the membership with a few specialized lenders providing financing on the basis of cumulative guarantys from financially responsible church members.

- Movies and Drive-In Theaters - The latter is almost arcane in nature surviving on the alternative use as a swap meet location to survive. In the case of movies, property rich exhibitors are now converting to renters of multiple screen facilities in shopping center locations turning from real property secured borrowers into personal property secured borrowers. Main lenders are the nation's commercial banks dealing on massive participation lines of credit with the major exhibitors. For example, the nation's largest exhibitor, General Cinema out of Boston is also the largest Coca Cola bottling franchise in the nation. These peripheral activities can create a profit center in themselves.

- Service Stations - Operators' leases are usually financed through commercial banks based upon a letter from the oil company which promises payment of the loan in full if the lease is canceled. Oil companies after dumping service locations by the carloads in the 1960s and 1970s finally realized that these locations were an impulse retail gold mine that had been untapped. This is after the mini-mall operators had taken these locations by the carloads during the earlier years. Now the trend is toward selling impulse items like snack food and candy with gas pumping as an incidental to the operation. Arco with its AM/PM operation led the way in this trend.

- Parking lots and Structures - It makes one wonder why urban area parking lots located in cities such as Los Angeles are not improved with high rise office buildings to meet their income potential. The reason is very simple. The operator can make more return on investment as a parking lot than can be made operating an office structure. This property is analyzed on a per space basis. The analysis determines how many business days there are in a year, say 252. Then the average stay per space is computed, say 3 hours. If you have a nine hour day the average number of turns in that space will be three. The average income per stay is then calculated, say $5.00. The formula for computing the income thus becomes $15.00 x 252, or $3,780 per space/year multiplied by the number of spaces equals the annual income for the entire facility. To these very gross numbers is applied a generous vacancy allowance, validation expense, personnel costs and the like to get to the bottom line number. Well managed parking facilities are highly desirable properties.

- Hospitals and other Medical facilities - These types of operations are usually highly personnel intensive and are analyzed on a per bed basis. The industry is in a state of transition with heavy emphasis on preventive medicine and Health Maintenance Organization formation. This, in turn, is escalating the cost of major medical insurance plans as they are being eased out of the picture. Most financing of these operations is done through fund raising and bond issues controlling financial statement performance in addition to the FHA project financing (under sections 231, 242 and Title XI) availability in certain instances.

- Mobile Home Parks - Again FHA has a financing program available under its project financing program under section 207. Mobile home park operators again have a high yielding form of operation, since minimal improvements have to be provided to the land. A recreation building, swimming pool, tennis courts and a few other amenities over an above the spaces prepared for the mobile homes together with utility and sewage hook-ups put the operator in business for a high yielding investment opportunity.

In reviewing each of these special purpose properties it is important to emphasize that no recommendation for investment is made to real estate investors. The property classifications above are but a few of a wide variety of special purpose uses that should only be considered for investment purposes if the individual investor has considerable exposure to the field.

Edmund Burke in his **Letter to a Noble Lord,** written in 1796 noted:

"... Economy is a distributive virtue, and consists not in saving, but selection. Parsimony requires no providence, no sagacity, no powers of combination, no comparison, no judgment . . ."

The astute real estate investor selects an appropriate vehicle, but is not stingy once the selection is made. Our next chapter devotes itself to performing due diligence on the selected property.

7
DUE DILIGENCE

Miguel De Cervantes' **Don Quixote** provides a wealth of time tested adages. One of these most familiar sayings is:

".. . Diligence is the mother of good fortune . . ."

De Cervantes must have had real estate in mind when he penned that phrase.

All of the capital in the world chasing the most lucrative of transactions is for naught in the case of real property if the investor has not done the necessary investigative home work required to test the uncertain waters of the property in question. No dedication of capital should be undertaken unless the investor or his agent have done the appropriate due diligence necessary in an effort to reduce the element of risk to the minimum.

In the previous chapter there were several projects that were analyzed relative to their profitability as an investment vehicle. In this chapter the methodology utilized by American Capital Investments, Inc. and other responsible syndicators for assemblage of an offering will be covered in detail.

FEASIBILITY STUDIES

In chapter six some of the factors of value making investments in a variety of real property applications were discussed at length. In order to determine that these factors are present in a given situation, considerable research is required. There are many properties now listed as scheduled items on financial statements of lenders throughout the Country. This publication has noted that one of the first things required is to pinpoint an area for investment concentration. Chapter four has pinpointed areas for concentration of the study. It was also observed that even in areas where generally economic recovery will lag the rest of the nation, there are still pockets of opportunity. The best examples of this observation are San Diego and San Francisco, California where the state's recovery is lagging, while these areas, for a variety of reasons will outperform the state as a whole.

Once the area of study has been identified, then it becomes a matter of moving from the community to a definite location within the community. First and foremost, one must determine what properties are available in a chosen category. As noted in previous chapters, commercial and industrial properties offer the most attractive terms from lenders who suffer from extreme regulatory pressure to convert these property into some form of earning assets on the corporate books. With this thought in mind, the next step is to determine availability of buildings which fit the overall investment criteria for return on equity, favorable leverage, and long term potential. Much of this is determined by the location of the property in question and the degree of anxiety on the part of the lender relative to real estate owned languishing on the balance sheet.

Keeping in mind the factors of value associated with commercial and industrial property covered in the previous chapter, a concerted search of the study area will begin. The first thing that one conducting a feasibility study will do is to visit the local Chambers of Commerce and obtain as much information as possible about the economic base of the community including a map of the metropolitan area as a means of orientation. Of prime importance is the discovery of how broad the economic base is in the area. Wide industry diversification is a robust economic signal. Dependence upon a single industry is a sign of vulnerability. Secondly, copies of all of the major newspapers in the area, particularly the Sunday editions, in order to get a feel for real estate values and the availability of properties in general in the area.

By driving the streets of the community and observing one can see by the real estate signs on properties which brokerage appears to handle the bulk of the properties in the study category. In Southern California major brokerages, such as CB Commercial, Grubb and Ellis, Cushman and Wakefield, The Seeley Company, et. al are extremely visible relative to commercial and industrial properties. Some of these firms, such as CB Commercial and Cushman and Wakefield have a national presence. Once the predominant local player has been identified, contact would be made to get a feel for vacancy levels, locational characteristics and the like. Care should be taken that the information provided should be taken with a "grain of salt" because the firm has a financial interest in steering the feasibility investigator in a certain direction. To a real estate professional this form of puffery can be filtered while obtaining useful information for the study area. Real estate professionals can ascertain very quickly, by observation, prime locations in a given area. Time, experience and "real estate sense" are excellent instructors in the area of sensing opportunity.

Following a trip to the local brokerage which should have provided the information concerning the leading commercial/industrial lender in the area, a trip to that institution's headquarters to speak to the chief credit officer is in order. It is poor form to write letters to financial institutions for REO lists or to call them on the phone to ask if they have any REO properties. Proper business form is to make an appointment with the chief credit officer or the person in charge of property liquidation in the firm. One can attain better results in that fashion. The approach to the lender should be on the basis that a study is being made of the area for potential investment. In this regard it would be appreciated if they could identify any properties available for sale in the commercial/industrial category. When the inquiry is made on a more professional basis, there is a higher degree of possibility for lender cooperation.

Sometimes a visit to the leading broker in the area is sufficient, since the leading lender may have already listed their REOs with them. In this case, the initial visit would be sufficient. The conductor of the feasibility study will then have a set up on the property showing the details relative to the site, its improvements, and financial details relative to the productivity of its occupancy levels including lease terms. From this array of data a specific site may be chosen for study.

Once a site has been selected, the investigative routine addresses a number of study areas. Some of the more critical areas of concern are:

- Adequacy of utilities - Even though there are improvements that are utility served on the site, expansion potential dictates concern over availability of water, in particular, in certain areas. Utility rates and their trending also have considerable impact on the desirability of office space both for the investor and the tenants.

- Labor force - Economic data gathered from census tract information and local sources can help the investigator determine the availability of qualified workers in the area as well as the wage levels they expect. One of California's burning economic problems that has plagued employers is the high cost of housing causing workers to expect higher wage levels than in other areas of the country.

- Adequacy of housing - Is there sufficient housing at affordable rates available to service the current population and expected future growth?

- Transportation - Can workers through means of well planned traffic circulation networks or public transportation commute from residential areas to the location in question within a reasonable time. 45 to 60 minutes would seem to be the outer limits in these situations. There will always be commuters who are willing to exceed this time, but this should not be the criteria. Employers who locate in the Elysian Park Industrial Complex along San Fernando Road in Los Angeles have chosen that location because they are able to attract workers for minimum wages to that area. These workers who generally live on the east side of town have public transportation, their mode of travel, available to the work site.

- Area amenities - Are there shopping, eating establishments and other features of convenience to the employee within easy access to the location? Workers enjoy diversion during lunch hours and breaks. In the case of the latter, is there an establishment on the property where employees can go on their coffee breaks? In office parks, such as the planned area of Irvine in Orange County, a separate food park was established for workers to spend their lunch hours as a means of social discourse.

- Building design - Windowless structures may have an aesthetic appeal, but the psychological effect on some workers may be devastating. Windows have some degree of assurance and contact with the outside world. Additionally, round buildings may also appeal to the eye, but a lot of practical usable space is lost in these applications. As a owner, you're concerned about efficiency. Maximum space utilization dictates a relatively square building. In the case of office buildings a rule of thumb is that the net rentable space should be minimally 80% of the gross space. This is referred to as the **efficiency ratio** of the building. One of the initial drawbacks of the problem plagued One Wilshire Building in downtown Los Angeles was the fact that its efficiency ratio was barely above 60% due to the wasted space of high ceilings and over wide hallways that dot the structure. If investment is contemplated in a Class A building (steel and concrete), the replacement costs are considerably higher than a frame and stucco Class D structure.

- Parking - Parking adequacy for employees, vendors and clients is always a concern. If you can't park where you are doing business, you're discouraged from doing business. The retail trade that exists in mini-malls in the Los Angeles area have learned that painful lesson. The city of Los Angeles requires one parking space for each 500 square feet of office space. This minimum requirement would be adequate if office tenants had minimal visits from customers and vendors. If the office houses a vocational school, this parking is totally inadequate to accommodate the users of the building. If the building under study has a heavy space user, such as a school, it is probably not a good investment candidate, since depreciation, repairs and maintenance items tend to escalate in that situation. Adequate parking is essential not only for the potential revenue but to assure the economic livelihood of the tenancy.

- Work Environment - Does the building provide a healthy work environment for the tenancy? Is it a building that is light and airy or one with dark dank halls providing an atmosphere of doom? Not only is the environment within the building where a safe and healthful work place should be afforded, but in the surrounding area as well. Are there security concerns in the immediate area? Is there a high incidence of crime that might pose a threat to employees, particularly female employees? A safe work environment provides the basis for a higher level of morade encouraging potential users as to the desirability of this location to office their firm.

- Competition - What is the degree of office space vacancy in the area? James Lang Wooten provides vacancy data for offices throughout the country. There will probably be local sources that can provide an accurate estimate of vacancy. Visual observation of competing buildings and their signage can also provide valuable clues as to the accuracy of the information provided. By conducting a rent survey of the area, one can determine whether the existing rent levels in the building are realistic relative to its competition. Due to the convoluted nature of lease arrangements, it must be determined how the rent is calculated in a given situation. Some buildings lease on a gross basis paying all utilities, while others may rent on a net basis with the tenant paying all charges including property taxes and insurance. It is important to convert these figures on a consistent basis to determine if the building under study fits a competitive profile.

- Tenant attitude - When dealing with an existing building one should find what features appeal to the tenants and what constitutes their concerns. This allows the feasibility conductor to determine the strengths and weaknesses of current management. It may also serve as the basis for a management plan once the building is acquired. Properly managed buildings result in the highest potential yields to investors.

SITE INVESTIGATION

When dealing with any REO situation, prospective purchasers need to be aware of environmental concerns that have been expressed on federal, state and municipal level. This concern is not just limited to the very visible air quality given daily readings by Air Quality Management Districts. The concern goes far beyond that compartmental enclave. Toxicity abounds in a variety of situations creating environmental hazards not readily discernable by the public at large. In certain areas of the country, particularly the south and midwest, the build up of radon gas in structures is of some concern. If a building was built prior to 1979, there is a definite possibility that carcinogenic forming asbestos was used either as wall insulation, in ceiling tiles, or on floor coverings in structures. Brick buildings in Los Angeles must comply with a Division 88 Ordinance dealing with proper reinforcement as a means of earthquake protection. In the case of properties that are within close proximity of a toxic waste dump, there may be soil and water pollution problems. Certain buildings in the Fairfax area of Los Angeles are fitted with valves to release the methane gas build up at regular intervals. Real estate brokers in California must advise their sellers to complete a seller disclosure form indicating all potential hazards or problems connected with residential property to a purchaser. The list seems endless.

Of particular interest to commercial/industrial investors is the Americans with Disabilities Act of 1990. Certain structural modifications of improvements as well as the work place within the improvements are required to accommodate handicapped workers and visitors to that location. These modifications might include ramps for wheelchairs, elevators adapted for braille to indicate the floors, telephones with hearing enhancement for the deaf along with special keyboards for their use, handicapped access rest rooms, and the like. Some of these modifications can be extremely expensive. If the building under study does not comply with this Act, this compliance should be a requirement in the negotiation process.

In performing a site investigation particular care should be given to construction quality and any evidence of possible contamination at the location. Deferred maintenance should get particular attention. Any needed repairs to roof systems, electrical systems or heating/air conditioning systems should be noted. Ease of access or lack of it is of some concern. If the site is keyed to traffic signals, that is a plus for ease of entry. Sometimes there may be a location that is on a busy business street, which is fine to attract business, but the traffic may be going at such a speed as to discourage customers from entry to the site. This is one of the problems locating next to a freeway offramp. In undertaking a thorough examination of the site and its features, the investigator obtains the necessary data essential in undertaking negotiations with the seller.

ENVIRONMENTAL CONCERNS

As noted above, environmental hazards can be costly and burdensome for property owners. Under the various Superfund acts, prior owners and users of property where hazardous materials have been found share joint responsibility for the clean up of these items. To a certain extent, the regulators have been insulated from the responsibility to replenish the cleanup fund for environmentally impacted properties that they acquire. This same benefit has not been conferred upon lenders in dealing with REO properties. Several leading cases involving lenders have required them to donate large sums to the Environmental Protection Agency to replenish clean up costs. For this reason, investors in commercial/industrial property in particular need some protection against potential environmental hazards that might exist on the property by requesting indemnification from the lender in this regard during the negotiation process. Lenders are almost universally requiring an environmental Phase 1 report. Included within this report, other than showing the intended recipient and a description of the property use, is the following:

- General field observation - evidence of:
  - ° Underground storage tanks - stained soil - vegetation damage - oily sheens on the water - polychlorinated Bipheryl (PCB's - usually in electrical storage vaults) - discarded batteries - oil/gas drums - above ground tanks - lead paint - asbestos - other evident hazards

- Storage tanks - Are there underground storage tanks on the property?
  - ° Any evidence visible or otherwise of soil or groundwater contamination?
  - ° Are any chemical manufacturing plants, gas stations or petroleum delivery/storage facilities located on surrounding properties?
  - ° Are any above ground storage tanks visible?

○ Is the subject or any neighboring property engaged in storing transporting or producing waste, chemicals or hazardous substances?

- Water Analysis - Is there evidence that water wells exist on the property?

  ○ Are these wells the primary or sole source of drinking water?

  ○ Are lead or lead soldered pipes visible on the property?

  ○ Chemical, gas and mineral analysis - Is there any evidence of asbestos on the property?

  ○ Was the structure built before 1979?

  ○ Are any suspected asbestos containing materials evident such as sprayed materials on fire proofed ares, pipe insulation, 12 x 12" floor tile, etc.?

  ○ Is there any evidence of Formaldehyde Foam insulation on the property?

  ○ Is there visible evidence of peeling, cracking or flaking paint? (lead deposits)

  ○ Is there any visible evidence of lead paint on the ceilings, walls or floors of any structures on the property?

  ○ Does it appear that pesticides or herbicides have been used in excess of normal household use?

  ○ Is the property used for agricultural purposes?

  ○ Are there any noticeable pesticide odors?

  ○ Are there any transformers, electrical devices or hydraulic equipment on the property? If yes, are there any labeled containing PCB's?

  ○ Does visible or other evidence exist of PCB contamination to the soil or groundwater on the property?

  ○ Does the property contain any fluorescent light ballasts? If yes, are any labeled containing PCB's?

  ○ Is there reason to suspect that radon may be a problem in the dwelling or the immediate property's locality.

  ○ Has radon screening been conducted which indicates that the property may have elevated levels of radon?

- General - Are there any conditions present not mentioned above that need to be corrected to remove any potential risks?
  - ° Could the activities of adjacent properties pose potential environmental risks to subject property?

After addressing each of the questions posed by the report, the environmental inspector then provides recommendations for further action environmentally with respect to the site in the summary and conclusion section. If the report recipient feels that further procedures are required, entry into Phase II environmental investigation is undertaken. In this phase further investigation in the form of chemical analysis and testing takes place leading to Phase III which involves recommendation of actions required of a remedial nature to offset the environmental hazards encountered. This phasing can be an expensive process in itself, let alone the actual cost of clean up. This is why it is essential to negotiate indemnification early on against hazards of this nature.

PROFITABILITY ANALYSIS

In forming any capital contribution to a real estate investment a proper return for the utilization of this money is expected. The negativity of cash flow as a means of offsetting tax liability on ordinary income is a thing of the past. A basic principal that has always driven prudent real estate investors in income producing property is the fact that it must do just that - produce income! This should be the prime concern in the negotiation process and this has driven American Capital Investments, Inc. in their assemblage of syndication packages for potential clients.

PRICE CONSIDERATIONS BASED UPON OCCUPANCY

A building that enjoys a sixty percent occupancy in the marketplace that charges market place rents does not attain the same value to an investor as one that enjoys consistent 90% occupancy over time. In the pressures of weak economic performance and limited resources to deal with real estate owned, lenders find themselves in the unique position of having to manage unwanted properties. Many cases these properties are not within the lenders service area and property managers are appointed to deal with these properties until proper disposal can be arranged.

Depending upon the latitude allowed property managers, foreclosed properties may deteriorate as far as proper servicing of the building tenants, thus impacting occupancy levels which can generally be improved just by upgrading management of the facility.

The hard realities of the negotiation process involve the fact that lower occupancy levels tend to lower expectations as to price, since price is **directly related to the income productivity of the building**. A building that is 60% occupied is worth considerably less than a building that is 90% occupied, particularly if that latter percentage figure involves long term financially responsible tenants.

Care must be taken in the negotiation process to study not only the quantity of the tenants in terms of number and space concentration, but the quality of the tenancy as well. If you have a building full of tenants whose rent check continually bounces, this is a sign of financial statement deterioration - this relates to tenant quality. Many times a key tenant in a building is the one that occupies the ground floor in a high rise structure. In the past this ground floor tenant has been a financial institution. This trend is changing rapidly with all of the closures, consolidations and the like in the financial community. Now this tenant may be computer related, a retailer or some other form of economic activity, but indicative of the type of tenant that may be attracted to upper floors. Loss of a ground floor tenant in a high rise can have serious implications for the balance of the tenancy. Thus, low rise buildings in an office park may serve as an attractive alternative choice.

In any event, negotiations as to price are directly related to occupancy. Bidders to lenders on commercial/industrial space are driven by negotiating a price that not only considers occupancy, but also derives an investment profit in consideration of the occupancy. Your examples in Chapter Six show exactly how consideration of occupancy affects purchase price and the concessions that lenders are willing to give in order to dispose of real estate owned properties.

PREPARING COMPREHENSIVE FINANCIAL ANALYSIS

In order to properly analyze any real estate investment, the true nature of the cash flows resulting from this capital infusion must be determined. Not only must the factors of income be examined through a detailed lease analysis and summation, but attention to expense and, in particular, **expense reduction**, lay an important foundation to the overall project itself. As noted in Chapter Six, property taxes do not necessarily go up, they may go down. An eight million dollar property that sells for three and a half million in California, Florida, or wherever, has a new assessment based upon purchase price, which establishes the market for that property. This means that there can be a considerable reduction in that sizeable expense item. Likewise, in the case of property management, the cost to the ownership may be excessive when outside property management firms are used. Vendors to financial institutions tend to charge higher fees with regard to real property management items ranging from the fees themselves to any necessary repair or maintenance items required. Through control of the building by real estate professionals, certain economies can be effected. A typical office purchase might be a building that is 65% occupied with an average monthly per square foot rental of $1.25 on a gross basis for the 60,000 sq. feet of leasable space. The analysis of this structure would be as follows:

Financial Analysis

39,000 square feet x $1.25 x 12 (annual rentals)	$ 585,000
Vacancy and management allowance - 5%	29,250
Effective income	$ 555,750
Expenses	115,500
Net operating income	$ 440,250
Capitalized at 10%	$4,402,500

At this point in time the investor has placed the upper limit on sales price on the property. As noted in the Wilshire Plaza transaction in Orlando shown in Chapter Six, it is possible not only to negotiate the price downward from an existing loan balance of much higher, but to arrange the terms on the purchase loan to fit the need to increase occupancy over time even to the point of a zero interest transaction during the period required to improve occupancy. The manner in which the leverage is negotiated allows the investor to not only receive an attractive return at lower occupancy levels but to maximize return possibilities through careful management and properly marketing the property to potential users. Our example above shows a purchase price that will provide an appropriate return on equity to the investor provided a proper interest rate can be negotiated for the leverage on the property. It is important to note that at some point in time the leverage could reach a point as being onerous. One should never purchase a commercial/industrial property on the basis of 100% leverage, as the property becomes vulnerable to repossession by the one granting this credit to a borrower. Normal down payment requirements on this type of property is 25%, but lower percentages are possible as in the case of Wilshire Plaza, the down payment is 18.5%.

THE IMPORTANCE OF CASH FLOW

Although prudent investment policy requires adequate cash reserves as back up, the objective of any real estate investment is for the property to pay for itself and provide and adequate return on investment. In any event, the tax consequences have to be considered in this decision making process. Cash flow represents the net operating income less debt service. In the example above considering an 18.5% down payment with a 8.75% loan available under 30 year amortization, the cash flow would be as follows:

Cash Flow Analysis

Proposed purchase price	$4,402,500
Down Payment required	815,000

(Purchase money loan — $3,587,500 at 8.75%
interest, 30 year amortization — annual payments
of $338,675.)

Net operating income from analysis above	440,250
Less annual debt service requirement	338,675
Net income after debt service	$ 101,575

Return on equity =
    $101,875 divided by $815,000 = 12.5% (rounded)

Proper attention to cash flow and appropriate financial analysis indicate that this investment is worthy of further pursuit. Before one goes charging off and spending money, a deeper economic analysis is required over and above the feasibility study calling for intensive field investigation.

COMPETITIVE FACTORS

Real property is in a constant state of flux ranging from demolitions to the creation of new competing improvements to the property in question.

One of the advantages of dealing with commercial/industrial properties is the fact that the likelihood of creation of new competition in the immediate future is somewhat remote. A better prospect is that of demolitions, which means that the remaining newer properties would gain economic advantage. There are several indicators which gauge to impact of competition in the area.

NEW BUILDING PERMITS

The planning department of the county or municipality where the property is located provides a wealth of information about projects contemplated for the community. This not only pertains to the property under study, but plans contemplated that would tend to compliment the property. In the case of commercial/industrial, a strong increase in residential permits is a healthy sign along with permits for any facilities which would help stimulate the need for space in the building in question, such as a restaurant in proximity to an office building location.

EXISTING VACANCY FACTORS

Existing vacancy factor figures can sometimes be deceiving. Sometimes it pays to study competing buildings that enjoy high levels of occupancy and their counterparts that do not have the same degree of success. In this study many times the difference may not only be in the amount charged for the space, but the level of management expertise of the building's ownership that is the principal factor for the difference. What is important about vacancy factors is the **trend** and **future potential**. If the factors have been moving downward with no indications of upward movement, it is a definite sign of economic deterioration in the area. If one is dealing in an area such as Orlando, Florida where there are many signs of upward economic mobility, future potential for reversal of vacancy rates can be positive.

VACANT LAND AVAILABLE FOR DEVELOPMENT

As long as there are competing parcels that are comparably zoned in the immediate area of the property under study, there is the potential of future competition which could impact occupancy levels. On the other hand, escalating construction and land costs may prevent developers to compete on an economic basis due to the fact that they must extract rent levels based upon a higher acquisition cost than one who has bought a property for considerably less than it would cost to replace it.

AREA TRENDS

As discovered in Chapter Two, the interaction of cycles and what cycles represent offer the charting of a course of investment strategy tied closely to key economic indicators in its path. There are a variety of economic publications which can guide real estate investors in the formation of a proper investment decision. In the case of a particular purpose, information about the community in which the potential investment is located is of particular importance. The ability of a metropolitan statistical area to **produce** more than it can **consume** allows it to grow and prosper. As one can note from the statistics shown relative to Orlando, Florida, this is an area which fits that economic pattern. In that chapter, certain economic factors were considered to reach that conclusion.

POPULATION

In the case of population, not only the numbers, but demographic factors have to be considered. Educational levels, population trends, ethnic mix and the like all factor into the study of population and what its trends represent. As previously noted, Orlando has a population mix of a youthful well-educated adult populace.

RETAIL SALES

Sales tax data on the various localities can show the trending of sales activity. By creating a trending module, predictions can be made concerning the salutary effect of these increases on the property in question.

CONSTRUCTION ACTIVITY

Healthy real estate development, particularly in the residential sector where absorption rates are high, can be a strong positive indicator that new job formation in the employment sector is occurring at a rapid pace.

INDUSTRIAL DISPERSION

As previously noted, a wide array of industrial activity free of concentration of one particular firm vis-a-vis the balance of the economic activity is a healthy economic barometer.

MEDIAN INCOME

Census data, particularly that closest to the census taking time, can be of great benefit in determining consumer purchasing power. It is also an indicator of compensation levels for industry and their future expansion needs.

Thucydides, the ancient greek philosopher in his **History of the Peloponnesian** noted:
"With reference to the narrative of events, far from permitting myself to derive it from the first source that came to hand, I did not even trust my own impressions, but it rests partly on what I saw myself, partly on what others saw for me, the accuracy of the report being always tried by the most severe and detailed tests possible. My conclusions have cost me some labor from the want of coincidence between accounts of the same occurrences by different eyewitnesses, arising sometimes from imperfect memory, sometimes from undue partiality for one side or the other. The absence of romance in my history will, I fear, detract somewhat from the interest; but I shall be content if it is judged useful by those inquirers who desire an exact knowledge of the past as an aid to the interpretation of the future, which in the course of human things eust resemble if it does not reflect it. My history has been composed to be an everlasting possession, not the showpiece of an hour."
As the potential investor investigates the past through economac observation, the door to the future opens wide offering in it opportunity or chaos. As Thucydides noted in his discourse we all suffer from the

fragilities of perception. One person perceives the glass as half full, while the other sees it as half empty. A half full building may lead to a seventy-five percent occupancy or a thirty percent occupancy. It lies in the hand of the skillful to determine the eventual result. Adroit syndicators have the innate ability to perceive the future by taking advantages of present trends. In the succeeding chapters the manner in which a syndicate is formed and the rationale behind it will be explored.

8
SYNDICATION — A MARRIAGE OF LEVERAGE AND EQUITY

DEFINING THE SYNDICATE

Noteworthy economist John Kenneth Galbraith observed in his work **The New Industrial State**:

"... Affluence adds to the need for ... stabilization of aggregate demand. A man who lives close to the margin of subsistence must spend to exist and what he spends is spent. A man with simple income can save ... Moreover, a rich society owes its productivity and income, at least in part, to large scale organization – to the corporation ..."

In syndication, the corporate form is but one vehicle for the amassing of capital for economic advantage. A leading syndication counsel, Samuel Freshman, defines a syndicate as: "... a joining together of two or more persons for the purpose of making and operating an investment...implying that one or more of the parties will take an active part in the operation of the investment and assume responsibility for managing the investment, and one or more of the parties will be completely passive investors. The parties who supply the investment capital will normally be the passive investors, although active investors may also supply a portion of the capital. The active investor may secure an override or management fee for his (sic) services in addition to the return on any cash he (sic) invests ..."

Within the scope of this broad definition of syndicate lie a number of ownership forms. With respect to ownership of real property, these forms might be:

- Limited partnership - the most commonly used vehicle with due regard to the implications of the Tax Reform Act of 1986 -

General partner(s) assume liability for the investment vehicle, while limited partners are limited to their capital contribution and/or proportionate future assessments, if applicable

- Tenancy in common - somewhat unwieldy for estate management
- Joint tenancy - usually when a small group of two or three are involved
- Joint Venture - a partnership vehicle designed for a single project with spousal community interest in the joint venturers (partnership equivalency)
- General Partnership - each of the partners has joint and several liability
- Common law trust - limited in scope
- By the structure of the document of creation
- Real estate investment trust - beneficial shares of interest are issued equivalent to shares of stock in a corporation
- Corporation - limited liability on the part of shareholders to the extent of their investment under normal circumstances

Irrespective of the nature of the ownership vehicle, it is essential that the basis for syndicate formation is a project that is viable. Confucius in his **The Confucian Analecta** noted: ". . . Learning without thought is labor lost, thought without learning is perilous . . ." Such it is with this text as a learning vehicle. It is up to each individual investor to apply thought to any project offering as a means of determining whether that project is an appropriate vehicle for the investment of capital.

THE ROLE OF THE SYNDICATOR

The advantage of syndication lies in the expertise of the syndicator. A syndicator is one who conceives and structures the project in such a fashion as to make investment in the venture attractive, whether it be to build a tract of homes or to purchase a New York skyscraper. Those who followed on the coat tails of Harry Helmsley in his Gotham syndicates enjoy comfortable estates today. The shrewdness and negotiation skills of this man in real estate transactions was almost unsurpassed in modern times. His structure of the acquisition of the Empire State Building was classic.

Today there are many who have learned from the activities of Helmsley, the Tishmans, Zeckendorfs and the like. The learning process consists not only of studying the successes, but the failure as well. In real estate there is as much to be learned from failure as success. The 1980s was a good case study in build-up for failure. When creation of housing stock with its commercial and industrial counterparts is based solely on the creation of supply without a careful **study** of demand, the results are predictable. Real estate development is a function of the availability of capital. If the necessary credit or investment capital is available to build the project, the developer will build it. Usually the developer is attuned to turnover of the project and go on to another one. In the late 1980s turnover took a screeching halt leaving developers with capital short - inventory long situations. Thus the domino effect of massive foreclosures took place with the resultant depression occurring heavily impacting the commercial/industrial market with rippling overtones in the residential market, particularly high-end merchandise.

A residual effect of this real estate "melt down" has been the creation of funds such as American Capital Investments, Inc. designed to take advantage of a down real estate market. Even in markets such as this, there are upsides. The Orlando, Florida and San Diego, California areas are just two examples of this. Sometimes these funds have been referred to as "bottom fishing" and "vulture funds." Whatever the label, these syndication vehicles through their ability to amass capital, management expertise and negotiation skills have structured unique investment opportunities designed to outperform other alternative devices available in the market place. Over the long term real estate investment has proven to outperform the growth of gross national domestic product in the case of well located projects in areas with a broad based viable economy.

REAL PROPERTY CANDIDATES FOR SYNDICATION

In Chapter Three various types of investment alternatives including real estate were explored in detail. The actual choice of investment vehicle is an amalgamation of factors dealing with comfort zones on the part of the syndicator and individual investors. Commercial and industrial property investment is not for an investment plebe. This area of investment lies with a person who has a certain degree of sophistication relative to income producing real estate and its attendant risks. Those who feel comfortable in this exclusive arena can reap the rewards of sound judgment based on solid information relative to a specific project.

Due to the wide variety of inventory available, attractive financing terms, motivated sellers and the like, commercial and industrial property acquisition under extremely favorable terms with **upside potential** has never been better. That is not to say that investment in residential property may not get similar results, but the regulators have an agenda concerning the disposal of residential inventory geared to making this merchandise available to low to moderate income families in the form of affordable housing. This, in effect, reduces the availability of investment opportunities in that area.

As noted in Chapter four, the location of the investment is equally important as the nature of the investment itself. Windows of opportunity exist throughout the country that only open themselves if the capital is dedicated to the project. Syndicators use a variety of devices not only to identify the area, but the property itself.

PROPER USE OF REAL ESTATE PROFESSIONALS

Real estate, due to the heterogeneity of location, is not like buying a uniform product, such as a stock or bond. It requires extensive investigation prior to the commitment of funds to any project. Even the most sophisticated of real estate investors needs to rely on the advice and assistance of others to literally serve as "eyes and ears" in the investigative process. One cannot be omnipresent. Reliance upon others with a greater familiarity either with location or logistics makes good sense. Some of the resources that are utilized on a consultancy basis are noted below.

REAL ESTATE BROKERAGE

Even those who possess "real estate sense" and can note the seemingly ideal locations in a given city after a cursory examination, understanding local real estate markets is essential. The nuances of how real estate business is conducted can be of vital assistance to the syndicator. Real estate brokerage representation to any seller, particularly if the buyer is a licensee, provides a layer of insulation taking away the emotionality of the buyer's real estate expertise allowing objective negotiation in a given transaction.

By dealing with a real estate broker who is extremely knowledgeable in **the desired investment category**, innumerable benefits can be derived.

It would be foolhardy to go to a brokerage that specializes in single family homes in upscale areas to discuss the purchase of an office building. What one needs is a member of the Society of Industrial Realtors, active in the marketplace, member of groups where the owners and users are members, such as a local chamber of commerce, in order to get a real feel for market activity. Another decided advantage to the use of brokerage, especially if the syndicator is located out of the area, is the knowledge that the real estate broker brings to the table about the general attitude of the lending fraternity in the area including those who are the most willing to negotiate on real estate owned projects.

It should be remembered that a commission is usually paid by the seller who is willing to absorb this expense if a buyer is available to take regulatory pressure off their corporate backs.

REAL ESTATE AND INVESTMENT COUNSEL

The structuring of a syndication involves considerable paperwork ranging from the formation of ownership instruments, such as partnership agreements together with the necessary publication documents, articles of incorporation and the like. Understanding of the legal aspects of real estate is best left to experts in the field. Most syndicators employ counsel thoroughly grounded in the legal requirements of establishing a proper syndication vehicle including preparation of the offering and the proper language to protect both the syndicator and investors. For example, the Tax Reform Act of 1986 has dictated that some form of percentage interest in the project be established for limited partners in a general partnership. For this reason limited partners are deeded a percentage interest which is then deeded to the limited partnership as a whole in order to attain tax benefits.

CERTIFIED PUBLIC ACCOUNTANTS AND TAX COUNSEL

It is not unusual for attorneys to assume the dual role of CPA as well as be a member of the state bar in these days of complex tax laws and regulations. The careful structuring, tax-wise of any syndicate, regardless of ownership entity can mitigate the effects of taxation on both the state and federal levels. The structuring of the agreement of purchase and the sale and escrow instructions prepared pursuant to the terms of a limited partnership agreement (the most common syndication device) are critical in providing maximized tax advantage in a given transaction. A typical offering circular, limited partnership agreement, agreement of purchase and sale and escrow instructions involving commercial property are shown as Illustrations 8-1, 8-2 and 8-3, respectively (see end of this chapter). Constant vigilance must be maintained by accountants and tax counsel to assure maximum tax benefits in a given transaction.

THE POSITIVE APPLICATION OF LEVERAGE AS AN ESTATE BUILDER

It should be noted that lenders deal in a non-traditional fashion when dealing with real estate owned. Rather than dealing in normal terms with either fixed or variable rate financing, the financing package used for real estate owned is a function of the degree of difficulty future purchasers would have in turning around the property to a profitable venture. In the case of buildings which are well located, but have lacked the management attention required to attain optimum tenancy, lenders may have a variety of methods applied to the leverage of the project to attract buyers. Some of these methods range from zero percent interest (and no payments) for a specified period to allow rent up of the structure with a gradual build up of interest to market rate over time.

LENDER'S ATTITUDES CONCERNING "LOANS TO FACILITATE" IN NEGOTIATING THE SALE OF "REAL ESTATE OWNED"

This prior description is a snapshot of the method used by American Capital Investments, Inc., in their Grand National Plaza project located in Orlando. It allows the dedication of capital to create a positive leasing posture without having to sacrifice heavy debt servicing requirements in the process. Another aspect of non-conventional leverage of commercial properties is the fact that less capital contribution is required from real estate investors creating opportunities to maximize return on investment in the process. As noted in Chapter five, lender attitude in the early 1990s reflects a combination of regulatory pressure and direct concern over a proliferation of non-performing assets and real estate owned that have accumulated on financial institution's books since the late 1980s. The only way to "clear off the books" is through having to deal with sharp negotiators with the necessary acquisitory capital to "wheel and deal" for the property. This is exactly the position that adequately capitalized buyers find themselves as 1993 rolls around. Lenders are highly motivated to convert non-performing assets into a performing mode. Their principal marketing tool is attractive leverage to loosen investor's wallets. The following example of an office building purchase using leverage can provide insight on how non-traditional mortgage terms can entice investors to purchase.

As an example, consider a 60,000 square foot four story curtain wall office building well located in one of the areas described as prime business prospects by Fortune Magazine. The efficiency ratio of this structure after taking out entry lobby, hallways, elevator shafts, bathrooms, storage and utility rooms equates to 48,000 square feet of net rentable space for a 80% efficiency ratio - the bare minimum. Adequate open paved parking surrounding the building is more than adequate to meet the needs of the tenants, their vendors and clients. The rents, all on five year leases (the expected time of carry for the project) average $12.00 per square foot/year on the net rentable space. No one tenant occupies more than 10% of the rentable space reducing the possibility of a dramatic loss in revenue due to unforseen departures. The current occupancy level of this building is not the idyllic 85 to 90 percent, but 65% due to absentee management not attending to their marketing homework, since subject is real estate owned of a financial institution. Operating expenses equate to 35% of the gross rents attained including vacancy and replacement reserves. The syndicator would then perform an internal analysis on this basis:

FOUR STORY BUILDING ANALYSIS

Current annual gross rents—$12.00 x 48,000 sq. ft.	$576,000
35% expenses, including vacancy and	
replacement reserves	201,600
Net income (current) available to service debt	$374,400

Assuming that an investor faced with this low occupancy building felt that a proper return on equity dollars runs a higher risk, a 11% capitalization rate would be attached to the net operating income to derive a bid to purchase the building based on the NOI divided by .11, or $3,400,000. Once the bid price is established, then the factor of leverage comes into play. It's time to get to some hard negotiations with the lender to structure a lending package which allows time to increase the occupancy to possibly 80% in one year. If one is operating in areas with considerable potential, such as the Greater Orlando Metropolitan area it is possible to attain with creative marketing and management expertise. Lenders in 1993 would normally want around a 9% fixed rate loan on a thirty year amortization with a seven to ten year call on the note. The latter maturity dates would pose no problem, since the syndicate would probably be disposing of the property within the time limitation taking advantage of an up cycle in the real estate market to transfer their tax base through a 1031 exchange to a property of greater value and defer capital gains taxes. For the sake of this problem, capital gains tax upon sale in five years will be considered.

After serious negotiations with the lender, they express their willingness to advance a loan based upon 80% of the proposed purchase price, or $2,720,000. All interest on this debt is at zero percent for the first year of the loan with monthly principal payments of $19,270, annualized to $236,640 principal reduction in the first year roughly equivalent to what the first monthly interest payment would be at an 8 and one half percent rate. After the first year, the annual payment would be $232,953 based upon the year end balance of $2,483,360 amortized at 8 and one half percent, roughly equivalent to what the principal reduction was in the first year alone! Based upon the worst case scenario for cash flow represented in the first year of operation, the return on equity to the syndicate based upon a $680,000 down payment (lender would pay all closing costs), would be calculated as follows:

Net income before debt service	$374,400
Annual debt service, first year — all to principal	236,640
Net income to syndicate after debt service	$137,760

Return on initial investment before
consideration of equity recapture = **20.3%!**

The above figure represents taxable income before consideration for depreciation. Consider the replacement cost of the building the same as the mortgage amount of $2,720,000 and using an annualized rate of 3.1746% in accordance with current straight line allowance under the Internal Revenue Code, for an annual rate of depreciation of approximately $86,349. Considering the investment on the basis of the current capital gains rate of 28%, the annual tax burden to the investment group would be:

Net income after debt service, but prior to depreciation	$137,760
Annual depreciation	86,349
Net taxable income	$ 51,411

28% tax burden on reportable income $ 14,395
Return after deducting the taxes from
   NOI after debt service $123,365

This still represents a 18.14% return on the down payment with adjustment for state taxes, if applicable. If the occupancy can be raised to the 80% level in the year grace period and maintained at that level for the remaining four years prior to sale, equity build-up and appreciation will provide a substantial capital base for acquisition and upward mobility.

Although the example is fictional, negotiations of this type are being negotiated with lenders on their real estate owned every day. It takes a great deal of sophistication and negotiation ability on the part of the syndicator in structuring transactions of this nature. This is where the syndicator establishes true value to the real estate investor by taking the investigative and negotiation steps necessary to structure transactions of this nature.

NON TRADITIONAL LENDING TERMS

Zero interest, 100% financing, the list goes on. Lenders with real estate owned on their books look toward creativity as shown in the above example to extract themselves out of a very large hole in the eyes of their regulators. Regulators place a full court press on those institutions who have a large inventory of real estate owned on their books. The club that they use is that if they don't liquidate, the alternative may be closure of the institution. It is also a way of regenerating dead capital tied up in an asset that deteriorates in value the longer that it is managed by absentee ownership who, many times, use outside vendors as caretakers for the property.

GETTING MORE "BANG" FOR YOUR "BUCK"

As one will note in the next chapter, the types of investment vehicles which can still provide some form of tax advantage are dwindling rapidly. Real Estate is still one of the remaining areas where cash flow can be sheltered maximizing return to the sophisticated investor.

Keynes so aptly pointed out in his 1933 **Essays in Biography** ". . . Of the maxims of orthodox finance, none, surely, is more antisocial than the fetish of liquidity. . . It forgets that there is no such thing as liquidity of investment for the community as a whole . . ."

Real estate has always been considered an illiquid investment, but the facile minds of real estate investors also realize that a tidy income stream can bolster the sparsest degree of liquidity. The devotion of capital to commercial real estate investments with due regard to the elimination of risk at capital loss through judicious choice of project and location can lead to the ultimate rewards of not only return **of** capital, but generous returns **on** capital. Some of the documents involved in the syndication process have been shown as examples in this chapter. The next chapter deals with how a syndicate works with the documentation to form the entity, deals with the tax issues involved and consummates the transaction.

Illustration 8-1

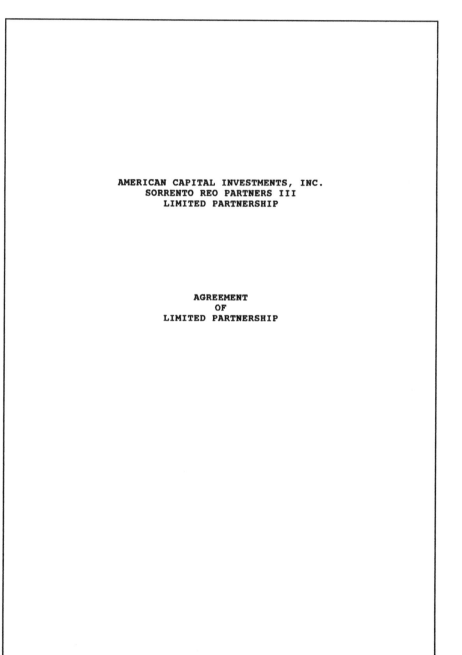

AMERICAN CAPITAL INVESTMENTS, INC.
SORRENTO REO PARTNERS III
LIMITED PARTNERSHIP

AGREEMENT
OF
LIMITED PARTNERSHIP

Illustration 8-1 (cont.)

TABLE OF CONTENTS

Illustration 8-1 (cont.)

AGREEMENT

OF

LIMITED PARTNERSHIP

OF

SORRENTO REO PARTNERS III,

A CALIFORNIA LIMITED PARTNERSHIP

This Agreement of Limited Partnership is entered into by and between· the party executing this Agreement on its signature page as the general partner, as the General Partner, and the parties executing this agreement on its signature page as the limited partners, as Limited Partners, with reference to the following facts:

A. The parties hereto desire to form a Limited Partnership pursuant to the California Revised Limited Partnership Act for the purpose of acquiring, holding, operating, managing and otherwise investing in the real property more particularly described on Exhibit "A" attached hereto, and all activities related thereto (the "Assets").

B. The parties agree that a limited partnership shall be formed in accordance with the following terms:

1. Formation and Name.

The parties hereby form a limited partnership under the California Revised Limited Partnership Act. The name of the partnership shall be SORRENTO REO PARTNERS III, A CALIFORNIA LIMITED PARTNERSHIP.

2. Definitions.

For the purposes of this Agreement, the following words and phrases shall have the following meanings:

2.1 "Act" shall mean the California Revised Limited Partnership Act, as it may hereafter be amended from time to time.

2.2 "Additional Capital Contribution" shall mean the amount of cash and the fair market value of property contributed by a Partner to the capital of the Partnership other than such Partner's initial Capital Contribution.

2.3 "Agreement" shall mean this Agreement of Limited Partnership, as it may hereafter be amended from time to time.

- 3 -

Illustration 8-1 (cont.)

2.4 "Assignee" shall mean a Person who has acquired a beneficial interest in the Partnership from a Partner, by "Assignment" as hereinafter defined, but who is not a substituted Partner pursuant to the requirements of Paragraph 14 of this Agreement. The term "Assignment" or "Assign" as used in this Agreement shall mean and refer to any assignment, sale, transfer, gift or other disposition by any Partner of all or any part of, or interest in, such Partner's Partnership Interest in this Partnership, including but not limited to any assignment by operation of law, inter vivos acts, testamentary disposition or otherwise, but excluding therefrom any pledge, hypothecation or encumbrance thereof.

2.5 "Capital Account" shall mean the account maintained for each Partner, which shall consist of that Partner's original Capital Contribution, (i) increased by the additional cash and the fair market value of any additional property contributions in addition to the Partner's initial Capital Contribution made by that Partner, (ii) increased by the amount of that Partner's allocation of Net Profits and gains, (iii) decreased by the amount of that Partner's allocation of Net Losses, (iv) decreased by the fair market value of property and any cash Distributions to that Partner, and (v) decreased by items described in Section 705(a)(2)(B) of the I.R.C. and Income Tax Regulations Section 1.704-1(b) (2)(iv)(1). With respect to any property Distributions, each Partner's Capital Account shall first be increased or decreased by the gain or loss that would have been realized had the Partnership sold the distributed property for its fair market value.

2.6 "Capital Contribution" shall be the sum of all money and the fair market value of other property, if any, contributed to the Partnership as capital by any Partner, and the assumption by a Partner of a Partnership liability.

2.7 "Code" shall mean the California Corporations Code, as amended.

2.8 "Distribution" shall mean any cash and/or the fair market value of property distributed by the Partnership to its Partners, and excludes payments to Partners of General Partner fees and expenses, if any, or other fees for services, and repayment to Partners of loans, if any, including interest accrued thereon.

2.9 "Expenses from Operations" shall mean all expenditures the General Partner determines in the exercise of the General Partner's discretion shall be necessary and reasonable for the operation of the Partnership, and sufficient reserves for contingent liabilities.

2.10 "General Partner" shall mean the original general partner hereunder and thereafter any Person succeeding the initial general partner as general partner in accordance with Paragraph 13 of this Agreement.

-4-

Illustration 8-1 (cont.)

2.11 "I.R.C." shall mean the Internal Revenue Code of 1954, as amended.

2.12 "Limited Partner" shall mean the initial limited partners so long as they shall remain a limited partner of this Partnership and any other Persons who become limited partners of this Partnership, including but not limited to any Assignee who becomes a limited partner by substitution in accordance with Paragraph 14 of this Agreement, and (to the extent provided in Section 15662(b) of the Code) a former General Partner who has ceased to be a General Partner.

2.13 "Majority-in-Interest of the Limited Partners" shall mean Limited Partners owning more than fifty percent (50%) of the aggregate interests of all Limited Partners in their respective capacities as Limited Partners in the current Net Profits.

2.14 "Net Profits" and "Net Losses" shall respectively mean all net profits and net losses of the Partnership for each accounting period as reflected on the federal income tax returns of the Partnership, adjusted to reflect any changes resulting from amendments to such returns or Internal Revenue Service audits which the Partners or the Partnership have accepted or with respect to which a final determination has been made.

2.15 "Partner" shall mean any Person who is a General Partner or a Limited Partner in this Partnership.

2.16 "Partner of Record" shall mean a Partner named on the list referred to in Paragraph 16.1.1 hereof.

2.17 "Partnership" shall mean the limited partnership formed by this Agreement.

2.18 "Partnership Interest" shall mean the entire right, title and interest owned by a Partner in the Partnership, whether owned by a General Partner or a Limited Partner.

2.19 "Partnership Interest Percentage" shall mean the percentage interest set forth next to such Partner's signature on the signature page of this Agreement.

2.20 "Person" shall mean an individual, partnership, limited partnership (domestic or foreign), trust, estate, association, corporation, or other entity.

2.21 "Proxy" shall mean a written authorization signed by a Partner or the Partner's attorney-in-fact giving another Person the power to vote with respect to the interest of that Partner. "Signed" for the purposes of this Paragraph 2.21 shall mean the placing of the Partner's name on the Proxy (whether by manual signature, typewriting, telegraphic

-5-

Illustration 8-1 (cont.)

transmission, or otherwise) by the Partner or the Partner's attorney-in-fact.

2.22 "Notice" shall be deemed "given" or "sent" as defined in Paragraph 21 hereof.

3. Principal Executive Office.

The principal executive office of this Partnership shall be as specified on the signature page hereof or such other place in California as the General Partner may, from time to time, designate by notifying all other Partners.

4. Purpose and Authority of Partnership.

The purpose of the Partnership is to acquire and own as an investment the Assets described in Exhibit "A" attached hereto. In order to carry out its purpose, the Partnership is empowered and authorized to do any and all acts and things necessary, appropriate, proper, advisable, incidental to or convenient for the furtherance and accomplishment of its purposes, and for the protection and benefit of the Partnership.

5. Filings.

5.1 The General Partner shall prepare, execute, acknowledge and take all actions necessary to assure prompt and timely filing of a Certificate of Limited Partnership ("Certificate"), and all appropriate amendments thereto, in the Office of the California Secretary of State, and shall record a certified copy thereof in the County Recorder's Office of each county in which the Partnership owns an interest in real property, in accordance with the Act. The Certificate shall be filed and recorded promptly following execution of this Agreement by the parties hereto, and shall provide that all amendments thereto and any Certificate of Dissolution or Certificate of Cancellation of Certificate of Limited Partnership required to be filed under the Act, when filed by the General Partner, may be executed and acknowledged by a single General Partner only.

5.2 The General Partner shall cause to be executed any and all assumed or fictitious business name statements required by law to be filed in connection with the formation or amendment of the Partnership and shall cause such statements to be filed and published as required by law.

5.3 The General Partner shall prepare, execute and take all actions necessary to assure prompt and timely filing in the Office of the California Secretary of State of (a) a Certificate of Dissolution and (b) a Certificate of Cancellation of Certificate of Limited Partnership, in accordance with the Act; unless, in either event, the dissolution occurred because a General Partner ceased to be a General Partner as provided under Paragraph 13.1 hereof by removal or otherwise, where (i) there is not at least one (1) remaining General Partner who is serving as

Illustration 8-1 (cont.)

General Partner in accordance with this Agreement and (ii) the Partners have not unanimously agreed in writing to continue the business of the Partnership and to admit one (1) or more General Partners, in which event the Limited Partners shall have such obligations as provided in Paragraph 18.2 hereof.

5.4 Any Partner may execute any certificate referred to in this Paragraph 5 by an attorney-in-fact, provided that the instrument appointing the attorney-in-fact has been recorded with the County Recorder's office of Los Angeles County and a recorded revocation of such appointment has not been recorded.

6. Term.

Subject to any contrary mandatory requirements of California law, the term of the Partnership shall commence as of the date of this Agreement, and unless extended by written consent of the General Partner and a Majority-in-Interest of the Limited Partners, shall terminate upon the earliest to occur of the following:

6.1 Five (5) years from the date of commencement; or

6.2 The Partnership is sooner dissolved in accordance with this Agreement.

7. Contributions to Capital and Capital Accounts.

7.1 As its initial Capital Contribution to the Partnership on account of its interest as General Partner, the General Partner shall contribute the sum or the property with its value which set forth opposite its signature on the signature page hereto. As his initial Capital Contribution to the Partnership on account of his interest as Limited Partner, each Limited Partner shall contribute the sum or the property with its value which set forth opposite his signature on the signature page hereto. Such Capital Contributions shall be paid as requested by the General Partner.

7.2 A separate Capital Account shall be maintained for each Partner in accordance with the provisions of Paragraph 2.5 hereof.

7.3 No Limited Partner shall be required to make any contributions or advances except as referred to in this Paragraph 7.

7.4 The Partners may (but shall not be obligated to) from time to time loan to c⁻ borrow on behalf of and for the account of the Partnership such sums as may be required by the Partnership to pay principal a⸱d/or interest on any indebtedness of the Partnership or for any other Partnership purpose. Any amount loaned by the Partners to the Partnership shall be upon

-7-

Illustration 8-1 (cont.)

the terms and conditions as the General Partner shall determine, provided that any such loan shall bear interest at a rate no greater than the maximum rate allowed by law; and further provided that, prior to the making of such loan, the amount and terms of and security for any loan by the General Partner or any affiliate of the General Partner to the Partnership shall have been approved in writing by a Majority-in-Interest of the Limited Partners. Such amounts shall be deemed loans and not capital contributions by the Partners.

8.   **Distributions of Cash**.

8.1   Each Partner shall receive from the Partnership income, an annual 16% interest payment on its original Capital Contribution amount, payable in monthly installments of 1.33% of the original Capital Contribution amount. Said payments shall be made within fifteen (15) days from the end of each month. Said interest payments shall continue until the Partnership is terminated in accordance with the terms of this Agreement. IF THE AVAILABLE CASH FROM THE PARTNERSHIP IS NOT SUFFICIENT TO MAKE THE PAYMENTS SET FORTH HEREIN, SAID PAYMENTS SHALL BE MADE BY AND ARE GUARANTEED BY THE GENERAL PARTNER.

8.2   The General Partner shall maintain a "reserve account" at a bank of its choice in an amount equal to one year's interest payments on one million dollars or one hundred sixty thousand dollars.

8.3 Subsequent to the payments set forth in Paragragh 8.1 hereof, additional cash shall be distributed to the Partners only in the event of a sale of the Assets, after paying all Expenses from Operations and after providing sufficient capital for other real and contingent obligations of the Partnership, all of the foregoing of which shall be determined in the judgment of the General Partner in acordance with good and sound business and accounting practices, in a manner which shall not substantially impair or affect the credit worthiness of the Partnership, in the following order of priority:

8.4   First, to Partners in payment of all accrued interest and the outstanding principal balance of their loans, if any, pursuant to Paragraph 7.4 hereof, and if there are not sufficient funds to repay all of the Partners who have made loans, then they shall receive repayment in proportion to the amount of their outstanding loans to the Partnership; and

8.5   Second, the remaining amount to be distributed, if any, shall be distributred first to the Limited Partners up to the amount of their original Capital Contribution and then to the General Partner up to the amount of its original Capital Contribution.

9.   **Allocations of Net Profits and Net Losses**.

9.1   **Net Profits**.

-8-

Illustration 8-1 (cont.)

9.1.1   Net Profits shall be allocated to the Partners in accordance with their Partnership Interest Percentages.

9.1.2   Notwithstanding Paragraph 9.1.1, however, in the event there are prior aggregate Net Losses after the first year, then Net Profits shall first be allocated to the Partners in the same manner and to the same extent as such prior Net Losses were so allocated, but in inverse order.

9.2   Net Losses.

9.2.1   After the first year of the expiration of the buy-out option set forth in Paragraph 14.10 herein, net Losses shall be allocated to the Partners in accordance with their Partnership Interest Percentages.

9.2.2   Notwithstanding anything to the contrary in this Paragraph 9.2, in the event of prior aggregate Net Profits, then Net Losses shall first be allocated to the Partners in the same manner and to the same extent as such prior Net Profits were so allocated.

9.3   In no event shall Net Losses be allocated to any Partner or Partners in any tax year of the Partnership if and to the extent that such allocation would cause the sum of such Partner(s)' deficit Capital Account balances (excluding any portion of such deficit Capital Account balances which are required to be restored to the Partnership upon liquidation pursuant to the terms of this Agreement) to exceed "Minimum Gain", as that term is defined in Paragraph 9.4 hereof, at the end of the tax year of the Partnership for which such allocation would otherwise be made. In addition, any Partner(s) having a deficit Capital Account balance in any tax year (subsequent to the first year) of the Partnership which deficit is attributable in whole or in part to allocations of Net Losses which are attributable to nonrecourse debt secured by Partnership property, shall, to the extent possible and at a time no later than the time at which Minimum Gain is reduced below the sum of such deficit Capital Account balances, be allocated Net Profits in an amount no less than the Minimum Gain determined at the end of the tax year to which such allocations of Net Losses relate.

9.4   "Minimum Gain" shall be defined for purposes of Paragraph 9.3 hereof as the excess of the outstanding principal balance on any nonrecourse debt secured by Partnership property over the adjusted basis for federal income tax purposes of such property.

10. Management Powers and Duties.

10.1 Except as otherwise explicitly set forth in this Agreement, the General Partner shall have full and exclusive authority for the management and control of the business and assets of the Partnership for the purposes herein stated, and

-9-

Illustration 8-1 (cont.)

shall manage and control the affairs of the Partnership and shall
use the General Partner's authority to carry out the purposes of
the Partnership. In so doing, the General Partner may take all
actions necessary or appropriate to protect the interests of the
Limited Partners and of the Partnership with respect to the
Partnership assets. The General Partner shall devote such time
as is necessary to the affairs of the Partnership, without salary
or compensation other than as expressly provided for in this
Agreement; provided, however, that the General Partner shall be
reimbursed by the Partnership monthly for any and all reasonable
out-of-pocket expenditures made by such General Partner on behalf
of or in connection with the business of the Partnership. This
reimbursement shall be considered to be an expense of the
Partnership in computing the Net Profits or Net Losses of the
Partnership.

10.2 By way of example, and not by way of
limitation or the authority of the General Partner, the General
Partner shall have the authority, right, power and privilege to
do or undertake any of the following:

10.2.1 Acquiring by purchase, lease or
otherwise any real property, on behalf of the Partnership, or
construct any buildings, structures or other capital improvements
on the property.

10.2.2 Granting or giving any options,
rights of first refusal, deeds of trust, mortgages, pledges,
ground leases, security interests, easements or other property
rights or otherwise encumbering property of the Partnership or
any portion thereof.

10.2.3 Obtaining, increasing, modifying,
consolidating, replacing or extending any loan or other
obligation, whether unsecured or secured, affecting any property
of the Partnership.

10.2.4 Selling, exchanging, or conveying
property of the Partnership or any portion thereof.

10.2.5 Causing or permitting the
Partnership to extend credit or to make any loans or become a
surety, guarantor, endorser or accommodation endorser for any
person or entering into any contracts with respect to the
Partnership, or any portion thereof.

10.2.6 Entering into or executing any
lease on behalf of the Partnership.

10.2.7 Releasing, compromising, assigning
or transferring any claims, rights or benefits of the
Partnership, in the ordinary course of business.

10.2.8 Filing with any governmental
authority any subdivision map or any amendment or modification

-10-

Illustration 8-1 (cont.)

thereto or consenting to any rezoning or other material change to the legal classification of any property of the Partnership.

10.2.9 Notwithstanding any other provisions of this Agreement, the General Partner shall have the right to take such action as the General Partner, in his reasonable judgment, deems necessary for the protection of life or health or the preservation of Partnership assets if, under the circumstances, in the good faith judgment of the General Partner, there exists an emergency or other situation requiring an immediate decision which should not reasonably be delayed until the approval of any other partner is obtained. The General Partner shall notify the other partners of such action contemporaneously therewith or as soon as reasonably practicable thereafter.

10.3 The General Partner may delegate any or all of such Partner's powers, rights, and obligations hereunder, and may appoint, employ, contract, or otherwise deal with any Person for the transaction of the business of the Partnership, which Person may, under supervision of the General Partner, perform any acts or services for the Partnership as the General Partner may approve. Any Person employed by the Partnership to act as managing agent, architect, engineer, attorney, accountant or any Person hired by the General Partner as an employee or independent contractor shall be paid such reasonable compensation as is determined by the General Partner.

10.4 Nothing contained herein shall prevent the General Partner, and Persons affiliated with, owning or controlling the General Partner, from engaging in business activities similar to those necessary or appropriate for this Partnership.

10.5 The General Partner shall not be liable, responsible or accountable in damages or otherwise to any of the Partners nor to the Partnership for any act or omission performed or omitted by the General Partner in good faith on behalf of the Partnership and in a manner reasonably believed by the General Partner to be within the scope of authority of the General Partner and in the best interests of the Partnership, except for gross negligence, willful misconduct or any breach of fiduciary duty with respect to such act or omission. The Partnership shall indemnify, but only from Partnership assets to the extent available, the General Partner for any loss or damage incurred (including but not limited to reasonable settlement costs made with a view to curtailment of costs of litigation, reasonable attorneys' fees and all other expenses incurred in settling or defending any claims or threatened action (including any disputes with the Internal Revenue Service or tax authorities) or final adjudicated legal proceedings) by reason of any act or omission performed or omitted by the General Partner in good faith on behalf of the Partnership and in a manner reasonably believed by the General Partners to be within the scope of the authority granted to the General Partner by this Agreement and in the best

-11-

Illustration 8-1 (cont.)

interests of the Partnership (but not in the case of gross negligence, willful misconduct or any breach of fiduciary duty with respect to such act or omissions); provided, however, that the Limited Partners shall not have any personal liability to the General Partner under any circumstances on account of any such loss or damage incurred by the General Partner or on account of the payment therefor.

        11.   **Restrictions on Management**.

       Notwithstanding the generality of Paragraph 10, the General Partner shall not be empowered, and shall have no authority, without the prior written consent of a Majority-in-Interest of the Limited Partners, to:

       11.1 Do any act in contravention of this Agreement;

       11.2 Do any act which would make it impossible to carry on the ordinary business of the Partnership;

       11.3 Confess a judgment against the Partnership;

       11.4 Possess Partnership property or assign its rights to specific Partnership property for other than a Partnership purpose;

       11.5 Admit a person as a general partner, except as permitted in this Agreement;

       11.6 Admit a person as a limited partner, except as permitted in this Agreement; or

        12.   **Rights and Obligations Of Limited Partners**.

       12.1 The obligation of each Limited Partner to make a contribution to the capital of the Partnership shall be limited to the Capital Contributions referred to in Paragraph 7 hereof. A Limited Partner shall not be bound by, or be personally liable for, the expenses, liabilities or obligations of the Partnership except to the extent of the Capital Contributions required to be made by him under the terms of this Agreement and any additional Capital Contributions actually made by him.

       12.2 Except for return of loans made by a Limited Partner and for Distributions made pursuant to Paragraph 15.5, no Limited Partner shall have any priority over any other Limited Partner as to return of contributions to the capital of the Partnership or as compensation as a Limited Partner by way of income.

       12.3 Except as provided in Paragraph 18.4 hereof, no Limited Partner shall have the right to receive property other than money upon any Distribution.

Illustration 8-1 (cont.)

12.4 The Limited Partners shall have the right to vote on and call a meeting of the Partners for any or all of the following matters:

12.4.1   The dissolution and winding up of the Partnership, as provided in Paragraphs 13.2 and 18.1.2 hereof. The required vote shall be that set forth in each of such respective Paragraphs.

12.4.2   Any change in the nature of the business of the Partnership. The General Partner shall not agree or commit to any change in the nature of the business of the Partnership without the prior affirmative vote of a Majority-in-Interest of the Limited Partners.

12.4.3   Transactions in which the General Partner does or might have an actual or potential conflict of interest with the Limited Partners or the Partnership. A Majority-in-Interest of the Limited Partners shall have the right to disapprove any such transaction(s) in writing and upon such disapproval the General Partner shall agree with a Majority-in-Interest of the Limited Partners as to the most efficient and inexpensive way to withdraw from such transaction(s), or from the other transaction(s) or relationship(s) which are the source or potential source of conflict.

12.4.4   The removal of a General Partner. A Majority-in-Interest of the Limited Partners may vote in writing to remove the General Partner, for any cause whatsoever, in such Limited Partners' sole discretion, and such removal shall be effective immediately upon such vote.

12.4.5   The admission of a General Partner or an election to continue the business of the Partnership after a General Partner ceases to be a General Partner under Paragraph 13.1 hereof (other than by removal) where there is no remaining or surviving General Partner. The required vote for such admission or election shall be an affirmative vote of all of the Limited Partners.

12.4.6   The admission of a General Partner or an election to continue the business of the Partnership other than under the circumstances described in Paragraph 12.4.5 hereof. The required vote for such admission shall be the affirmative vote of a Majority-in-Interest of the Limited Partners.

12.4.7   Extension of the term of the Partnership as set forth in Paragraph 6 hereof. The required vote shall be that set forth in Paragraph 6 hereof.

12.4.8   Certain acts of the General Partner as set forth in Paragraph 11 hereof. The required vote shall be that set forth in Paragraph 11 hereof.

-13-

Illustration 8-1 (cont.)

12.4.9   Selection of a liquidating Limited Partner as set forth in Paragraph 18.2 hereof. The required vote shall be that set forth in Paragraph 18.2 hereof.

12.4.10   Any other matters provided for under this Agreement.

12.5 Nothing contained herein shall prevent the Limited Partners, and Persons affiliated with, owning or controlling them, or owned or controlled by them in the past, from engaging in real estate and other business activities in addition to their investment in the Partnership.

13.   Changes in General Partner; Transfers of Its Partnership Interest.

13.1 A Person shall cease to be a General Partner of the Partnership upon the happening of any of the following events, subject to Paragraph 13.3 hereof:

13.1.1   Subject to Paragraph 11.2 hereof, the General Partner withdraws from the Partnership (other than by way of Assignment), or is removed by the Limited Partners in accordance with Paragraph 12.4.4 hereof;

13.1.2   An order for relief against the General Partner is entered under Chapter 7 of the federal bankruptcy law;

13.1.3   The General Partner:

13.1.3.1 Makes a general assignment for the benefit of creditors;

13.1.3.2 Files a voluntary petition under the federal bankruptcy law;

13.1.3.3 Files a petition or answer seeking for that Partner any reorganization, arrangement, composition, readjustment, liquidation, dissolution or similar relief under any statute, law or regulation;

13.1.3.4 Files an answer or other pleading admitting or failing to contest the material allegations of a petition filed against that Partner in any proceeding of the nature set forth in Paragraph 13.1.3.3; or

13.1.3.5 Seeks, consents to, or acquiesces in the appointment of a trustee, receiver, or liquidator of the General Partner, or of all or any substantial part of that Partner's properties;

13.1.4   Sixty (60) days after the commencement of any proceeding against the General Partner seeking reorganization, arrangement, composition, readjustment,

-14-

Illustration 8-1 (cont.)

liquidation, dissolution or similar relief under any statute, law or regulation, such proceeding has not been dismissed, or if within sixty (60) days after the appointment without that Partner's consent or acquiescence of a trustee, receiver or liquidator of the General Partner or of all or any substantial part of that Partner's properties, the appointment is not vacated or stayed, or within sixty (60) days after the expiration of any such stay, the appointment is not vacated;

13.1.5   In the case of a General Partner who is an individual, either the death of such Partner or the entry by a court of competent jurisdiction of an order adjudicating the Partner incompetent to manage such Partner's person or estate;

13.1.6   In the case of a General Partner who is acting as a General Partner by virtue of being a trustee of a trust, the termination of the trust (but not merely the substitution of a new trustee, in which case the new trustee automatically becomes the new General Partner);

13.1.7   In the case of a General Partner that is a separate partnership, the dissolution of the separate partnership;

13.1.8   In the case of a General Partner that is a corporation, the filing of a Certificate of Dissolution, or its equivalent, for the corporation;

13.1.9   In the case of a General Partner that is an estate, the distribution by the fiduciary of the estate's entire interest in the Partnership; and

Notwithstanding the provisions of this Paragraph 13.1, a Person who ceases to be a General Partner of the Partnership shall be deemed to be acting as a General Partner with respect to a third party doing business with the Partnership until an amended Certificate of Limited Partnership is filed with the Secretary of State pursuant to section 15622 of the Code.

13.2 If a General Partner ceases to be a General Partner as provided in Paragraph 13.1 above, the Partnership shall not be terminated unless there is no remaining or surviving General Partner and the Limited Partners fail to elect in writing to continue the business of the Partnership and to admit at least one (1) successor General Partner within one hundred eighty (180) days thereafter, in accordance with Paragraph 12.4.5 hereof; but if they do not so elect to continue the Partnership and designate a General Partner within such time, the Partnership shall be dissolved and terminate and shall be wound up in accordance with Paragraph 18 hereof.

13.3 The General Partner shall not be empowered and shall have no authority, without the prior written consent of a Majority-in-Interest of the Limited Partners, to withdraw from

-15-

Illustration 8-1 (cont.)

the Partnership for any reason whatsoever, or to Assign, hypothecate, pledge, encumber or otherwise transfer any part of its Partnership Interest. The General Partner shall not Assign or otherwise transfer all or any part of its Partnership Interest, except to (i) an Assignee approved by a Majority-in-Interest of the Limited Partners or (ii) a successor corporation in connection with a merger, consolidation or corporate reorganization of the General Partner. Upon any Assignment permitted under this Paragraph 13.3, the Assignee shall (i) be substituted as General Partner in place of the assigning General Partner, and (ii) subject to any contrary mandatory requirements of California law or this Agreement, be entitled to all rights and be subject to all obligations of the assigning General Partner as of the date of the Assignment. A General Partner who Assigns its Partnership Interest in compliance with this Paragraph 13.3 shall not be deemed to have "ceased" to be a General Partner under Paragraph 13.1 hereof, and accordingly shall not have the rights in the Partnership under Paragraph 15.3 hereof.

14. Admission of Additional and Substituted Limited Partners and Transfers of and Restrictions on Transfers of Their Partnership Interests.

14.1 Each Partner's Partnership Interest is personal property and such Partner has no interest in specific Partnership property.

14.2 Except as otherwise provided in this Paragraph 14, no Limited Partner shall voluntarily or involuntarily (whether by operation of law or otherwise) assign, pledge, hypothecate, encumber or in any manner transfer (herein collectively "Transfer") all or any part of his Partnership Interest, nor shall any third party be admitted as a substituted Limited Partner nor to any participation herein or to any rights hereunder, without the prior written consent or approval of the General Partner, which consent or approval may be given or withheld in the sole discretion of the General Partner. Any purported Transfer without such consent shall be void. Notwithstanding the foregoing, a Limited Partner may Transfer all or a portion of only its Partnership Net Profits (and related cash Distributions) interest as follows:

14.2.1   To the Partnership or any other Partner;

14.2.2   If an individual, by succession or testamentary disposition upon his death;

14.2.3   If an individual, to his spouse, his lineal ascendants or descendants or their respective spouses, or to a trustee or custodian for the benefit of any of them; or

14.2.4   To a corporation, partnership or other legal entity if, immediately following the Transfer and for

-16-

Illustration 8-1 (cont.)

as long thereafter as such Assignee is a partner of this Partnership, the Partner making the transfer owns or controls, directly or indirectly, more than fifty percent (50%) of the partnership's capital and profits, or more than fifty percent (50%) of the total ownership interest of any other entity.

14.3 The Assignment of all or any portion of a Limited Partner's Partnership Interest shall not in and of itself cause a dissolution of the Partnership and the Partnership and its business shall nevertheless continue uninterrupted.

14.4 Upon any permitted Assignment of all of a Limited Partner's Partnership Interest to an Assignee, (i) such Limited Partner shall cease to be a Limited Partner as to the Partnership Interest so assigned and (ii) such Assignee may be admitted to the Partnership as a substituted Limited Partner, from time to time, only upon the terms and conditions of this Paragraph 14.

14.5 Subject to the other provisions of this Paragraph 14, any Assignee of all or any part of a Limited Partner's Partnership Interest shall be deemed admitted as a substituted Limited Partner of the Partnership only upon the satisfactory completion of the following:

14.5.1 The Assignee shall have accepted and agreed in writing to be bound by the terms and provisions of this Agreement and shall have assumed in writing each of the obligations of the Assignor;

14.5.2 The Assignor shall have filed with the Partnership a duly executed and acknowledged written assignment in a form satisfactory to the General Partner, specifying the interest being Assigned and setting forth the intention of the Assignor that the Assignee succeed to the Assignor's interest as a Limited Partner;

14.5.3 The Assignor and Assignee shall have executed and acknowledged any other instruments reasonably required by the General Partner in order to effectuate the transfer and substitution;

14.5.4 A counterpart signature page of this Agreement (including any amendments) shall have been executed by such Assignee and a spousal consent executed by such Assignee's spouse, if any, to evidence the consents and agreements above.

14.6 Except as provided in this Paragraph 14 and as required by operation of law, the Partnership shall not be obligated for any purpose whatsoever to recognize the Assignment by any Limited Partner of all or any part of his Partnership Interest until the Partnership has received actual notice thereof. Any Person who is the Assignee of all or any part of a Limited Partner's Partnership Interest and desires to make a

-17-

Illustration 8-1 (cont.)

further Assignment of all or any part of such Partnership Interest shall be subject to all the provisions of this Paragraph 14 to the same extent and in the same manner as any Limited Partner desiring to make an Assignment of such Limited Partner's Partnership Interest.

14.7 No Limited Partner may withdraw from the Partnership without the prior written consent of the General Partner. The mere Assignment of a Limited Partner's Partnership Interest does not entitle the Assignee to become or to exercise any rights of a Partner. An Assignment entitles the Assignee to receive, to the extent assigned, only the Distributions to which the assignor would be entitled. A Limited Partner remains a Partner upon Assignment of all or part of the Limited Partner's Partnership Interest, subject to the Assignee becoming a substituted Limited Partner in accordance with the provisions of Paragraph 14.

14.8 The bankruptcy, dissolution, withdrawal, death or adjudication of incompetence of a Limited Partner shall not cause the termination or dissolution of the Partnership, and the business of the Partnership shall continue. Upon any such occurrence, the trustee, receiver, executor, administrator, committee, guardian, conservator or other legal representative of such Limited Partner shall have all the rights of such Limited Partner for the purpose of settling the estate of or administering the property of such Limited Partner, or to Assign all or any part of such Limited Partner's Partnership Interest and to join with the Assignee in satisfying conditions precedent to the admission of the Assignee as a substituted Limited Partner, as provided in this Paragraph 14.

14.9 An Assignee who has become a Limited Partner shall have, to the extent assigned, the rights and powers of, and shall be subject to the restrictions and liabilities of, a Limited Partner under this Agreement and the Act. An Assignee who becomes a Limited Partner is also liable for the obligations of the assignor to make contributions to the capital of the Partnership as provided in Paragraphs 7 and 18 hereof and Section 15652 of the Code. However, the Assignee is not obligated for liabilities unknown to the Assignee at the time he became a Limited Partner and which could not be ascertained by the Agreement. Additionally, if the Assignee of a Limited Partner's Partnership Interest becomes a Limited Partner, the Assignor is not released from the Assignor's liability under Paragraph 15.7 of this Agreement and Sections 15622(d) and 15666 of the Code.

14.10 **GUARANTEED ONE TIME 100% BUY-OUT OPTION.** Each Limited partner shall have a one time right to require the General Partner to purchase the Limited Partner's Partnership Interest. If the General Partner receives written notice from a Limited Partner not less than 60 days and not more the 90 days from the date which is twelve months following the date of purchase of the Limited Partner's Partnership Interest, the

-18-

Illustration 8-1 (cont.)

General Partner shall be required to purchase the Limited Partner's Partnership Interest at the **original purchase price** payable within 120 days from the date which is twelve months following the date of purchase. The General Partner may either purchase the Limited Partner's Partnership Interest with its own funds in which case the Interest shall be credited to the General Partner's Capital Account or it may be purchased with Partnership funds in which case a Capital Account shall be established for the Partnership and the Partners shall each have a pro rata share in accordance with their Partnership Interest Percentage in the Partnership Capital Account.

15. Distributions and Withdrawals.

15.1 Except as provided in this Paragraph 15, a Partner is entitled to receive Distributions from the Partnership before the withdrawal of that Partner from the Partnership and before the dissolution and winding up thereof, subject to the limitations contained in Paragraph 15.7 hereof, only to the extent and at the times or upon the happening of the events specified in this Agreement.

15.2 A withdrawal by a General Partner prior to the expiration of the term of the Partnership set forth in Paragraph 6 hereof shall not be a breach of this Agreement unless such withdrawal violates Paragraph 13.3 hereof.

15.3 Subject to any liability created under Section 15662(a) of the Code, a General Partner who ceases to be a General Partner under Paragraph 13.1 hereof, or such Partner's executor, administrator, trustee, guardian, receiver or other legal representative, as the case may be, shall:

15.3.1 Retain the same interest in that Partner's Capital Account, and entitlement to Net Profits, Net Losses and Distributions as if such Person were still a General Partner, but such Person shall actually have the status of a Limited Partner;

15.3.2 Not be personally liable for Partnership debts incurred after the Partner ceases to be a General Partner other than any debts incurred by reason of that Person's being deemed to be acting as a general partner pursuant to Section 15642 of the Code;

15.3.3 Be entitled to vote as a Limited Partner on all matters ; and

15.3.4 Have its interest in Net Profits, Net Losses and Distributions reduced pro rata with all other Partners to provide compensation, or an interest in the Partnership, or both, to a new General Partner.

19-

Illustration 8-1 (cont.)

15.4 A Limited Partner may withdraw from the Partnership only upon the terms and conditions provided in Paragraph 14 hereof.

15.5 Notwithstanding anything to the contrary contained in the Act, upon withdrawal a Limited Partner is only entitled to receive Distributions to which that Partner is entitled as a Limited Partner under this Agreement and not the fair value of such Partner's Partnership Interest at the time of such withdrawal.

15.6 Subject to Paragraph 18.3 hereof, at the time a Partner becomes entitled to receive a Distribution, that Partner has the status of, and shall be entitled to all remedies that would be available to, a creditor of the Partnership with respect to the Distribution.

15.7 Notwithstanding anything in this Agreement to the contrary, a Partner is obligated to return a Distribution from the Partnership to the extent that, immediately after giving effect to the Distribution, and notwithstanding the compromise of a claim referred to in Section 15636(c) of the Code, all liabilities of the Partnership, other than liabilities to Partners on account of their Partnership Interests and liabilities as to which recourse of creditors is limited to specific property of the Partnership, exceed the fair value of the Partnership assets, provided that the fair value of any property that is subject to a liability as to which recourse of creditors is so limited shall be included in the Partnership assets only to the extent that the fair value of the property exceeds this liability.

16. Books and Records, Accounting and Tax Elections.

16.1 The Partnership shall adopt such accounting basis as the General Partner shall select for purposes of keeping the Partnership's books and records, preparing its federal, state and local income tax returns or information reports, and for purposes of maintaining the Partners' Capital Accounts, all in accordance with generally accepted accounting principles. The following documents shall be kept at the principal executive office of the Partnership:

16.1.1 A current list of the full name and last known business or residence address of each Partner set forth in alphabetical order, together with the contribution to the capital of the Partnership and the share in Net Profits and Net Losses of each Partner;

16.1.2 A copy of the Certificate referred to in Paragraph 5.1 above and all certificates of amendment thereto, together with executed copies of any powers of attorney pursuant to which any certificate has been executed;

-20-

Illustration 8-1 (cont.)

16.1.3   Copies of the Partnership's federal, state and local income tax or information reports, if any, for the six (6) most recent taxable years;

16.1.4   Copies of this Agreement (including all amendments hereto);

16.1.5   Financial statements of the Partnership for the six (6) most recent fiscal years; and

16.1.6   The Partnership books and records for at least the current and past three (3) fiscal years.

16.2 As soon as is practicable during each year after the date hereof, the General Partner shall send to the Limited Partners annual financial statements prepared by the Partnership's accountant for the preceding fiscal year. Such statement need not be certified, except that any Partner, at his own expense, shall be entitled to request, at a regular accounting period, that said statement be certified.

16.3 The General Partner shall promptly furnish to a Limited Partner a copy of any amendment to this Agreement which is executed by the General Partner pursuant to a power of attorney from that Limited Partner,

16.4 The General Partner shall send to each of the Partners within ninety (90) days after the end of each taxable year such information as is necessary to complete federal and state income tax or information returns, and a copy of the Partnership's federal, state and local income tax or information returns for the year.

16.5 Each Limited Partner has the right, upon reasonable request, to (i) inspect during normal business hours any of the Partnership records required to be maintained under Paragraph 16.1 above, and (ii) obtain from the General Partner, promptly after becoming available, a copy of the Partnership's federal, state and local income tax or information returns for each year.

16.6 Upon the request of any Limited Partner, the General Partner shall promptly deliver to such Limited Partner, at the expense of the Partnership, a copy of any of the information required to be maintained under Paragraphs 16.1.1, 16.1.2 and 16.1.4 above.

16.7 The General Partner shall have fiduciary responsibility for the safekeeping and use of all funds and assets of the Partnership, whether or not in the immediate possession or control of the General Partner. The funds of the Partnership shall not be commingled with the funds of any other Person, and the General Partner shall not employ such funds in

-21-

Illustration 8-1 (cont.)

any manner except for the benefit of the Partnership. All funds of the Partnership not otherwise invested shall be deposited in one or more accounts maintained in such banking institution as the General Partner shall determine, and withdrawals shall be made upon such signatures as the General Partner shall determine. All assets of the Partnership shall be held in the name of the Partnership.

16.8 The General Partner shall retain accountants for the Partnership. The accountants shall prepare for execution by the General Partner all tax returns of the Partnership and shall perform such other services as the General Partner shall, in such Partner's discretion, determine.

16.9 The fiscal year of the Partnership shall end December 31st of each year of the term hereof.

16.10 The Partnership may, in the sole discretion of the General Partner, make an election pursuant to Section 754 of the I.R.C., to adjust the basis of the Partners' property as allowed by Sections 743(b) and 734(b) of the I.R.C. Any and all tax elections and decisions of the Partnership, including but not limited to the rate and method of depreciation, shall be made to maximize current tax deductions and to minimize the current tax liability of the Partners, unless in the judgment of the General Partner a different decision is in the best interest of the Partnership and the Partners.

16.11 The General Partner shall be the "tax matters partner" pursuant to Section 6321 of the I.R.C.

17. Meetings of Partners and Voting Requirements.

The following procedures shall govern meetings of Partners and voting of Partners:

17.1 Meetings of Partners shall be held at the principal executive office of the Partnership, or such other place as all of the Partners shall agree to in writing.

17.2 A meeting of the Partners may be called by the General Partner, or by Limited Partners representing more than ten percent (10%) of the aggregate interests of all Limited Partners in their respective capacities as Limited Partners in Net Profits from operations of the Partnership, for any matters on which the Limited Partners may vote pursuant to this Agreement and mandatory requirements of the Act.

17.3 Whenever Partners are required or permitted to take any action at a meeting, a written notice of the meeting shall be given not less than ten (10), nor more than sixty (60), days before the date of the meeting to each Partner entitled to vote at the meeting. The notice shall state the place, date, and

-22-

Illustration 8-1 (cont.)

hour of the meeting and the general nature of the business to be transacted, and no other business may be transacted.

17.4 Notice of a Partners' meeting, or any report, shall be given either personally or by Mail or other means of written communication, which Mail shall be, notwithstanding provisions to the contrary in Paragraph 21 of this Agreement, addressed to the Partner at the address of the Partner appearing on the books of the Partnership or given by the Partner to the Partnership for the purpose of notice in accordance with Paragraph 21 of this Agreement, or, if no address appears or is given, at the place where the principal executive office of the Partnership is located or by publication at least once in a newspaper of general circulation in Los Angeles County. Notwithstanding Paragraph 21 of this Agreement, (i) the notice or report shall be deemed to have been given at the time when delivered personally or deposited in the Mail or sent by other means of written communication; (ii) an affidavit of mailing of any notice or report in accordance with the provisions of this Agreement, executed by the General Partner, shall be prima facie evidence of the giving of the notice or report; and (iii) if any such notice or report addressed to the Partner at the address of the Partner appearing on the books of the Partnership is returned to the Partnership by the United States Postal Service marked to indicate that the United States Postal Service is unable to deliver the notice or report to the Partner at such address, all future notices or reports shall be deemed to have been duly given without further mailing if they are available for the Partner at the principal executive office of the Partnership for a period of one (1) year from the date of the giving of the notice or report to all other Partners.

17.5 Upon written request to the General Partner by any person entitled to call a meeting of Partners, the General Partner immediately shall cause notice to be given to the Partners entitled to vote that a meeting will be held at a time requested by the person calling the meeting, not less than ten (10), nor more than sixty (60), days after the receipt of the request. If the notice is not given within twenty (20) days after receipt of the request, the person entitled to call the meeting may give the notice or apply to the Superior Court of Los Angeles County for an order summarily requiring the giving of notice, as provided in Section 15637 of the Code.

17.6 When a Partners' meeting is adjourned to another time or place, except as provided in this Paragraph 17.6, notice need not be given of the adjourned meeting if the time and place thereof are announced at the meeting at which the adjournment is taken. At the adjourned meeting the Partnership may transact any business which might have been transacted at the original meeting. If the adjournment is for more than forty-five (45) days or if after the adjournment a new record date is fixed for the adjourned meeting, a notice of the adjourned meeting shall be given to each Partner of Record entitled to vote at the meeting.

-23-

Illustration 8-1 (cont.)

17.7 The transactions of any meeting of Partners, however called and noticed, and wherever held, are as valid as though had at a meeting duly held after regular call and notice, if a quorum is present either in person or by Proxy, and if, either before or after the meeting, each of the Persons entitled to vote, not present in person or by Proxy, signs a written waiver of notice or a consent to the holding of the meeting or an approval of the minutes thereof. All waivers, consents, and approvals shall be filed with the Partnership records or made a part of the minutes of the meeting. Attendance of a Person at a meeting shall constitute a waiver of notice of the meeting, except when the Person objects, at the beginning of the meeting, to the transaction of any business because the meeting is not lawfully called or convened and except that attendance at a meeting is not a waiver of any right to object to the consideration of matters required by this Agreement or the Act to be included in the notice but not so included, if the objection is expressly made at the meeting. Neither the business to be transacted at nor the purpose of any meeting of Partners need be specified in any written waiver of notice, unless otherwise provided in this Agreement, and except as provided in Paragraph 17.8 below.

17.8 Any Partner approval (other than unanimous approval by those entitled to vote) at a meeting pursuant to any of the matters listed in Paragraph 12.4 hereof shall be valid only if the general nature of the proposal so approved was stated in the notice of the meeting or in any written waiver of notice.

17.9   A Majority-in-Interest of the Limited Partners represented in person or by Proxy shall constitute a quorum at a meeting of Partners.

17.10   The Partners present at a duly called or held meeting at which a quorum is present may continue to transact business until adjournment notwithstanding the withdrawal of enough Partners to leave less than a quorum, if any action taken (other than adjournment) is approved by the requisite vote of Partners specified in this Agreement.

17.11   In the absence of a quorum, any meeting of Partners may be adjourned from time to time by the vote of a majority of Partnership Interest Percentages represented either in person or by Proxy, but no other business may be transacted, except as provided in Paragraph 17.10 above.

17.12   Any action which may be taken at any meeting of the Partners may be taken without a meeting if a consent in writing, setting forth the action so taken, shall be signed by Partners having not less than the minimum number of votes that would be necessary to authorize or take that action at a meeting at which all entitled to vote thereon were present and voted. In the event the Limited Partners are requested to consent on a matter without a meeting, each Partner shall be given notice of the matter to be voted upon in the same manner as

-24-

Illustration 8-1 (cont.)

described in Paragraphs 17.3, 17.4 and 17.5 hereof. In the event any General Partner or Limited Partners request in accordance with Paragraph 17.2 hereof a meeting for the purpose of discussing or voting on the matter the notice of a meeting shall be given in accordance with Paragraphs 17.3, 17.4 and 17.5 hereof and no action shall be taken until the meeting is held. Unless delayed in accordance with the provisions of the preceding sentence, any action taken without a meeting will be effective fifteen (15) days after the required minimum number of voters have signed the consent; however, the action will be effective immediately if the consent is signed by the General Partner and Limited Partners representing at least ninety percent (90%) of the aggregate interests of all Limited Partners in their respective capacities as Limited Partners in Net Profits from operations of the business of the Partnership.

17.13   Every Partner entitled to vote shall have the right to do so either in person or by one or more agents authorized by a written Proxy executed by such Partner or his duly authorized agent and delivered to the General Partner. Any Proxy duly executed is not revoked and continues in full force and effect until: (i) an instrument revoking it or a duly executed Proxy bearing a later date is delivered to the General Partner prior to the vote pursuant thereto, (ii) a subsequent Proxy is executed by the Partner executing the prior Proxy and is presented to the meeting, (iii) the Partner executing the Proxy attends the meeting and votes in person or (iv) written notice of the death or incapacity of the maker of such Proxy is received by the General Partner before the vote pursuant thereto is counted; provided that no such Proxy shall be valid after the expiration of eleven (11) months from the date of its execution, unless the Partner executing it specifies therein the length of time for which such Proxy is to continue in force. Notwithstanding the foregoing, a Proxy may be made irrevocable pursuant to the provisions of Section 705(e) of the Code. The form of Proxy shall be governed by the provisions of Section 604 of the Code, where applicable.

17.14   In order that the Partnership may determine the Partners of Record entitled to notices of any meeting or to vote, or entitled to receive any Distribution or to exercise any rights in respect of any other lawful action, the General Partner, or Limited Partners representing more than ten percent (10%) of the aggregate interests of all Limited Partners in their respective capacities as Limited Partners in Net Profits from operations of the Partnership, may fix, in advance, a record date, which is not more than sixty (60) or less than ten (10) days prior to the date of the meeting and not more than sixty (60) days prior to any other action. If no record date is fixed:

17.14.1   The record date for determining Partners entitled to notice of or to vote at a meeting of Partners shall be at the close of business of the business day next preceding the day on which notice is given or, if notice is

Illustration 8-1 (cont.)

waived, at the close of business on the business day next preceding the day on which the meeting is held;

17.14.2   The record date for determining Partners entitled to give consent to Partnership action in writing without a meeting shall be the day on which the first written consent is given;

17.14.3   The record date for determining Partners for any other purpose shall be at the close of business on the day on which the General Partner adopts it, or the sixtieth (60th) day prior to the date of the other action, whichever is later; and

17.14.4   The determination of Partners of Record entitled to notice of or to vote at a meeting of Partners shall apply to any adjournment of the meeting unless the General Partner, or the Limited Partners who called the meeting, fix a new record date for the adjourned meeting, but the General Partner, or the Limited Partners who called the meeting, shall fix a new record date if the meeting is adjourned for more than forty-five (45) days from the date set for the original meeting.

18.   Sale, Dissolution and Liquidation.

18.1 The Partnership shall be dissolved and its affairs shall thereupon be wound up only upon the first to occur of the following:

18.1.1   The expiration of the term of the Partnership;

18.1.2   The election in writing of the General Partner and a Majority-in-Interest of the Limited Partners to dissolve the Partnership;

18.1.3   A General Partner ceases to be a General Partner under Paragraph 13.1 hereof, by removal or otherwise, unless (i) at the time there is at least one (1) other General Partner who is serving as General Partner in accordance with this Agreement, or (ii) all Partners agree in writing to continue the business of the Partnership and to admit one (1) or more General Partners, as provided in Paragraphs 12.4.5 and 13.2 hereof.

18.1.4   The passage of thirty (30) days after sale or other disposition of all of the Partnership property;

18.1.5   Entry of a decree of judicial dissolution under Section 15682 of the Code; or

18.1.6   Any other event requiring the dissolution of the Partnership under mandatory provisions of the Act, or other laws of the State of California.

-26-

Illustration 8-1 (cont.)

18.2 Upon the dissolution of the Partnership, the Partnership shall engage in no further business other than that necessary to wind up the business and affairs of the Partnership and liquidate the assets of the Partnership. The General Partner shall manage the liquidation and winding up of the Partnership. If there are no remaining or surviving General Partners and the Limited Partners have elected not to continue the business and replace one (1) or more General Partners as provided in Paragraph 13.2 hereof, then a Majority-in-Interest of the Limited Partners shall promptly designate in writing a representative Limited Partner who shall assume such duties, and all references to the rights and obligations of the liquidating General Partner in this Paragraph 18 shall be deemed to refer to such Limited Partner, as appropriate. Notwithstanding any of the foregoing, if the dissolution occurs by court order pursuant to Section 15681(d) of the Code, the winding up shall be conducted in accordance with the decree of dissolution.

18.3 The proceeds from the liquidation and the winding up of the Partnership, net of the expenses of liquidation (after all gains, profits and losses from operations and sale of all Partnership assets have been credited and/or charged to each Partner's Capital Account), shall be distributed in the following order:

18.3.1   First, to provide for or pay creditors of the Partnership, including Partners who are creditors to the extent permitted by law, in satisfaction of the liabilities of the Partnership other than liabilities for Distributions to Partners under Paragraphs 15.1, 15.5 or 15.6. Should there be insufficient funds to pay such creditors in full, first all creditors who are not Partners shall be paid and then each Partner who is a creditor shall be repaid in the ratio which the amount owed to such Partner bears to the aggregate amount owed to all such Partners.

18.3.2   Second, to pay Partners and former Partners in satisfaction of liabilities for Distributions to Partners under Paragraphs 15.1, 15.5 or 15.6. Should there be insufficient funds to pay Partners in full, each Partner shall be repaid in the ratio that the amount owed to such Partner bears to the total owed to all such Partners.

18.3.3   Third, subject to Section 15636 of the Code, to each Partner, in proportion to each Partner's Capital Account and, to the extent that there is a negative balance in any Partner's Capital Account, such Partner(s) shall contribute to the Partnership an amount of cash sufficient to bring the balance of such Capital Account(s) to Zero Dollars ($0.00), which contribution shall be distributed among the Partners with positive balances in their Capital Accounts, and/or in payment of partnership creditors. In no event, however, shall a Limited Partner be responsible to fund more than an amount equal to the amount of Additional Capital Contributions as

-27-

Illustration 8-1 (cont.)

described in Paragraph 7.1 hereof, less the amounts, if any, previously contributed to the Partnership by such Partner.

18.4 At the discretion of the General Partner, any or all of the Partnership assets may be distributed in kind during liquidation rather than sold and different Partnership assets may be distributed to each Partner. The General Partner shall establish the value of the Partnership assets distributed in kind, and such assets shall be treated as though the assets were sold and the cash proceeds distributed. For purposes of this Paragraph, the difference between the established value of assets distributed in kind and their book value is to be treated as a gain or loss on the sale of the assets and shall be respectively credited or charged to the Partners in proportion to their interests in Net Profits or Net Losses as set forth in Paragraph 9 hereof.

18.5 After dissolution, the General Partner can bind the Partnership as follows:

18.5.1 By any act appropriate for winding up Partnership affairs or completing transactions unfinished at dissolution; and

18.5.2 By any transaction which would bind the Partnership if dissolution had not taken place, if the other party to the transaction:

18.5.2.1 Had extended credit to the Partnership prior to dissolution and had no actual knowledge or notice of the dissolution; or

18.5.2.2 Though not so extending credit, had nevertheless know of the Partnership prior to dissolution, and, had no actual knowledge or notice of dissolution, and a Certificate of Dissolution has not been filed pursuant to Section 15623(a) of the Code.

19. Sale of Partnership Assets and Interests.

A Majority-in-Interest of the Limited Partners (collectively "Sellers" in this Paragraph 19) may cause the Partnership to sell all its assets, subject (i) to compliance with applicable restrictions on transfer of any such assets pursuant to the partnership agreement or other such document evidencing or establishing such assets, (ii) compliance with applicable restrictions on transfer of Partnership Interest pursuant to Paragraph 14 hereof and (iii) to the right of any Limited Partner(s) disagreeing with such sale to purchase the interests of Sellers in the Partnership, all by complying with the following provisions.

19.1 Sellers shall give written notice ("Notice" in this Paragraph 19) to the Partnership and to the other Partners of their intention to cause the Partnership to sell its

-28-

Illustration 8-1 (cont.)

assets, which Notice shall set forth the minimum price in cash which Sellers would approve if the Partnership were to agree to sell all its assets. If all the other Limited Partners agree to such sale (for which purpose the failure of any Limited Partner to state in a writing delivered to the Partnership and all the other Partners its disagreement within thirty (30) days of such Notice shall conclusively be deemed agreement to such sale), then the General Partner is hereby instructed to attempt to sell the assets of the Partnership for the best available price, but not less than the price stated in the Notice, any such sale to be negotiated and consummated as soon as possible thereafter consistent with the General Partner's reasonable efforts to maximize the price received by the Partnership for its assets; if the General Partner is unable to consummate a sale of the Partnership's assets within one (1) year of such Notice, then the Notice shall be of no further force and effect and the General Partner shall be under no further obligation to sell the Partnership's assets pursuant to this Paragraph 19, unless and until another Notice be given by a Majority-in-Interest of the Limited Partners. If within thirty (30) days of such Notice any of the other Limited Partners state in writing to the Partnership and each of the other Partners that they do not agree that the Partnership sell all of its assets for the price stated in the Notice, then such other non-agreeing Partners (collectively "Buyers" in this Paragraph 19) shall have the right to purchase the Sellers' Partnership Interests, and the Partnership Interests of all other Limited Partners agreeing to such sale (such other Partners also "Sellers" for purposes of the procedures which follow), upon the following terms and conditions.

19.2 The purchase price of Sellers' Partnership Interests shall be that amount which would be distributed to Sellers pursuant to Paragraph 18.3 if the Partnership assets had been sold for the price stated in the Notice, the Partnership had been liquidated, and the proceeds thereof had been applied in the order there specified. Such purchase price shall be calculated by the General Partner and confirmed in writing to each Limited Partner, within thirty (30) days after the election of Buyers pursuant to this Paragraph 19 to acquire the Sellers' Partnership Interests.

19.3 If Buyers elect to purchase the Sellers' Partnership Interests pursuant to this Paragraph 19, the purchase and sale shall close on the ninetieth (90th) day after the Notice (or the next business day thereafter) at the offices of the Partnership, or at such other time and place as Buyers and Sellers may agree. At the closing Sellers shall assign to Buyers, in such proportions as Buyers may instruct, their entire Partnership Interests, free and clear of all liens and encumbrances; Buyers shall pay the entire purchase price for the Sellers' Partnership Interests, as determined by the General Partner, in cash; and the parties shall execute any and all documents reasonably necessary to effectuate such purchase and sale.

-29-

Illustration 8-1 (cont.)

19.4 If Buyers or any of them shall for any reason other than default of any Seller fail to complete the purchase of Sellers' Partnership Interests in the time and manner aforesaid, then all Buyers shall thereupon conclusively be deemed to have offered to sell their Partnership Interests to Sellers at any time during the ninety (90) day period commencing upon such failure to purchase, for a purchase price determined in the manner described in Paragraph 19.2, except that, if accepted, ten percent (10%) of the purchase price for such Partnership Interests shall be paid by Sellers in cash and the balance of the purchase price shall be in the form of a Note, made jointly by all Sellers, secured by a pledge of the Partnership Interests thereby acquired by Sellers, bearing interest at a per annum rate of the lower of (i) ten percent (10%), or (ii) the so-called reference rate of interest announced by Bank of America, N.T.&S.A. at Los Angeles, California, fixed as of the closing date of such purchase and sale, payable in three (3) equal annual installments of principal, which, together with interest thereon, shall be due the first, second and third anniversaries of the closing of such purchase and sale. The closing of such purchase and sale shall be held thirty (30) days after the election by Sellers or any of them to accept such offer and to purchase the Buyers' Partnership Interests. Upon the failure of Sellers or any of them to accept such deemed offer of Buyers to sell provided in this Paragraph 19.4, and to consummate the purchase and sale as herein provided, such offer to sell shall lapse.

19.5 At any time prior to the closing of a transaction under Paragraph 19.3 or 19.4, the purchasing Partner(s) may nominate or designate another person to receive the Partnership Interests of the selling Partner(s) in the Partnership.

20. Miscellaneous.

20.1 The General Partner shall not be required to devote its full time and attention to the business of the Partnership and it may, without liability to the Partnership, or to any of the Partners hereunder, and without any consent whatsoever, engage directly or indirectly, independently or with others, in businesses similar to that of the Partnership and neither the Partnership nor any of the other Partners shall have any right in and to any such business venture or ventures or the income or profits derived therefrom, by virtue of this Agreement. The General Partner shall devote so much of its time and attention to the Partnership as may be reasonably necessary for the Partnership's purposes.

20.2 Each of the Partners hereby waives any right which he may have against other Partners who may capitalize on, or take advantage of information learned as a consequence of his association with the affairs of the Partnership. The Partners agree that this Partnership Agreement only refers to the Assets, and that none of the Partners shall have any fiduciary obligation

-30-

Illustration 8-1 (cont.)

to make available other business or real estate opportunities to the Partners or to the Partnership.

20.3 Each of the Partners hereby waives his right, if any, to institute any legal action or proceeding for partition with respect to the Property of the Partnership, during the term of the Partnership, or during any period of dissolution of the same, and upon any breach of the provisions of this Paragraph by any Partner, the other Partners (in addition to all rights and remedies at law and in equity they might have) shall be entitled to a decree or order restraining or enjoining such action or proceeding.

21. Notices.

The time a notice is "given" or "sent", unless otherwise expressly provided in this Agreement, shall mean the time a written notice, demand, consent or other communication required or desired to be given under this Agreement (collectively "Notices") to a Partner or the Partnership is deposited in the United States mails; or the time any other written Notice is personally delivered to the recipient or is delivered to a common carrier for transmission, or actually transmitted by the Person giving the notice by electronic means, to the recipient; or any time any oral notice is communicated, in person or by telephone or wireless, to the recipient or to a Person at the office of the recipient who the Person giving the notice has reason to believe will promptly communicate it to the recipient. "Mail" for the purposes of this Paragraph, except as otherwise expressly provided in this Agreement, shall mean first class, certified or registered mail, postage prepaid, return receipt requested, and addressed to the party to whom the Notice contained therein is to be given at the address provided in the list referred to in Paragraph 16.1.1 hereof (which address may be changed upon the giving of written Notice thereto to all other Partners and the Partnership in the manner provided in this Paragraph 21).

22. Successors and Assigns.

Subject to the restrictions on transfer set forth in Paragraphs 13 and 14 hereof, the covenants and agreements contained herein shall be binding upon and inure to the benefit of the heirs, executors, administrators, successors and assigns of the respective parties hereto.

23. Applicable Law and Severability.

This document shall, in all respects, be governed by the laws of the State of California applicable to agreements executed and to be wholly performed within the State of California. Nothing contained herein shall be construed so as to require the commission of any act contrary to law, and wherever there is any conflict between any provision contained herein and any present or future statute, law, ordinance or regulation

-31-

One Up On Trump

Illustration 8-1 (cont.)

contrary to which the parties have no legal right to contract, the latter shall prevail but the provision of this document which is affected shall be curtailed and limited only to the extent necessary to bring it within the requirements of the law.

24. Attorneys' Fees.

In the event any action be instituted by a party to enforce any of the terms and provisions contained herein, the prevailing party in such action shall be entitled to such reasonable attorneys' fees, costs and expenses as may be fixed by the Court.

25. Captions.

The captions appearing at the commencement of the paragraphs hereof are descriptive only and for convenience in reference. Should there be any conflict between any such caption and the paragraph at the head of which it appears, the paragraph and not such caption shall control and govern in the construction of this document.

26. Number and Gender.

In this Agreement whenever the context so requires, the masculine gender includes the feminine and/or neuter, and vice versa, and the singular number includes the plural.

27. No Obligation to Third Parties.

The execution and delivery of this Agreement shall not be deemed to confer any rights upon, nor obligate any of the parties hereto to, any person or entity other than each other and the Partnership.

28. Exhibits, Schedules and Other Documents.

All exhibits attached hereto and referred to herein are hereby incorporated herein as though set forth at length.

29. Modifications or Amendments.

No amendment, change or modification of this Agreement shall be valid unless it is in writing, is signed by all of the parties hereto, and expressly states that an amendment, change or modification of this Agreement is intended.

30. Separate Counterparts.

This document may be executed on separate signature pages, which the General Partner may attach to a copy of this Agreement, and when so attached shall be deemed to be an original document which the General Partner may file or record.

-32-

Illustration 8-1 (cont.)

31. **Entire Agreement**.

This document constitutes the entire understanding and agreement of the parties with respect to the subject matter of this Agreement, and any and all prior agreements, understandings or representations are hereby terminated and cancelled in their entirety and are of no further force or effect.

IN WITNESS WHEREOF, the parties hereto have executed this Agreement on the _____ day of _____, 19__.

General Partner Signature Page

GENERAL PARTNER	INITIAL CAPITAL CONTRIBUTION	PARTNERSHIP INTEREST PERCENTAGE
AMERICAN CAPITAL INVESTMENTS, INC.	An undivided one half (1/2) interest in the Property. Value = $1,136,500	50%

Address:
330 Washington Boulevard
Penthouse Suite
Marina del Rey, CA 90292

(which shall constitute the principal executive office of the Partnership referred to in Paragraph 3 hereof)

-33-

Illustration 8-1 (cont.)

Limited Partner Signature Page

       The undersigned, desiring to become a Limited Partner in Sorrento REO Partners III, a California Limited Partnership, do hereby agree to be bound by all the terms and provisions of this Agreement of Limited Partnership.

LIMITED PARTNER	INITIAL CAPITAL CONTRIBUTION	PARTNERSHIP INTEREST PERCENTAGE
_____ Name _____ _____	An undivided ____ interest in the Property. Value = $ _____	____%
Address		
Home phone number		
Work Phone number		
Soc. Security Number		
_____ Signature		

Illustration 8-1 (cont.)

EXHIBIT A

MESA VIEW OFFICE CENTER
6725 MESA RIDGE ROAD
SAN DIEGO, CALIFORNIA

Lot 19 of Resubdivision of Mesa Rim Industrial Park, in the City of San Diego, County of San Diego, State of California, according to Map thereof No. 10668, filed in the Office of the County Recorder of San Diego County, June 30, 1983.

-35-

Illustration 8-2

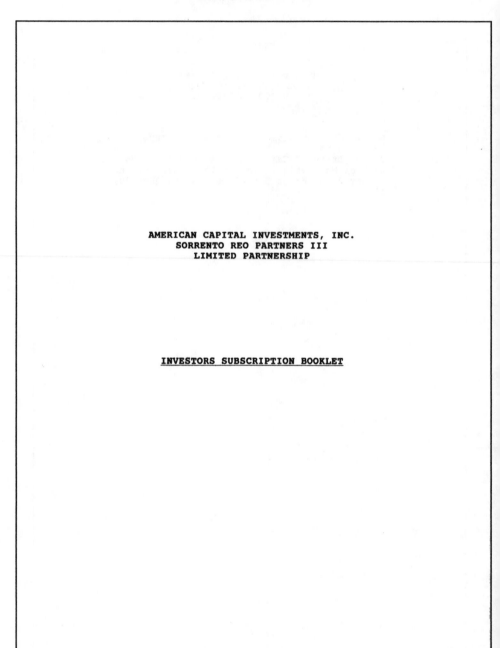

AMERICAN CAPITAL INVESTMENTS, INC.
SORRENTO REO PARTNERS III
LIMITED PARTNERSHIP

INVESTORS SUBSCRIPTION BOOKLET

Illustration 8-2 (cont.)

SUBSCRIPTION INSTRUCTIONS

Subscription Agreement **Complete and sign.**	On the signature page of the Subscription Agreement indicate the property interest in the Mesa View Office Center owned by American Capital Investments, Inc. that you wish to purchase. The purpose of the questions in the Subscription Agreement is to obtain the information necessary to determine whether a prospective investor satisfies the "accredited investor" requirements under Regulation D promulgated under the Securities Act of 1933.
Payment	Make a check in an amount equal to your total purchase price for the property interest you wish to purchase payable to: American Capital Investments, Inc.
Send all documents and payment to:	American Capital Investments, Inc. 330 Washington Street, Penthouse Marina del Rey, CA 90292

2

Illustration 8-2 (cont.)

SUBSCRIPTION AGREEMENT

Dear Sir or Madam:

American Capital Investments, Inc., a California corporation ("Company") hereby agrees with you as follows:

1. **Sale and Purchase of Limited Partnership Interest**. The Company, in reliance upon your representations and warranties set forth herein and subject to the conditions and in accordance with the terms set forth herein, will sell to you, and you, subject to the conditions and in accordance with the terms set forth herein, will subscribe for and purchase from the Company, an interest in the Property commonly known as Mesa View Office Center (the "Property") and then transfer that interest to Sorrento REO Partners III, a California Limited Partnership where a capital account will be established for you as a Limited Partner ("Securities), at a purchase price equal to Twenty Five Thousand Dollars ($25,000) per 1.09992 interest in the Property. Subject to the conditions and in accordance with the terms set forth herein, your obligation to subscribe and pay for the Securities shall be complete and binding upon the execution and delivery of this Subscription Agreement. Upon your payment of the purchase price as provided in Section 2, and the Company's acceptance of your subscription, your purchase of the Securities will be completed. This subscription may be accepted or refused in whole or in part by the Company in its sole and absolute discretion.

2. **Payment**. Payment for the Securities shall be made in cash or cashier's check. Payment shall be delivered to the Company or to the custodian for the Company's funds.

3. **Agreements with Investors**. The other Investors in the Securities have executed and delivered or will execute and deliver subscription agreements substantial identical to this Subscription Agreement in which such other Investors agree (or have agreed) to subscribe for and purchase the Securities and make (or have made) substantial the same representations and warranties as are made by you in Section 4 hereof. The purchases of the Securities made by you and the other Investors are to be separate purchases from the Company and the sales of the Securities to you and the other Investors are to be separate sales by the Company. This Subscription Agreement and such other subscription agreements are sometimes collectively referred to herein as the "Subscription Agreements."

4. **Your Representations and Warranties**. You represent and warrant as follows:

(a) You and your investment representative, if any, have received copies of the Agreement of Purchase and Sale and Escrow Instructions and Agreement of Limited Partnership of Sorrento REO Partners III, a California Limited Partnership. You had immediately

3

Illustration 8-2 (cont.)

prior to receipt of any offer regarding the Company, such knowledge and experience in financial and business matters as to be able to evaluate the merits and risks purchasing the Securities.

(b) You are able now, and were able at the time of receipt of any offer regarding the Company, to bear the economic risks of your purchase or investment.

(c) You or your investment representative, if any, have had the opportunity to ask questions of and receive answers from representatives of the Company concerning the terms and conditions of the offering of the Securities in the Company and to obtain any additional information necessary to verify the accuracy of the information furnished to you concerning the Company and such offering. In evaluating the suitability of this investment, you have not relied upon any representations or other information (whether oral or written) other than as contained in this Subscription Agreement, the Agreement of Purchase and Sale and Escrow Instructions and Agreement of Limited Partnership of Sorrento REO Partners III, a California Limited Partnership.

(d) You are acquiring the Securities for your own account for investment purposes only and not as a nominee or agent for any other person and not with the view to, or for resale in connection with, any distribution of any part of the Securities. If you are a corporation, trust, partnership or other organization, you were not organized for the specific purpose of acquiring the Securities.

(e) If you have utilized an investment representative, you have previously given the Company notice in writing of such fact or will list such person at the end of this Agreement, specifying in such notice that such investment representative would be acting as your "purchaser Securities Act of 1933 (the "Act").

(f) You have been informed that the offer of the Securities is being made pursuant to the exemption from the registration requirements of the Act afforded by Section 4(2) thereof and Regulation D promulgated thereunder, relating to transactions by an issuer not involving any public offering, and that, consequently, the materials relating to said offer have not been subject to the review and comment of the staff of the Securities and Exchange Commission or the National Association of Securities Dealers, Inc.

(g) You understand that you must bear the economic risks of your investment for an indefinite period because the Securities have not been registered under the Act or any applicable state securities laws and, therefore, the Securities may not be sold or otherwise transferred by you unless the Securities are registered or qualified under the Act and applicable state securities laws or an exemption from such registration or qualification is available.

4

Illustration 8-2 (cont.)

(h) Please provide the following information:

    (i)   Name: _____

             Address: _____

             _____

             Marital Status: _____ Age: _____

             Social Security or Fed. I.D. No.: _____

    (ii)   Employment and Business Information

             Occupation or Profession: _____

             Nature of Business: _____

    (iii) Educational Background

School	Major	Degree (if any)	Year Degree Received

    (iv)   Professional licenses or registration, including bar admissions, accounting certification, real estate brokerage licenses, if any:

    (v)   Investment in private placement or public offerings during the past five years:

Name of Investment	Type of Investment (oil/gas, real estate, corporate stock	Amount of Investment	Date of Investment

5

Illustration 8-2 (cont.)

(vi)   As of today's date, is your net worth in excess of ten (10) times the total purchase price of the Securities you are purchasing? (For purposes of net worth, the principal residence you own must be valued (i) at cost, including the cost of improvements net of current encumbrances or (ii) in accordance with its appraised value pursuant to a written appraisal.)
Yes _____ No _____ .

(vii)   As of today's date, is your net worth or you joint net worth with your spouse in excess of $1,000,000?

Yes _____ No _____ .

(viii)   (a) Has your income (exclusive of your spouse's income) in each of the last three years been in excess of $200,000?

Yes _____ No _____ .

(b) Do you expect your income (exclusive of your spouses income) in the current year to be in excess of $200,000?

Yes _____ No _____ .

(ix)   Do you have a pre-existing business or personal relationship with the Company or any of its officers or directors? (A pre-existing relationship means that the duration and nature of the relationship should be such as to enable a reasonably prudent purchase to be aware of the character, business acumen and general business and financial circumstances of the person with whom the relationship exists.)

Yes _____ No _____ .

5. Conditions to Closing. Your obligation to purchase and pay for the Securities to be purchased by you is subject to the representations and warranties contained in Section 4 hereof being true and correct.

6. Expenses. Each party hereto will pay its own expenses relating to this Subscription Agreement and the purchase of the Securities, except as set forth in the Agreement of Purchase and Sale and Escrow Instructions and the Agreement of Limited Partnership of Sorrento REO Partners I, a California Limited Partnership.

6

Illustration 8-2 (cont.)

---

7. **Amendments**. This Subscription Agreement may only be changed, waived, discharged or terminated with the written consent of you and the Company.

8. **Counterparts**. This Subscription Agreement may be executed in any number of counterparts, each of which shall be an original but all of which when taken together shall constitute one Subscription Agreement.

9. **Governing Law**. This Subscription Agreement and all amendments hereto shall be governed by and construed in accordance with the laws of the State of California.

If you are in agreement with the foregoing, please sign where indicated below and then return this Agreement to the Company, whereupon this Agreement shall become a binding agreement between you and the Company.

Very truly yours,

American Capital Investments, Inc., a California corporation

By: _____
Stephen Murphy, President

The foregoing Subscription Agreement is hereby accepted and agreed to as of the date thereof. I hereby acknowledge that the information provided in this Subscription Agreement is complete and accurate and may be relied upon by you. I will notify you immediately of any material change in any of such information occurring prior to the termination of this offering.

By_____   _____
   (Signature)   (Please Print Name)

Interest in Property _____   Indicate type of ownership:

$25,000 per 1.09992 interest   [ ] Individual
$_____ I wish to purchase   [ ] Joint Tenants
                                        [ ] Tenants in Common
Total Subscription Amount   [ ] Community Property
$_____   [ ] Corporate
                                        [ ] Partnership
                                        [ ] Trust

7

Illustration 8-3

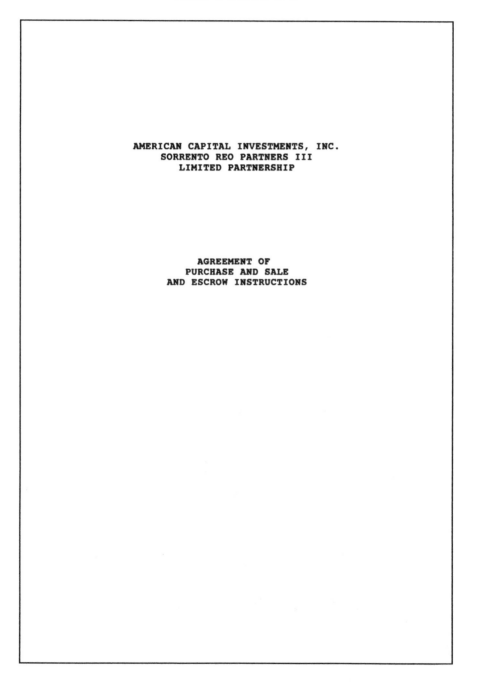

AMERICAN CAPITAL INVESTMENTS, INC.
SORRENTO REO PARTNERS III
LIMITED PARTNERSHIP

AGREEMENT OF
PURCHASE AND SALE
AND ESCROW INSTRUCTIONS

Illustration 8-3 (cont.)

AGREEMENT OF PURCHASE AND SALE
AND ESCROW INSTRUCTIONS

This Agreement of Purchase and Sale and Escrow Instructions (the "Agreement") is made and entered into as of _____ __, 1992, by and between _____ ("Buyer") and American Capital Investments, Inc., a California corporation ("Seller").

R E C I T A L S

A. Seller is the owner of the real property and improvements commonly known as the Mesa View Office Center located at 6725 Mesa Ridge Road, San Diego, California, more particularly described in Exhibit "A" attached hereto and incorporated herein by this reference (the "Property"). The Property consists of 1.52 acres and a two-story garden style office exists on the site.

B. It is the intent of the Seller to sell an undivided one half (1/2) interest in and to the Property to no more than thirty-five (35) persons. Simultaneous with the execution of this Agreement the Buyer shall execute a Limited Partnership Agreement entitled Sorrento REO Partners III, a California Limited Partnership (the "Partnership"), and transfer its Property interest to the Partnership.

C. The current amount of money the Seller has invested in the property is $2,273,000. A breakdown of the components of this purchase price are attached hereto as Exhibit "B" and incorporated herein by this reference. Accordingly, Seller is willing to sell a one half interest in the property for the purchase price of $1,136,500. Seller shall sell no less than a 1.305 interest in the property for a purchase price of $25,000 and Seller shall have no more than 35 purchasers. A total of 45.46 interests of an undivided 1.0992 interest in the Property are offered for sale.

D. Under the terms of the Partnership Agreement, the Buyer shall receive a 16% annual return on the purchase price and shall also receive a pro rata share of the equity in the Property. A condition of entering into this Agreement is the simultaneous contribution of the Property interest purchased under this Agreement to the Partnership and the execution of the Partnership Agreement.

A G R E E M E N T

NOW, THEREFORE, for and in consideration of the mutual covenants and conditions set forth herein, the parties hereto agree as follows:

1. **Purchase and Sale**. For the purchase price and upon and subject to the terms and conditions herein set forth, Seller hereby agrees to sell to Buyer, and Buyer hereby agrees to

Illustration 8-3 (cont.)

purchase from Seller an undivided _____% interest in the
Property.

        2. Purchase Price. The purchase price for the
interest purchased hereunder (the "Purchase Price") shall be
_____ ($_____) and shall be payable in cash,
cashier's or personal check.

        3. General Conditions.

        3.1 The Real Property is subject to a loan in
favor of Coast Federal Bank, Federal Savings Bank, in the
principal amount of One Million Five Hundred Thousand Dollars
($1,500,000.00). The income from the Property shall be paid to
the Partnership.

        3.2 Buyer agrees that, simultaneous with the
execution of this Agreement, Buyer shall transfer the interest in
the Property purchased hereunder to Sorrento REO Partners III, A
California Limited Partnership, and agrees to be bound by the
terms and conditions of said Partnership Agreement. The Buyer's
interest purchased hereunder shall be credited to Buyer's capital
account as set forth in the Partnership Agreement.

        4. Title.

        4.1 An undivided _____% interest in and to the
Property shall be conveyed to Buyer by grant deed in fee ("Deed
I") (which Deed I shall be duly executed and acknowledged and
shall be deposited by Seller into escrow at least one (1)
business day prior to the Close of Escrow). Buyer shall then
convey its interest in and to the Property to the Partnership by
grant deed in fee ("Deed II"), which Deed II shall be duly
executed and acknowledged and shall be deposited by Seller into
escrow at least one (1) business day prior to the Close of
Escrow), subject only to the following conditions of title (the
"Conditions of Title"):

        (a) a lien to secure payment of real estate
taxes not delinquent;

        (b) the Deed of Trust securing the Coast
Federal Bank loan;

        (c) matters affecting the condition of title
suffered or created by, or with the written
consent of Buyer or Seller;

        (d) any other matters disclosed by a
Preliminary Title Report, a copy of which shall be
available to Buyer upon request. AT ANY TIME
PRIOR TO THE CLOSE OF ESCROW, SAID PRELIMINARY
TITLE REPORT SHALL BE AVAILABLE TO BUYER FOR
BUYER'S INSPECTION AND APPROVAL.

3

Illustration 8-3 (cont.)

---

5. Escrow.

5.1 As used herein, the term "Opening of Escrow" shall mean the date executed counterparts of this Agreement are delivered to Beverly West Escrow, 433 N. Camden Drive, Beverly Hills, California (the "Escrow Holder"). The Opening of Escrow shall be on or before a date which is five (5) calendar days after the date this Agreement and the Partnership Agreement is executed by both Buyer and Seller. This Agreement, together with the General Conditions attached hereto as Exhibit "C" and incorporated herein by this reference (the "General Conditions"), shall be considered as the escrow instructions between the parties, with such further escrow instructions as Escrow Holder shall require to clarify the duties and responsibilities of Escrow Holder. If such further escrow instructions prepared by Escrow Holder are inconsistent with the terms of this Agreement, the escrow instructions shall be modified to the extent necessary to give full effect to the terms of this Agreement. If Escrow Holder shall require further instructions, Escrow Holder shall promptly prepare such further escrow instructions, which shall promptly be signed by Buyer and Seller. Such further escrow instructions shall provide that in the event of any conflict between the terms and conditions of this Agreement and said further escrow instructions, the terms and conditions of this Agreement shall control.

5.2 As used herein, the term "Close of Escrow" shall be the date the Escrow Holder receives the Purchase Price from Buyer and causes both Deed I and Deed II to be recorded, and shall be no later than thirty (30) calendar days after the Opening of Escrow. Upon Close of Escrow, Escrow Holder shall release the Purchase Price to Seller.

5.3 In the event the Close of Escrow shall fail to have occurred as provided for in Paragraph 4 hereof, either party not then in default may terminate escrow and its obligations hereunder upon three (3) days prior written notice to the other party and Escrow Holder. In the event of such termination, all sums and documents deposited in escrow (less applicable escrow fees) shall be returned to the depositing party.

6. Title Insurance. At the Close of Escrow, the Title Company shall furnish to the Partnership a CLTA standard coverage joint protection policy of title insurance, insuring title to the Property as vested in the Partnership, and insuring the lien of the Deed of Trust securing the Coast Federal Bank Loan as a first deed of trust lien on the Real Property subject only to the Conditions of Title (the "Title Policy"). The Title Policy shall be in an amount equal to the value of the Property and shall be dated as of the date and time of recordation of the Deed, and shall be issued and delivered to the Partnership as promptly as practicable following such recordation. Seller shall bear the costs of the issuance of the CLTA standard coverage title insurance policy. It shall be a condition precedent to the Close of Escrow and Buyer's and Seller's obligations hereunder that the Title Company be committed to issue the Title Policy.

4

Illustration 8-3 (cont.)

7. Expenses/Prorations.

7.1 Seller shall pay the escrow fees. Seller shall pay all costs in connection with the recordation of the Deed.

7.2 In the event escrow fails to close due to the default of either party hereto, such defaulting party shall be responsible for all escrow fees and costs, including, without limitation, reasonable cancellation or termination fees charged by Escrow Holder.

8. Notices. All written notices and demands of any kind which either party may be required or may desire to serve on the other in connection with this Agreement may be served by personal delivery or registered or certified mail, return receipt requested. Any notices or demands so served by registered or certified mail shall be deposited in the United States mail, with postage thereon fully prepaid, addressed to the other party to be so served as follows:

To Seller: American Capital Investments, Inc.
                    330 Washington Boulevard, Penthouse
                    Marina del Rey, California 90292

To Buyer: _____
                    _____
                    _____

Copy to: Cindy Casteel Watkins, Esq.
                    Law Offices of Philip A. Kramer
                    12100 Wilshire Boulevard, Suite 350
                    Los Angeles, California 90025

Any such communication shall be deemed to have been given at the time of such personal delivery or forty-eight (48) hours after to mailing thereof as hereinabove provided. Any party may change the address at which it is to receive notices by so notifying the other party at this Agreement in writing.

9. No Waiver. The waiver by either party of any term, condition or provision of this Agreement shall not be construed as a waiver of any other or subsequent term, condition or provision of this Agreement.

10. Time Is Of The Essence. Time is of the essence of the parties' obligations hereunder.

11. Gender. Whenever the context of this Agreement so requires, the masculine gender includes the feminine and neuter, the singular in number includes the plural, and the plural number includes the singular.

12. Attorneys' Fees. If either party hereto commences an action against the other to enforce any of the terms hereof, the losing or defaulting party shall pay to the prevailing party

5

Illustration 8-3 (cont.)

reasonable attorneys fees and costs incurred in connection with the prosecution of such action (and upon any appeal).

13. **Agreement**. This Agreement and all documents referred to herein constitute (i) the entire agreement between the parties hereto with respect to the subject matter hereof, (ii) supersede all prior or simultaneous negotiations or agreements, and (iii) may not be modified, amended or otherwise changed in any manner except by a writing executed by the party to be charged.

14. **Representations and Warranties**. All representations and warranties made by either party in this Agreement or any of the documents delivered to the other party in accordance with the terms of this Agreement shall be deemed remade as of the Close of Escrow and, together with the agreements made by Buyer and Seller hereunder to indemnify the other, shall survive the Close of Escrow.

15. **Governing Law**. This Agreement shall be governed by and construed in accordance with the laws of the State of California.

16. **Successors and Assigns**. This Agreement shall be binding upon and shall inure to the benefit of the successors and assigns of the parties hereto.

17. **Interpretation**. This Agreement is the product of arms length negotiations and shall not be construed for or against either party.

18. **Counterparts**. This Agreement may be executed in one or more counterparts, each of which shall be deemed an original, but all of which together will constitute one and the same instrument.

IN WITNESS WHEREOF, the parties hereto have executed this Agreement as of the date first written above.

"SELLER":   "BUYER"

AMERICAN CAPITAL
INVESTMENTS, INC.

By: _____   _____
     STEPHEN MURPHY, President

6

Illustration 8-3 (cont.)

EXHIBIT A

MESA VIEW OFFICE CENTER
6725 MESA RIDGE ROAD
SAN DIEGO, CALIFORNIA

Lot 19 of Resubdivision of Mesa Rim Industrial Park, in the City of San Diego, County of San Diego, State of California, according to Map thereof No. 10668, filed in the Office of the County Recorder of San Diego County, June 30, 1983.

EXHIBIT B

1.	Purchase Price From Coast Federal Bank	$ 1,800,000
2.	Closing Costs	31,878
3.	Administrative and Legal Fees	25,000
4.	Improvements to Property (Breakdown Attached)	416,275
		$ 2,273,153

7

Illustration 8-3 (cont.)

IMPROVEMENTS FOR 6725 MESA RIDGE ROAD

Revitalize existing landscape and replace with new as necessary.	$ 27,500
Replace sprinklers, valves and timer box.	2,900
Repave parking lot.	31,800
Restripe parking lot.	2,100
Elevator repair including pumps, valves, rollers, muffler and feed line.	11,200
Replace alarm module, bells and perimeter contacts. Install integrated key card access system.	10,455
Split power panel to separate suites. Add additional service for new HVAC. Rewire 3 suites to isolate individually. Update GFI's.	15,815
Provide tenant improvement for Suites 200 and 202 from shell space, 3,483 square feet at $18.40 per SF.	64,087
Provide tenant improvements to vacant suites for drop ceiling, HVAC and light grids.	33,321
Revamp entry, interior corridors and provide plants and pictures.	22,400
Replace 10 HVAC units and repair 7 HVAC units, including condensate lines and power stubbed out. Haul away unusable units. Install new ducting for separate suites. Update existing duct network.	91,380
Reglaze 31 glass panels and weatherize.	25,600
Update all interior and exterior lighting.	7,700
Replace stairwell doors.	4,488
Replace stairwell rails and recoat steps.	3,026
Replace 3 restroom stalls, 4 toilets, 1 urinal and 4 lav fixtures. Install new counter tops and mirrors.	18,150
Retile all restrooms, coat and seal entry tile.	17,800
Install new carpet in 6 suites including color matched base.	10,333
Repair all roof leaks, HVAC bases and reflash as necessary.	14,920
General clean up and debris removal.	1,500
Total	$416,275

8

9
FORMING THE
SYNDICATION

INCOME TAX IMPLICATIONS

From the 1904 Federal Court case of **Compania de Tabacos v. Collector of Internal Revenue** came a cogent quote:

". . . Taxes are what we pay for a civilized society . . ."

In the civilized society that greets the dawn of the 21st century, taxes are first and foremost on the minds of all United States citizens. On the one hand there is the hue and cry for better infrastructure; increased fire and police protection; aid for the aged and indigent; bolstering our defense; reduction of the high cost of health services; reduction of a staggering deficit; more jobs; affordable housing; improved environment; and so forth. The other fist shaking at Washington rankles at excessive spending, the thrift bailout, corruption, high taxes, pork barrel legislation, congressional perks, jobs lost through environmental concerns, etc. No matter what side may be taken, the inevitability of it all is that taxes required for the government to meet the needs of the people are an inevitable event in our lives. Strangely enough, the people that demand the services may be some of the same voices that complain about higher taxes. It's an anomaly of our society.

One of the issues that our government is facing head on is the problem of escaped assessments by the taxpayers. This problem is being addressed in a very aggressive fashion through a reporting form known as the 1099. Many who provide services in excess of $500 to individuals or companies during the year where there is no retention of the billing for income tax purposes will receive a 1099 form from the recipient of these services at year end. The duplicate of this form is filed with the IRS. In real estate transactions this 1099S form is rendered by the closing agent to the IRS noting the sales price received by seller(s) in transfers of real estate. This then becomes a cross check with the seller(s) tax return to determine that the sale was reported for capital gains purposes. This enables the government to track those who are subject to a capital gain and don't report the sale. 28% tax on the gain can add up to billions of lost revenue to the government that was unreported before the new 1099 reporting requirements. This requirement is just the tip of the iceberg. Eventually closing agents will probably be required to report broker's commissions, insurance premiums, title insurance fees, **their own fees**, structural pest control billings, contractor payments, and the like paid out of the closing transaction on a 1099 form. This will, again, close up some loopholes that have existed for many years where payment is made for services which remains unreported.

Yet to be resolved by the government is that vast army of individuals who works on the basis of cash only. Many of these, particularly in states bordering Mexico, are illegals who do not interface with financial institutions and deal on a cash basis. This underground economy avoids billions of dollars of tax assessments each year from a society that provides them with health and welfare services from tax dollars in return for their nonpayment.

Taxes are a responsibility of all citizens, yet preservation of capital is also a strong motivator. In order for one to establish any form of estate in this society, it is important to create some sort of vehicle which will mitigate taxation while still contributing a fair share and, at the same time, allow capital to grow through a well placed investment portfolio. Our government waffles between programs to encourage investment and those designed to discourage investments in certain areas. One of the programs designed in the latter area was the Tax Reform Act of 1986.

THE TAX REFORM ACT OF 1986

One of the principal provisions of the Tax Reform Act of 1986 effectively strips the ability of the taxpayer to charge real estate losses and allowable deduction credits against ordinary income. In a case where the real estate investor actively participates in the investment, credits of up to $25,000 are allowed against non-passive income of the taxpayer each year. Before applying the $25,000 credit, passive income is deducted from passive losses with the net loss figure being the upper limit of the deduction. In the case of individuals with $100,000 to $150,000 of adjusted gross income, the $25,000 limitation is reduced ratably without regard to passive losses. There are special tax credits involved with respect to investments involving low income housing in order to stimulate FHA project financing investments together with similar programs adopted by individual states to encourage affordable housing availability.

The Code defines passive activities as: 1) trade or business activities in which the taxpayer or spouse does not materially participate, that is, is not involved on a regular, continuous and substantial basis, and 2) rental activities where payments are primarily for the use of tangible property. Essentially this means if the investor is not involved in the day to day activities involving a syndication entity, the income derived from that entity would be considered passive. The law states, with the exception of residential interest deductions, income derived from an investment as a limited partner in a syndication is considered passive and if the losses from the investment in the way of expenses and depreciation exceed the income derived, only limited tax benefits as a deduction from other forms of income can be obtained as noted above. The losses can be accumulated, however, for a five year period in the expectation that passive income may be created to offset them. In the case that a limited partner is paid for personal services provided to a passive activity, such as a limited partnership in real estate, this is not considered passive income and cannot be sheltered with passive losses from the partnership.

These provisions of the Act were designed to offset some of the abuses of the 80s where limited partnerships were formed for cattle feeding, tank cars, real estate showing a negative return for tax reporting purposes (in some cases the investment also produced negative cash flows as well), and other devices designed for high income individuals to offset substantial income gained from their principal business endeavors.

In order to qualify for the maximum deduction, the taxpayer has to prove active participation in an investment activity. The definition of active participation involves establishing the fact that the taxpayer holds at least a 10% interest in the activity.

For this reason, limited partnerships are now formed on the basis of proving the limited partners **material** participation in the investment. The device used to accomplish this objective is to grant a percentage interest to the investor **individually** which the investor then, in turn, deeds to the partnership as evidence of active participation in the activity of the partnership.

Material participation requires involvement in the activity on a regular, continuous and substantial basis. If investors are actively involved in a variety of activities in a management capacity, such participation is likely to be considered materially participating in these activities. The reason for acquisition of a percentage interest in the project prior to deeding the property to the limited partnership by a limited partner is to avoid the provision if the code that states a limited partnership interest is not considered as materially participating. By showing an actual interest in the property, the limited partner then gains the status of material participation by establishing the percentage interest in the project.

Syndicators, such as American Capital Investments, Inc., have carefully studied the provision of the Tax Reform Act of 1986. With the aid of tax and investment counsel, the offerings have been structured in such a manner to create investments where the passive income **exceeds** passive losses through negotiating the price of the project and the leverage vehicle to effect purchase. To the real estate investor the true meaning of investment has returned since income property was designed to do just that, produce income. Today this objective can become a reality through judicious negotiation with the lending fraternity involving the real estate owned languishing in their portfolios.

In any balanced portfolio situation, investment should be considered using a variety of investment vehicles ranging from stocks and bonds to depository devices to real estate investments for those who have substantial capital to devote to these activities. An investment rule of thumb is that real estate capital, once invested, should continue to be devoted to that activity. There comes some point in time where the syndicate, for one reason or another, feels that it is appropriate to dispose of the investment. At this point in time, the issue of capital gains emerges. It may be preferential to defer such capital gains and the appropriate device for this is section 1031 of the Internal Revenue Code.

SECTION 1031 OF THE INTERNAL REVENUE CODE

Income property investors often use the method of exchanging property equities as a method of capital gains tax deferment. The gain recognized on sale can be deferred if the following conditions prevail:

- The properties must be held for productive use in a trade or business, or for investment.

- The properties exchanged must be of a like kind or their nature or character must be similar. In the case of real estate it means that other real estate would have to be exchanged for it. If personal property were involved in the exchange, this would be considered "boot" and a taxable portion of the exchange for capital gains purposes.

- An exchange must be effected.

As long as the real estate exchanged is compatible with the investment objective, it would qualify as "like kind." This means, in some cases, that a lot for an industrial building might qualify as well as an apartment for an office building, if the objective was compatible.

Some of the unlike kind property, or **boot**, could be cash, precious gems, motor vehicles, precious metals or other forms of personal property used as a portion of the consideration.

Recent regulations have placed further qualifications on the exchange transaction itself for purposes of qualification under Section 1031 of the Internal Revenue Code:

- The exchange will not qualify if:

  1. The parties are related - for purposes of this qualifications this is defined as immediate family members, lineal descendants, corporations in which the exchangers own more than 50% of the stock, two corporations that are members of the same holding group, and a grantor or fiduciary of a trust.

  2. Either party sells the property within two years of the exchange. (waived in the event of death or involuntary conversion, i.e. foreclosure, bankruptcy, etc.)

  3. A property in the United States is exchanged for a property outside the country.

Exchanges go through a series of mathematical computations for purposes of establishing equity positions and calculating the tax impact of the transaction. In order to best illustrate the procedure, a step by step description of the methodology will be performed.

Initially there will be a computation of the equities to be exchanged in the transaction. For purposes of illustration, consider a 10% interest in Project A to be exchanged for a similar interest in project B. The 100% price established for Project A is $1,000,000, while project B has a $1,500,000 price tag. There is an existing mortgage on Project A of $600,000, while project B has a mortgage of $800,000.

This is best described by showing the balancing of 10% of the equities as follows:

Project A		Project B
$100,000	Exchange Price	$150,000
-60,000	Existing Mortgage	-80,000
40,000	Owner's equity	70,000
+30,000	Cash Required	

The next procedure in the process is to determine the gains realized from the transaction:

$100,000	Exchange Price	$150,000
-70,000	Adjusted basis	-90,000
30,000	Realized Gain	60,000

Once realized gains are computed, then recognized gains (taxable) are then worked into the formula:

o	Cash Required	$30,000
o	Boot	-0-
o	Mortgage Relief	20,000*
o	Recognized Gain	$50,000

*Recognizes the $20,000 difference between the mortgage on Project A and the one on Project B.

Taxable income on this transaction would be based on the realized gain or the recognized gain, whichever is less. The calculations would be:

$30,000	Realized Gain	$60,000
-0-	Recognized Gain	50,000
-0-		$50,000

The second party who owns Project B exchanging with the first party who owns Project A will have no tax liability, while the other party will have a $50,000 gain subject to a potential 28% capital gains tax.

Once the two projects are exchanged, the book basis of each property is re-established predicated upon the tax impact of the transaction:

$ 70,000	Old Basis	$ 90,000
+ 80,000	New Mortgage	+60,000
+ 30,000	Cash and boot paid	-0-
+ -0-	Recognized Gain	+50,000
$180,000	Total	$200,000

LESS

$ 60,000	Old Mortgage	$ 80,000
+ -0-	Cash and Boot Received	+30,000
$ 60,000		$110,000

$120,000	New Basis	$ 90,000

Once the new basis has been established for the exchange properties, then the taxpayer would then allocate between land and improvements to establish a depreciation schedule. Normally depreciation would be established on some form of depreciated value on the improvements. In the case of real estate owned that is being purchased, there may be instances where buildings are being purchased at **below** the depreciated value of the improvements. This creates a unique situation, tax-wise and one that would require competent tax counsel to resolve.

Historically exchanges were intended to occur on a concurrent basis. In recent years the issue of concurrency has been challenged, more specifically in the case of a decision rendered in the United States District Court in Portland, Oregon in the case of **Starker v. United States (602 F.2CD 1341, 9th Circuit)** where the principal of deferred exchange was first introduced. That decision involved an exchange of real estate between the plaintiff and the Weyerhauser Lumber Company wherein Weyerhauser did not immediately have the exchange property and took some time in accumulating the property to effect an exchange. During the period that the proceeds credited to Starker were on Weyerhauser's books, the company gave the Starkers a 6% credit on their money. By the time the entire exchange had taken place, it was seven years after Weyerhauser had purchased the Starker property. The judge, Solomon by name, rendered the decision that the transaction fell within the guidelines of Section 1031 of the IRC. Even after this decision, the IRS continued to resist the principle of deferred exchanges. In a later Starker case involving another transaction with Weyerhauser, Judge Solomon again got the bench call and reversed his position in the earlier case by disallowing the transaction making it subject to capital gains tax.

This confusion and the Internal Revenue Service's intractable position relative to delayed exchanges has now been resolved by a clarification of the law. Now the law allows exchange properties to be identified within 45 days after the exchange has been established through the initial closing of say, Project A, in our example above. The taxpayer then has the earlier of 180 days after the initial closing has occurred, or the due date of the exchanger's tax returns for the year of transfer. Usually the second date can be adjusted through the filing of an extension. For all intents and purposes, the transaction must be closed 180 days after the closing of the initial sale. With this new deferred exchange ruling, a spate of exchange accommodators have been established to act as independent third parties to hold the proceeds of the first sale to complete the deferred exchange within the prescribed time limits. If the proceeds of the initial transaction come within the **possession and control** of the taxpayer, all tax benefits of the transaction are lost.

Other ways of mitigating tax liability for real estate investors lies in two other areas:

o Tax free gift giving through the allocation of $10,000 bequests to donees ($20,000 in the case of husband and wife) by the donors is allowed federally with certain states, including California, imposing taxes on gifts above these levels.

o Establishing living trusts to manage the assets of the investor. This second procedure requires considerable advice from both tax and legal counsel before undertaking. In the case of a married couple, it may be prudent to have the trust initiated after the death of one or the other party instead of establishing it while both are alive. Remember that inheritance taxes are not a factor until the net asset value of the estate exceeds $600,000 per person federally. The tax rate above that amount is a sliding scale running from 37% to 55%, depending upon the size of the estate. Remember that personal property is probated in the estate of **domicile** of the deceased, while real property is probated in the state where the property is **located.** When the estate of the late Howard Hughes was admitted to probate, a considerable jurisdictional dispute was created between the states of Florida, Nevada and California who each claimed to be the estate of domicile for the reclusive billionaire. The reason for this legal brouhaha was the fact that a large part of the estate involved personal property, in particular stock ownership in the Hughes Tool Company, which controlled Trans World Air Lines, and casino interests in Las Vegas, Nevada.

1099 TAX REPORTING

As previously noted, sale transactions of real estate are now being reported by closers on a 1099 form throughout the country as a means of identifying potential taxable events. Probably where this process gets most confusing is in the case of tax deferred exchanges. These transactions may involve no tax liability whatsoever, but the Internal Revenue Service obtains a report of the transfer which allows them to question whether or not a taxable event has occurred. It was further noted that the 1099 reporting requirements for closers involving the payees receiving remuneration through closings will probably expand allowing the IRS to view more potential unreported taxable events in the future.

One other method of obtaining tax free dollars without the necessity of the reporting process is through the vehicle of refinancing property.

Leverage can not only free up dollars for other real estate investments, it can serve to obtain better loan terms in the relatively low rate atmosphere of the early 1990s. One note of caution, if one borrows above the actual acquisition cost of the property, a portion of the interest allowance for income tax purposes may be lost in the case of residential property. This is important to note when one is negotiating lines of credit that are secured by a personal residence. As taxpayers know painfully well, interest paid on installment credit, such as a personal unsecured loan or credit card debt is no longer allowed as a deduction for income tax purposes. This is the reason why the personal residence has become such a popular borrowing device.

Once all aspects of the transaction have been examined from a tax standpoint, then the partnership agreement is in a position to be drafted. In the analysis of this agreement, please refer to the form shown as an illustration in the previous chapter.

FORMING THE PARTNERSHIP

The partnership agreement is the basic device used in a limited partnership to spell out the duties and responsibilities of the general and limited partners as well as clearly define the objective and purpose of the partnership itself. Each state, such as California, normally has an Act which clarifies how a limited partnership can conduct its affairs. In order for a limited partnership to be able to conduct its business in the state, certain legal steps must be taken over and above the recordation of the limited partnership agreement itself. Initially, a fictitious name filing must be made with the county clerk and an advertisement of the existence of the partnership must be placed in a newspaper authorized to accept legal advertising in the state in the area where the partnership is located. It must be done in compliance with requirements set forth in the Corporations Code of the State of California. For this reason, such agreements are usually drafted by counsel and not undertaken by the syndicator, unless the syndicator happens to be a qualified member of the bar.

The agreement itself will set forth the name of the partnership and the definitions of the terms to be used in conjunction with the agreement itself. It will also identify the principal place of business of the partnership for purposes of legal process of service and other requirements. Some of the more important provisions are:

- Purpose and authority - Usually the language in this section is worded in the broadest of terms in order to allow the partnership latitude in its operation.

- Filings - In this section the general partner will affirm that it will perform the necessary filings and required advertisements in connection with partnership formation as well as the documents required for its cancellation with allowance for the use of a power of attorney, if appropriate.

- Term - This figure varies dependent upon the investment objective of the partnership. Many syndicates are designed for a five year term to allow investment maturity and appreciation.

- Contributions to capital - In this section the ground rules are set for the limited and general partner's contribution of capital to the partnership. All of the capital is eventually contributed for the general partner's use in the conduct of partnership business. A separate accounting for each limited partner's capital account is established in this section. There are also provisions for lending to the partnership for partnership purposes, such as making payments on existing indebtedness.

- Distributions of cash — This is the section that piques any investor's interest. This answers the burning question of how much return will be derived on capital. A specific return may be identified along with an amount of monthly payment based upon the partner's initial capital contribution plus distribution of any other monies derived from partnership activity over and above working capital requirements necessary to continue partnership operations.

- Allocation of net profits and net losses — Investors never want to hear about the latter category, although many of the abortive real estate partnership investments of the 1980s fell into hard times. In the cases of net losses, most agreements will provide that it is the limited partners' responsibility to proportionately replenish that portion of the capital account required to keep proper working capital levels. In the event there are profits, such losses will be charged against unallocated profits. Profits would be allocated in accordance with the cash distribution section.

- Management duties and powers — Normally the management and conduct of the business would be allocation among the general partner(s). Among these duties in the case of a syndicate dealing with financial institutions and their real estate owned portfolio to negotiate the transaction including all leverage aspects and enter into all documentation necessary to effect closing. In addition the general partner(s) would have the power to dispose of partnership assets and conduct partnership affairs, including property management, on a daily basis. Within this broad language is usually an exculpatory clause concerning the general partner(s) business conduct vis-a-vis limited partners as long as such partner dealt in good faith within the scope of authority.

- Changes in the general partner; transfers of its partnership interest - This section deals with the numerous possibilities that could occur relative to the general partner's position including transfer of its interest, death, insolvency or partnership dissolution.

- Admission of additional and substituted limited partners and transfers of and restrictions on transfers of their partnership interests — This section lays the ground rules on transfer of limited partners' interests and the circumstances that might arise to cause such transfer.

- Guaranteed one time 100% buy-out option — In certain instances the general partner may offer to purchase from the limited partners, on a prorata basis, the balance of their capital account.

- Distributions and withdrawals — Entitlement to distributions is established for limited partners in this section as well as the conditions attached to early withdrawal from the partnership.

- Books and records, accounting and tax elections — This section establishes the necessary record keeping and reporting devices to be used by the partnership.

- Meetings of partners and voting requirements — This section deals with establishing a meeting and voting procedure including establishing what represents a quorum for the partnership to constitute a valid voting vehicle.

- Sale, dissolution and liquidation — When the partnership affairs are wound down, this section notes procedures to be followed in each instance.

- Sale of partnership assets and interests — If a majority of the limited partners opt for sale of the partnership, the procedure for conducting such sale is set forth in this section.

- Miscellaneous sections dealing with the legal rights of the parties are usually tacked on at the end of the partnership agreement relative to legal notices, binding agreement on successors and assigns of the partners, which state law will apply, attorneys fees, etc. are covered in omnibus fashion.

The agreement is then signed in counterparts by the individual limited partners as they sign their particular subscription form representing individual contributions to the partnership.

It should be noted to potential investors in limited partnerships that some limited partnership interests may be assessable, which means that liability may go beyond just the initial capital contribution. For this reason, appropriate cash flowing projects that have the potential of continued cash flow are preferable to those where the property is located in an area of decline where prospects for lost tenancy are higher.

SYNDICATION DOCUMENTS

- Documents to form the transaction — Initially if the offer is made through a real estate licensee, the initial document utilized will be a purchase agreement and deposit receipt form. This form sets forth the conditions of purchase along with the proposed buyer's earnest money deposit. If the terms and conditions of this document are unconditionally accepted by the buyer, it forms a contract and the basis for the purchase. Within the four corners of this document, the following is considered:

1. Receipt of the earnest money deposit to remain uncashed until accepted.

2. Identifying the property to be purchased by street address and legal description noting the real property with improvements as well as any personal property included in the transfer.

3. A time limit within which the offer must be accepted.

4. Identification of a closing (escrow) agent.

5. Establishing the length of the escrow.

6. Naming the ownership entity and acceptable title conditions.

7. Dealing with any owner's or merchant's association and the handling of their assessments, dues, etc., if any.

8. Disposition of fire insurance coverage.

9. Determination of prorations required, if any, for taxes, insurance, rents, etc.

10. Provisions for collateralization of any real or personal property if financing of such is required together with provision for a bill of sale on any personal property.

11. Any structural pest control requirements.

12. Due diligence requirements (including environmental matters and inspection of the premises) that are of concern of the purchaser.

13. Retrofit requirements on the part of the seller (smoke detectors, etc.)

14. Maintenance of the property in good condition by seller during escrow.

15. Including fixtures in sales price.

16. Destruction of the premises invalidates the sale and the buyer's obligation to perform under the agreement.

17. Willingness of the seller to accommodate a 1031 exchange if the buyer so requires.

18. Allowance to the broker to disclose the terms of the sale to affiliate groups.

19. Provision for brokerage commission, if applicable.

20. Delivery of possession requirements.

21. Any specific condition of transfer prescribed by the nature of the transaction, such as assignment of leases, approval of authorities, etc. Typical of this would be a lease on Indian land where approval by the Bureau of Indian Affairs might be required.

    In addition to the purchase agreement and deposit receipt, once the document has been accepted, other forms will follow. In the case of the deposit receipt and purchase agreement, the first offer may not be accepted. It is not unusual for an offer to be accompanied by as many as two to five counter-offers before finally being accepted or not accepted at all. In the case where a variety of counter-offers have been produced, usually the real estate licensee who is involved in the negotiation will then prepare a new deposit receipt incorporating the terms of the original offer as modified by the various counter-offers for signature by the buyer and seller.

ESSENTIAL PROVISIONS OF THE LIMITED PARTNERSHIP AGREEMENT

As noted above in going through the various clauses of a typical limited partnership agreement, it is essential that the limited partners feel comfortable with the arrangement that is being made with the general partner. These are essentially set forth in the partnership agreement. It is essential that real estate investors study the instrument of creation carefully in order to determine that this investment tax-wise and devotion of capital-wise meets specific investment objectives. In the case of real estate owned, unusual transactions are being created allowing property to be bought at far less than replacement cost allowing positive cash flow. This is an unusual investment "window" in the real estate cycle. The unusual lending terms available on real estate owned also allow for the investment group to improve cash flow while concurrently enjoying the advantage of lowered payments during the early acquisition stages. With this in mind, one steps from the purchase agreement into the closing.

CLOSING THE TRANSACTION

Once the transaction is established the parties will then engage an escrow or closing agent to close the sale. In some cases the purchase agreement may also serve as the escrow instruction, but most closers prefer a separate escrow instruction since certain items, such as transferring of possession and the handling of keys, etc. are not necessary to effect the legal transfer of the property and create the condition of title bargained for. The courts of California have established that, when prepared separately, the deposit receipt and purchase agreement will be superseded by the escrow instruction only in those provisions where they are contrary in nature to the earlier document. All other provisions, including the liquidated damages clause that prevails in many deposit receipts today, would remain.

Usually, if the clients are represented by agents, the closing process is initiated by the agent. It should be remembered that throughout the country, the closing process varies due to local laws and historical development of methodology. For example, in Northern California escrows are basically handled by title companies who use unilateral instructions that are not prepared until the time that loan approval has been obtained on the property. On the other hand, Southern California processes its closings on the basis of a bilateral instruction that is signed in counterparts by the parties. In order to see how the documentation in escrow evolves, here are some helpful illustrations:

- New escrow information sheet Illustration 9-1 — This is used by the escrow officer to take down the basic information of transfer in order to convert this information into an instruction fulfilling the intent of the parties. It should be remembered that the escrow officer is an impartial independent third party who merely follows the principals instructions. The escrow holder is also bound to the confidentiality of the transaction and, as such is a limited agent to both buyer and seller to carry out the intentions of the parties. If the escrow officer is unclear of the contractual obligation created by the escrow instruction, then there must be clarifying instructions obtained.

- Documentation check sheet — Illustration 9-2 provides a tracking of documents through the escrow process and serves as an auditing device at the close of escrow to determine that all documents required on the given transaction have been received.

- Information sheet — Illustration 9-3. This is used by escrow to obtain information on the various parties of interface during the transaction such as homeowner's groups, insurance agents, lenders of record, etc.

- Escrow instructions — Illustration 9-4 represents the transfer of the information shown on Illustration 9-1 into the form of a formal contractual arrangement between the parties. There are other items that may be addressed by the escrow for the escrow's protection and they may fall within the general provisions of the escrow instruction. Also of consideration are the various statutes that affect the clearing of checks at the title company; Foreign Investors Reporting Tax Act (FIRPTA), both on federal and state level; 1099 reporting requirements, exculpatory clauses relative to the rendering of legal and tax advice; and environmental conditions that may exist on the property.

- Broker's commission — By the way of a third party instruction, shown as Illustration 9-5, the allocation of broker's commission is established, usually by the seller. In certain instances the buyer may pay the broker's commission. Although there are characteristic ways that closing charges are paid by the principals, there is no requirement that they paid in that fashion with the exception of FHA/VA financing which has certain limitations to charge allocation under certain circumstances. Their allocation of charges is **by agreement of the parties**.

- Structural pest control instructions — Illustration 9-6 demonstrates a typical structural pest control instruction. The delivery of the report itself is the responsibility of the selling broker.

- Proration instructions — Illustration 9-7 shows how various items are to be handled relating to proration, preliminary change of ownership report which accompanies the deed for recording, various federal and local requirements and the good funds compliance by the parties.

- Agreement to furnish insurance — This form shown as Illustration 9-8 is used to assure lenders that adequate fire insurance is being obtained on the property being acquired by the buyer.

- Special instructions re: deposit — When a good faith deposit is in excess of $10,000 and will be retained in escrow in excess of thirty days, the depositing party may, by the use of Illustration 9-9, use this instruction as a means of transferring this deposit to an interest bearing account.

- Lender's instructions — Illustration 9-10 is a typical lender escrow instruction form which will outline the conditions of disbursement of the lender's loan proceeds when remitting loan documentation.

- Title company transmittal — This document, shown as Illustration 9-11 is used to submit documentation (reconveyances of existing trust deeds, deeds, trust deeds, partnership agreements for recording, etc.) together with instructions relative to the condition of title required. This transmittal also may serve as a recording instruction to the title company upon receipt of the lender's funds.

- Settlement check sheet and check register — Illustration 9-12. This is used for figuring prorations and the checks to be disbursed by the appropriate parties. Actual settlement is effected through a closing statement which will not necessarily equate the total consideration due to the effect of prorations and closing costs on the buyer's and seller's allocation of escrow proceeds.

Once settlement is effected, your partnership now owns the property!

In the **Encyclical on the Condition of Labor** rendered on May 15th, 1891, Pope Leo XIII noted:

> ". . . Every man has by nature the right to possess property of his own . . ."

As real estate investors you have now entered the sanctum of property ownership. In order to sustain value and improve yields on your investment, a key ingredient is the use of proper management techniques to accomplish that objective. In the concluding chapter the subject of property management will be discussed in detail as a capital enhancement device.

Illustration 9-1

NEW ESCROW INFORMATION SHEET
Initial Deposit $_____
Bal of Cash thru $_____
Pd. O/S/ Escrow $_____
New Loan Amt. $_____
T.D. & Note $_____
Other $_____
Total: $_____
Commission: ____% _____ Split
Broker Address: _____

Tel No._____ Agent_____

Broker Address: _____
_____
Tel No._____ Agent_____

SELLER:_____
_____
Address:_____
_____
Home Ph: _____ Bus Ph:_____
Forwarding:_____
Address at c.o.e. _____
BUYER:_____
Vesting:_____
Address:_____
Home Ph:_____ Bus. Ph:_____
Will Occupy: Yes____ No____

TRUST DEED AND NOTE/PAYOFF
(1) In favor of _____
Address:_____
_____
Loan No. _____
(2) In favor of _____
Address:_____
_____
Loan No. _____
(3) In favor of _____
Address:_____
_____
Loan No. _____

ESCROW INSTRUCTIONS — TERMS
Termite: Yes____ No____
P.R. Approval: Yes____ No____ #Days__
New Insurance: Yes____ No____
Buyer/Property: Yes____ No____
Personal Property Included: _____

ESCROW NO._____ DATE_____
OPENED BY _____
TITLE CO. _____
CLOSING DATE _____
PROPERTY ADDRESS _____
_____
LEGAL DESCRIPTION: _____
_____
_____
_____
_____

PARCEL # ____ - _____ -
Broker Address: _____
_____
Tel No._____ Agent_____

PRORATES:
Interest to_____ RENTS:
Insurance to_____ $_____
Taxes to _____ Per_____
Adjust Sec./Cleaning Dep. $_____
Yes____ No____ Per_____

TRUST DEED AND NOTE (to file)
For $_____ In favor of _____
_____
Vesting:
Interest fr:_____ @ ____%
Payable: _____
_____
_____
Maturity Date: _____
Clauses: _____
_____
_____

TRUST DEED & NOTE (of record/to remain)
For $_____ In favor of: _____
_____
Payable: $_____ per _____
Including ____% all due: _____
Impounds: Yes____ No____
Give____ Buy____
Adjust: Cash____
T/D____
S/P____
ADD'L TERMS AND INSTRUCTIONS
_____
_____

Illustration 9-2

ESCROW OFFICER: _____

TITLE CO: _____ PHONE: _____ TRANSACTION TYPE:_____

ORDER NUMBER: _____ TITLE OFFICER: _____

ESCROW NO._____ DATE OPENED: _____ CLOSE OF ESCROW:_____

LIST BROKER: _____ SELLER: _____

_____ PHONE: _____ _____ PHONE: _____

SELL BROKER: _____ BUYER: _____

_____ PHONE: _____ _____ PHONE: _____

BUYER TO OCCUPY: YES____ NO____ PROPERTY: _____

CHECK LIST

	Req.	Rec'd.		Req	Rec'd.
ESCROW INSTRUCTIONS			PRELIMINARY REPORT		
Seller			Copies to Lender		
Buyer			Copies to Brokers		
Brokers			Buyer Approval		
Lender			Supplement		
GRANT DEED			Supplement		
Seller			PEST CONTROL REPORT		
Title Co.			Completion		
TRUST DEED & NOTE			Buyer Approval		
Buyer			DEMAND:		
Title Co.			Loan #		
COMMISSION			Address		
Seller			Phone		
Broker			DEMAND:		
Broker			Loan #		
I.D. STATEMENT			Address		
Seller			Phone		
Buyer			BENE. STATEMENT		
AMENDMENT RE:			Loan #		
Seller			Address		
Buyer			Phone		
Brokers			NEW INSURANCE		
Lender/T.C.			Phone		
AMENDMENT RE:			Agent		
Seller			Ordered		
Buyer			Effective		
Brokers			Premium		
Lender/T.C.			LOAN SUBMITTED		
RENT STATEMENT			LOAN APPROVED		
Seller			LOAN DOCUMENTS		
Buyer			Received		
CONTINGENCIES			Signed by Borrower		
1.			Returned to Lender		
2.			AUTHORIZED FUNDING		
3.			AUTHORIZED RECORDING		

COMMENTS: _____

LENDER: _____

ADDRESS: _____

PHONE: _____

LOAN REP/LOAN PROCESSOR: _____

TYPE OF LOAN: _____

MANAGER APPROVAL: _____

ESCROW INSTRUCTIONS: _____

FUNDING REQUESTED: _____

CLOSING: _____

Illustration 9-3

ESCROW NO._____

PROPERTY ADDRESS:_____

_____

PLEASE FURNISH THE FOLLOWING INFORMATION

FIRST TRUST DEED LOAN HELD BY:

_____

_____

_____

LOAN NO.: _____

SECOND TRUST DEED LOAN HELD BY:

_____

_____

_____

LOAN NO.: _____

NAME AND ADDRESS OF HOMEOWNER ASSOCIATION:

_____

_____

ACCOUNT NO.: _____

NAME AND ADDRESS OF INSURANCE AGENT CARRYING FIRE/HOMEOWNER POLICY:

_____

_____

_____

POLICY NO.: _____

AGENTS NAME: _____

Illustration 9-4

Paid Outside Escrow $	
Cash Thru Escrow	
Loan of Record-1st	
Loan of Record-2nd	
Loan of Record-3rd	
New 1st Loan	
New 2nd Loan	
New 3rd Loan	
Total Consideration $	

ESCROW INSTRUCTIONS TO _____
ESCROW TYPE _____
ESCROW OFFICER _____ ESCROW NO. _____
DATE _____
TO COMPLETE A TOTAL CONSIDERATION OF $_____
I/We will hand you_____
and will deliver to you any notes, instruments and additional funds required from buyers to
enable you to comply with these instructions on or prior to_____ all of which you
are authorized and instructed to use and deliver provided instruments have been filed for
record entitling you to procure assurance of title in the form of a Standard Policy of Title
Insurance covering property in the County of _____State of California Records of
said County described as follows: _____

Property Address (not verified) _____
showing title vested in _____

Free from encumbrances except (1) General and Special taxes, including any special district
levies, payments for which are included therein and collected therewith for the current fiscal
year, not delinquent, including taxes for the ensuing year, if any, not yet payable.
(2) Covenants, conditions, restrictions, reservations, rights of way, easements and
exceptions of minerals, oil, gas, water, carbons, and hydrocarbons on or under said land now
of record, and in deed to file, if any, affecting the use and occupancy of said property.

THESE INSTRUCTIONS ARE CONTINUED ON ADDITIONAL INSTRUCTIONS
ATTACHED HERETO AND MADE A PART HERETO. If above encumbrance in a
purchase money trust deed, endorse interest on notes as of date of recording deed. In event
unpaid balance of trust deed(s) or record are more or less that the sum(s) set forth above
adjust difference (   ) in cash (   ) thru deed of trust to file (   ) in the
selling price. Prorate taxes on real property only based on the latest tax bill in your
possession or on latest available tax figures furnished by the title company as of _____.
Prorate interest on loans of record as of _____. Prorate rents as of _____ based
on rent statement handed you. Any rents in arrears to be disregarded in your prorations.
Prorate insurance as handed you as of _____ and in the event the lender requires
additional insurance to cover new loan, this is your authorization to order same and pay
premium, if any, from buyers funds. As of _____ credit seller and debit buyer the
amount of impounds, if any, as disclosed by beneficiary statement from the holder of the
loan of record.

> **EACH PARTY SIGNING THESE INSTRUCTIONS HAS READ THE ADDITIONAL
> ESCROW CONDITIONS AND INSTRUCTIONS ON THE REVERSE SIDE HEREOF
> AND APPROVES, ACCEPTS, AND AGREES TO BE BOUND THEREBY AS
> THOUGH THE REVERSE SIDE HEREOF APPEARED OVER THEIR SIGNATURES.**

The undersigned hereby agrees to pay on demand charges for drawing, recording, and
notarizing all documents, charges of title company, if any, charges of lending institution, if
any, and the buyer's and/or borrower's customary escrow fees, necessary to complete this
escrow.
Lender's or
Buyer's Signature_____   Lender's or
Buyer's Signature_____   Buyer's Signature_____
Address   Buyer's Signature_____

The foregoing terms, provisions, conditions and instructions are hereby approved an
accepted in their entirety and concurred in by me. I will hand you necessary documents
and/or funds called for on my part to cause title to be shown as above, which you are
authorized to deliver when you hold for my account the sum of $_____ together with
any documents due the undersigned as described above, within the time as above provided.
Pay your escrow charges, my recording fees, charges for evidence of title as called for,
whether or not this escrow is consummated, except those the buyer agreed to pay. You are
hereby authorized to pay bonds, assessments, taxes, and any liens or encumbrances of
record, plus accrued interest, charges and bonus, if any, Pay Documentary Transfer Tax as
required on Deed to property I am conveying. You are also authorized to reimburse party
advancing money for cost of building report.

Borrower's or
Seller's Signature_____   Borrower's or
Seller's Signature_____   Seller's Signature_____
Address   Seller's Signature_____

Illustration 9-4 (cont.)

GENERAL INSTRUCTIONS

1. Time is of the essence of this escrow. If, for any reason, this escrow cannot be closed by the date set forth on page one of these instructions, you shall nevertheless close it as soon as possible thereafter unless notice of cancellation is given by either party. Any notice of cancellation affecting this escrow, for whatever reason and whenever given, may be given only in writing, delivered to you in duplicate. On receipt of such notice you shall within three days mail one copy to the other party. Unless written objection thereto from such other party shall be received by you within ten days after such mailing, you are authorized to comply with any instructions in such notice and to cancel the escrow upon payment of your cancellation charges. In the event written objection is received within the time stated or in the event conflicting claims are made upon you in this escrow, you may refuse to take any further action hereunder or you may interplead the parties in any court of competent jurisdiction, in which case you shall be entitled to your costs including reasonable attorney's fees incurred therein. If you become a party to any civil action by reason of this escrow, you shall be entitled to recover your attorney's fees and costs, as may be allowed by the court.

2. You are hereby authorized to deposit any funds or documents handed you under these escrow instructions or cause the same to be deposited with any subescrow agent, subject to your order at or prior to close of escrow in the event such deposit shall be necessary or convenient for the consummation of this escrow.

3. Unless specifically instructed to the contrary, all prorations and adjustments shall be effected on a 30-day basis, and close of escrow is the day instruments are recorded.

4. Prorate taxes, on real property only, based on latest tax bill available to you.

5. Seller warrants that premiums on existing insurance have been paid.

6. All disbursements shall be made by regular escrow check. All disbursements of funds and/or instruments of this escrow shall be mailed, unregistered, to the designated party in accordance with subject escrow instructions, address of whom is incorporated herein. Deliver title policy to buyer and to holder of first and/or new encumbrances.

7. You shall make no physical examination and'gr representation of the real and/or personal property described in any document deposited in said escrow.

8. All provisions, instructions and conditions mentioned in these General Instructions shall govern, without reservation, any amended and/or supplemental instructions furnished in this escrow unless amended by specific reference.

9. You are authorized to furnish a copy of these instructions, any amendments thereto, and/or final closing statement to the Real Estate Broker representing any of the parties in this transaction, also any lender holding or contemplating a loan against subject property.

10. Unless specifically instructed to the contrary, prepare the Deed providing for the Tax Bills to be forwarded to the buyers at the address of the property that is the subject of this escrow.

Illustration 9-5

Escrow Instructions to:

Escrow No. _____ Escrow Officer _____ Date _____

You are advised that the commission be paid for services in connection with this transaction is the sum of $ _____
Said amount is to be paid as follows:

$ _____ to _____ Lic. # _____

address _____ Phone _____

$ _____ to _____ Lic. # _____

address _____ Phone _____

$ _____ to _____ Lic. # _____

address _____ Phone _____

$ _____ to _____ Lic. # _____

address _____ Phone _____

I have read and hereby approve the foregoing, and you will pay said commission at the close of this escrow and charge my account with the amount thereof, or if necessary, I will hand you funds required to pay the same.

_____

_____

Illustration 9-6

PAGE _____

Escrow Instructions to:

Escrow No. _____ Escrow Officer _____ Date _____

The seller herein agrees to furnish, at his expense, an inspection report by a licensed structural pest control operator and a notice that all measures recommended in the report have been completed. Such report is to affect the premises known as _____

Escrow holder is instructed to deliver, as soon as possible, a copy of the structural pest control inspection report to the buyer(s) herein prior to the close of escrow. Also, if the completion report is received by the escrow holder prior to the close of escrow, you are instructed to deliver, as soon as possible, a copy of said completion report to the buyer(s) herein prior to the close of escrow.

Delivery means delivery in person to any one of the buyers (if there is more than one buyer) or mailing, by ordinary mail, at least two working days prior to the close of escrow, to any one of the buyers.

From the seller's funds you are authorized to pay, upon presentation, invoices purporting to be from a licensed structural pest control operator for the inspection, report and recommended work.

Illustration 9-7

PAGE ....

Escrow Instructions to:

Escrow No. .... Escrow Officer .... Date ....

Prorate taxes on the basis of $_____ for one year, which is the tax information presently available, and it is satisfactory that the title policy reflect same. You are not to be concerned with any supplemental bills which either party may receive after the close of escrow.

Unless buyer furnishes you with a Preliminary Change of Ownership Report to attach to the grant deed prior to close of escrow, you are to charge buyer and pay the additional $20 fee for recording said deed.

The parties acknowledge that they are aware of Section 1445 of the Tax Reform Act of 1984 and will comply with same outside of escrow, and you are not to be concerned in any way.

City or County Ordinances requiring special reports or inspections, if any, will be handled outside of escrow and you are not to be concerned.

The parties are aware that Sections 12413 and 12413.5 of the California Insurance Code, which became effective January 1, 1985, provide that funds deliverable through or by a title insurance company, underwritten title company or controlled escrow company shall not be disbursed until such funds have cleared. You are relieved of all liability and responsibility in the event that close of escrow is delayed pending clearance of said funds.

Signature _____   Signature _____

Signature _____   Signature _____

Illustration 9-8

AGREEMENT TO FURNISH INSURANCE

TO:
_____

DATE_____

I, the undersigned purchaser/borrower, agree to furnish the insurance coverage checked:

AUTOMOBILES, TRUCKS AND RECREATIONAL VEHICLES:
_____Comprehensive, including fire, theft and collision coverage.
_____Loss Payable Endorsement

MACHINERY AND EQUIPMENT OR
REAL PROPERTY:
__XX___Fire and extended coverage
__XX___Lender's Loss Payable Endorsement

BOATS:
_____All-Risk Hull Insurance
_____438BFU Lender's Loss Payable Endorsement
_____Breach of Warranty Endorsement

AIRCRAFT:
_____All-Risk Ground and Flight Insurance
_____Lender's Loss Payable Endorsement
_____Breach of Warranty Endorsement

MOBILE HOMES:
_____Fire, Theft and Combined Additional Coverage
_____Lender's Loss Payable Endorsement.

for the property which is the subject of a conditional sale contract/security agreement dated_____19_____.

I have, or will instruct the insurance agent for such insurance to provide at the _____Office, located at_____ with proof of insurance in the form of a policy or policy binder, including the endorsements checked above.

I Understand and agree that the proof of insurance must be delivered to Sterling Bank within ten days from this Agreement, and upon the failure to so deliver proof of insurance or upon the lapse or cancellation of such insurance, I agree that the Bank MAY procure Lender's Single Interest Insurance on the property, which insurance shall cover only the Bank's interest as a secured party. In the event that the Bank at its sole option secures the Lender's Single Interest Insurance, it shall become effective as of the earliest of:

The date funds were advanced by the Bank for purchase of the property, OR
The expiration date of the insurance, OR
The date the insurance was cancelled.

I agree that the amount of the premium for Lender's Single Interest Insurance plus interest MAY be added to my contract/loan balance and I will pay said sum in addition to all other sums due under the loan. The interest on the premium will be the annual percentage rate applicable to the contract/loan from the effective date of the insurance.

Insurance Agent:

_____   _____

_____   _____

_____   _____

Phone No._____

FOR BANK USE ONLY
INSURANCE VERIFIED: Date_____
Person Talked to_____
Insurance Co./Agent_____
Policy No._____
On Year/Make _____
Effective from_____to_____

Illustration 9-9

Escrow Instructions to:

Escrow No. .... Escrow Officer .... Date ....

The undersigned hereby agree:

1. That the sum of $_____ delivered, or to be delivered, to you by _____
_____in subject escrow shall
be deposited in an interest bearing Money Market Account in your office, in the name of
_____ by STERLING BANK, as Escrow Agent;

2. That interest earned on said Money Market Account, if any, shall be reported as
required by governmental regulations. For reporting of such interest Bank shall use the
social security number or taxpayer identification number of _____
_____;

3. That the sum of $10 shall remain on deposit in said Account through the end of the
satement cycle period within which this escrow closes;

4. That the Account shall be governed by applicable banking laws, customs and rules
printed pertaining to Money Market Accounts, and the undersigned shall execute such
additional authorizations or other documents that may be required by Bank;

5. That the Account shall be handled by you in accordance with your usual procedures
for holding funds deposited with you as an escrow agent, and you are to disburse the
funds in said Account as directed herein and in joint escrow instructions delivered to
you by the undersigned. It is hereby agreed that you are to hold any evidence of
deposit and you shall have exclusive authority to withdraw or otherwise handle such funds
until you have made all disbursements;

6. That when you make disbursements you are to pay all interest earned on the deposit to
_____. This instruction is not
subject to change with respect to any amounts that Bank has reported to tax authorities
as required by law or regulation;

7. That the deposit shall be subject to Bank's rules and regulations and pricing
structure for insured Money Market Accounts, as provided in the disclosure statement
delivered to the undersigned, receipt of which is hereby acknowledged;

8. That federal regulations also permit the Bank to require 7 days prior written notice
for any withdrawal or transfer, and, Bank rules provide that interest accumulated during
a statement cycle period is lost if the account is closed prior to the end of the period.
You shall have no responsibility for any delay in closing escrow arising from imposition
of the 7-day notice requirement, nor for any loss of interest arising from closing escrow
and making disbursements prior to the end of a statement cycle period; and

9. That funds deposited pursuant to this instrument shall at all times be considered
deposited in this escrow subject to all prior or amended escrow instructions, except that
this instrument may not be amended or changed without the Bank's written consent.

Date_____   _____   _____
                                              (Buyer)   SS or ID #

Date_____   _____   _____

Date_____   _____   _____
                                              (Seller)   SS or ID #

Date_____   _____   _____

Illustration 9-10

Real Estate

_____Office

_____, California
Telephone No._____

Date:_____
Your Escrow No._____
Title Order No._____
Our Escrow No._____

Gentlemen:

We forward herewith our deed of trust executed by _____
securing a note for $_____ in our favor, and covering the following described
property:

_____

You are authorized to record the above First Trust Deed through your escrow subject to the
following conditions:

1. Show title to the above described real property vested in the name(s) of _____

_____
FREE FROM ENCUMBRANCES EXCEPT:
     1)_____ general and special taxes for fiscal year 19____ to 19____;
     2) Covenants, conditions and restrictions, rights, rights of way and easements of
       record, if any;
     3) Our deed of trust to file.

2. Furnish us a policy of Title Insurance, ALTA from issued by _____,
_____ insuring us with liability of $_____.

3. Furnish us with Realty Tax Service designated _____ for _____ years, notices in this
connection TO BE ADDRESSED TO US AT OUR ADDRESS AS SHOWN ABOVE
AND REFER TO LOAN NUMBER GIVEN HEREON.

4. Obtain for us an original Fire Insurance policy (acceptable to us) issued in names of
record owners, IN COMPLETED FORM WITH ALL ENDORSEMENTS ATTACHED,
3 year period, premium paid, with Extended Coverage Endorsement, Special Form, and
Loss Payable clause in favor of _____
affixed thereto for at least $_____, covering premises known as: _____.

5. THERE IS TO BE NO JUNIOR LIEN TO OURS UNLESS SPECIFICALLY
APPROVED BY US.

6. A satisfactory report and certificate of completion, if necessary, issue by a licensed
termite or pest control operator showing subject property free from termite infestation,
dry rot or fungi.

7. A certified copy of your escrow statement to our borrower within 5 days after closing
of your escrow which will show receipt of our loan funds an the disposition of these funds.

8. Unless you have done so, please forward us a certified copy of your escrow instructions
and any amendments thereof. Also, any supplements to the title report.

When you are ready for funds and can comply with our instructions herein, please advise us
(by telephone and followed by written instructions) and we will forward our remittance to
your escrow in the amount of $_____, being the net proceeds of loan after
deducting the loan service of $_____, said net amount will be remitted to you by:

____ Our Cashiers Check payable to your order, upon your request.
____ Our Cashiers Check payable to your Title Company with our authorization for them
      to accept your instructions for disbursement with title policy insuring our deed of
      trust can be issued.

Illustration 9-10 (cont.)

WE ARE NOT TO BE CHARGED WITH ANY EXPENSES IN CONNECTION WITH THIS TRANSACTION.

If the request for our loan is canceled, you are to collect and remit to us a cancellation fee of $_____. If the deed of trust is not filed for record to complete this loan within 30 days form the date hereof, our commitment may be canceled and our papers withdrawn. We reserve the right at our option to cancel all instructions and recall papers and/or remittance at any time prior to your compliance with these instructions. Please acknowledge receipt of this letter. Thank you.

Received the above described documents and original of foregoing instructions.

Date:_____ By:_____
By:_____

Illustration 9-11

TITLE COMPANY		COUNTY (Office)	If in connection with order already opened, please check here	☐
DATE	ESCROW OR LOAN NUMBER	TITLE OFFICER	ORDER NUMBER	NEW

Please enter } order for policy or policies of title insurance as checked below:
THIS CONFIRMS

CLTA OWNER'S/LENDERS ..... Standard Coverage Form ..... ☐ with liability in the amount of .... $ _____

CLTA JOINT PROTECTION ..... Standard Coverage Form ..... ☐ with liability in the amount of .... $ _____

ALTA LENDERS ..... American Land Title Association Form ..... ☐ with liability in the amount of .... $ _____

CLTA ENDORSEMENT .... ☐ _____

——————➤ IF ALTA POLICY IS REQUESTED   ☐ SINGLE RESIDENCE☐ MULTIPLE RESIDENCE☐ COMMERCIAL

THIS INFORMATION WILL EXPEDITE YOUR REPORT➤   ☐ STREET ADDRESS _____

The property to be covered is described as

Present Owner's Name _____

We Enclose the Following:

Deed from _____ To _____ D.T.T. $ _____

Deed from _____ To _____ D.T.T. $ _____

Deed of Trust by _____ Amount $ _____

Deed of Trust by _____ Amount $ _____

Deed of Trust by _____ Amount $ _____

Recon _____ Item _____ of your report dated _____

Note _____ Deed of Trust _____ Request for Recon _____ Item _____ of your report dated _____

Miscellaneous _____

Statement of Information _____ Buyer _____ Recent Owner _____

UPON FURTHER AUTHORIZATION you will record all instruments without collection when you can VEST TITLE IN:

Subject to:
1. ☐ All ☐ 2nd ½ ☐ None   General and Special Taxes for fiscal year 19 _____ 19 _____.
2. Bonds and/or Assessments _____
3. Covenants, conditions, restrictions, reservations, easements and rights of way of record.
4. Items numbered _____ as shown on preliminary report dated _____
5. Deed of Trust of record - to record for $ _____
6. _____
7. _____

Additional Instructions:

Send _____ copies of report to _____ COMPANY

_____

Street _____

City _____ Zip _____

Order Tax Service: _____ Type _____ Years

Please Forward: (check items requested, if any.)

☐ 1. _____ Copies of covenants, conditions and restrictions.

☐ 2. _____ Copies of plat map.   BY _____

☐ 3. Amount of _____ taxes for proration purposes

Illustration 9-12

PASTE OR STAPLE RECEIPT

AND CHECK COPIES HERE

TAX PRORATION	INTEREST PRORATION
INSURANCE PRORATION	RENTS

1st T/D FIRST PAYMENT DUE $

2nd T/D FIRST PAYMENT DUE $ ESCROW NO.   DATE

THIRD PARTY STATEMENT

ADDRESS

	CHARGES	CREDIT
TOTALS		

	CHECK #	REC. TOTALS

TITLE INSURANCE

ESCROW FEE

SETTLED BY	DATE	CHECKS DRAWN BY	DISBURSEMENT TOTALS

10
PROPERTY MANAGEMENT — THE KEY TO MAINTAINING POSITIVE CASH FLOW

FORMING A MANAGEMENT PLAN

Black's Law Dictionary describes manage in this fashion:

> ". . . To control and direct, to administer, to take charge of. To conduct; to carry on the concerns of a business or establishment. Generally applied to affairs that are somewhat complicated and that involve skill and judgment. . ."

In order to effectively manage any enterprise, whether it be a real estate project or General Motors, some form of gamesmanship is involved. That means one has to formulate a strategy by which the operation can be conducted in the most efficient and meaningful manner.

In the case of a majority of real estate syndications the person who is responsible for the day-to-day affairs of the enterprise is the general partner. As such, the general partner must formulate a plan which best meets the partnership objectives. These objectives can be one or more of the following:

- Income

- Appreciation

- Leverage (through judicious use of financing)

- Tax Benefits

- Equity Buildup

- Potential Income Increase

- Diversification

- Pride of Ownership

When dealing in the area of real estate owned on the books of financial institutions or their regulators, automatic satisfaction of a majority of these objectives might be accomplished in a single transaction. Each aspect requires further examination.

Income through the guise of positive cash flow which manifests itself into positivity even after the consideration of depreciation on properties that are not fully leased is a function of purchase price and financing terms. If the right transaction is negotiated - and we assume that the transactions' closing as described in the prior chapter is evidence of a proper negotiation - the preservation of income then becomes the concern of the general partner. In order to preserve income, the plan would be to develop a marketing strategy that will not only preserve current tenancy, but enhance occupancy through judicious marketing efforts.

Appreciation becomes a function of the manager's ability to enhance occupancy levels which translates into more value, therefore the strategy followed to enhance income will automatically create appreciation in the property.

Leverage is one of the tools used not only to minimize capital investment, but a device where a wide degree of latitude can be exercised with a seller who is taking back paper as a means of disposing of property ownership. This, again, would have been negotiated before any closing took place. Future leverage, however, becomes a concern of the general partner as a way of returning capital to the limited partners with monies not impacted by taxes and to take advantage of reasonable loan rate windows as they develop in the real estate cycle.

Tax benefits are naturally high up on the pecking order of a real estate investor, particularly the sheltering ability of depreciation, a non-cash item. Transactions should be structured by a general partner as part of the management plan to mitigate the effect of income taxes as much as possible.

Equity buildup is somewhat contrary to leverage, although they can be complimentary. For example, as the rent level increases and the building increases in value, leverage can be used to reduce initial capital investments, as noted earlier.

Potential income increase is only possible when the property is managed efficiently in a professional manner. This area is paramount in the management pecking order and requires the greatest degree of attention from a management standpoint. It involves identifying potential markets for the space and what is expected from the market place as a consumer of space. The management plan would then be devised to offer the space, as desired, at a competitive rental rate while being responsive to tenant requirements weighing the cost factors involved.

Diversification provides an investor with a risk allocation umbrella. If one devotes all investment capital in one area of concentration, any serious deterioration of that area could represent financial disaster. William Zeckendorf found that out when his New York City house of cards fell down upon him. He totally lacked the diversification (and the liquidity) to bail himself out.

Pride of ownership has a price tag attached to it. If an investor acquires a property in the penultimate condition, a purchase price tag is attached accordingly. Sometimes the "runt of the litter," which requires some cosmetology which is well located can expand the value of an investment by light years. It is important, once a property has been acquired to maintain the property in such a fashion that it will be attractive to tenants. As part of the management plan there must be concern about maintenance and replacement reserves for equipment established.

Within these objectives, some management parameters can be established. First, the functions of property management to be established for a particular project must be allocated. The initial responsibility for **all** property management functions lies with the general partner, but some of these duties may be delegated, depending upon the size and scope of the project. In any event, there are some functions, particularly in maintenance, where it may be less expensive to use outside vendors than to keep an elaborate staff. This usually depends upon the type of building under management. In the case of office space, generally a building superintendent would be required to handle maintenance chores in order that the tenants could have access to a management representative for any maintenance problems. Some of the other functions to be considered are:

- Marketing — What type of media should be used to advertise space? Should the owner handle leasing directly or use an agent familiar with the area?

- Merchandising vacancies — Leasing agents on premises, signage and other considerations fall within this function.

- Screening tenants — Policies relative to establishing an idyllic tenant profile, how to deal with lease applicants, what financial data would be required, deposits desired, credit checks to be performed and the like all need to be addressed.

- Collecting rents — Will payment be made directly to the owner or the owner's representative? Will a lock box be established at the owner's bank as a means of using an automated accounting system for the building?

• Paying bills — Will accounts payable be handled at the site or at the owner's office. What types of checks and balances are to be established to avoid misapplication of funds?

• Supervising maintenance — Which type of maintenance will be handled by outside vendors and which will be done by staff personnel?

• Hiring and training staff — Will employment agencies be utilized? Will outside resources or in-house training be conducted? What type of personnel policies are required in conjunction with the building in question?

• Bookkeeping — Will data processing or ledgers be used? How will checks and balances be established? How many signatures will be required on company checks? What is needed to satisfy investor and tax reporting authority requirements? Will payroll be processed by outside vendors? Who should be selected as an outside auditor?

• Reporting to owners — Certain types of financial reports need to be rendered to limited partners in a limited partnership in accordance with the terms of the limited partnership agreement. It is the duty of the bookkeeping function to provide the records necessary to provide this data and should be part of the management plan in establishing the overall management objectives for the building in question.

ESTABLISHING THE MANAGEMENT TEAM

As a property manager, one sits in an island surrouded by entities requiring interface on a continuous basis. In the case of a limited partnership, the general partner performs this function. The general partner serves a dual purpose of being a communications hub between the tenants and staff with the limited partners while serving as insulation between these parties and the ownership dealing with matters involving the management of the property on a day-to-day basis.

If the limited partnership is physically located in one state, while the property is located in another, the general partner may opt to hire a professional manager to handle the day to day affairs of the operation with the "back office" functions of bookkeeping and personnel matters handled at the general partner's business location. This represents an important personnel decision on the part of the general partner, since property management costs amount to 5 to 10% of the gross rent levels. If the property manager does a proper job, this function is well worth the rate charged. Some thought should be given to providing incentives to the property manager for cost reduction and increases in occupancy levels. There are various methods of remuneration that may be considered in that regard. It might be in the form of a bonus or commission arrangement.

Hiring a professional manager is a key business decision. Failure to properly screen candidates can impact future earnings of the investment group. The ideal manager not only has the management attributes of coordinating, directing and controlling the activities of the property management function, there must be accountability to the ownership as well as exceptional communication skills in the make up of this individual. In real estate positive thinkers who are willing to take innovative approaches to dealing with the problems of the market place are definitely preferable to those who tend to look at things through jaundiced eyes. People oriented persons make the best managers, since they possess the communication skills necessary to get things done. Since property management is a specialization, the search would be directed toward professionals, such as Certified Property Managers to deal with large buildings. It is important to determine that the manager selected has **experience** in the management of the property type. For example, don't hire a property manager with residential experience to deal with commercial and industrial property, which is a whole different ball game altogether. Another thing to investigate in states outside of California is the requirement for property managers to have a real estate license, as they do in the Golden State.

Property managers must be screened as to their attitude toward professional conduct. The Real Estate Commissioner of the state of California has specific ground rules concerning the professional conduct of licensees under Commissioner's Regulation 2785 dealing with the sale, lease and exchange of real property (shown as Illustration 10-1). Owners as well as property managers should be aware of these regulations and be guided by them.

Once the decision has been made relative to management of the property, the conduct of the management function is then undertaken. In any event, annual operating budgets should be established as a means of cost effectiveness and as a measure against management performance prepared in a similar fashion to net operating statements shown earlier in this book. The only difference being the fact that the figures provided for budgetary purposes would be on a pro-forma basis.

Illustration 10-1

CODE OF PROFESSIONAL CONDUCT—COMMISSIONER'S REGULATION 2785

Commissioner's Regulation 2785, formerly known as "Code of Ethics and Professional Conduct," was revised as of June 9, 1990 as a "Code of Professional Conduct." The new "Code" consists of two major parts: essentially a review of unlawful activities as decreed by the Real Estate Law, and, secondly, a statement of "Suggestions for Professional Conduct" to "encourage real estate licenses to maintain a high level of ethics and professionalism in their business practices."

Commissioner's Regulation 2785.
PROFESSIONAL CONDUCT

In order to enhance the professionalism of the California real estate industry, and maximize protection for members of the public dealing with real estate licensees, whatever their area of practice, the following standards of professional conduct and business practices are adopted:

(a) Unlawful Conduct in Sale, Lease and Exchange Transactions. Licensees when performing acts within the meaning of Section 10131 (a) of the Business and Professions Code shall not engage in conduct which would subject the licensee to adverse action, penalty or discipline under Sections 10176 and 10177 of the Business and Professions Code including, but not limited to, the following acts and omissions:

Comm. Reg. 2785. (a)(1)

Knowingly making a substantial misrepresentation of the likely value of real property to:

(A)   Its owner either for the purpose of securing a listing or for the purpose of acquiring an interest in the property for the licensee's own account.

(B)   A prospective buyer for the purpose of inducing the buyer to make an offer to purchase the real property.

Comm. Reg. 2785. (a)(2)

Representing to an owner of real property when seeking a listing that the licensee has obtained a bona fide written offer to purchase the property, unless at the time of the representation the licensee has possession of a bona fide written offer to purchase.

Comm. Reg. 2785. (a)(3)

Stating or implying to an owner of real property during listing negotiations that the licensee is precluded by law, by regulation, or by the rules of any organization, other than the broker firm seeking the listing, from charging less than the commission or fee quoted to the owner by the licensee.

Comm. Reg. 2785. (a)(4)

Knowingly making substantial misrepresentations regarding the licensee's relationship with an individual broker, corporate broker, or franchised brokerage company or that entity's/person's responsibility for the licensee's activities.

Comm. Reg. 2785. (a)(5)

Knowingly underestimating the probable closing costs in a communication to the prospective buyer or seller of real property in order to induce that person to make or to accept an offer to purchase the property.

Comm. Reg. 2785. (a)(6)

Knowingly making a false or misleading representation to the seller of real property as to the form, amount and/or treatment of a deposit toward the purchase of the property made by an offeror.

Comm. Reg. 2785. (a)(7)

Knowingly making a false or misleading representation to a seller of real property, who has agreed to finance all or part of a purchase price by carrying back a loan, about a buyer's ability to repay the loan in accordance with its terms and conditions.

Comm. Reg. 2785. (a)(8)

Making an addition to or modification of the terms of an instrument previously signed or initialed by a party to a transaction without the knowledge and consent of the party.

Comm. Reg. 2785. (a)(9)

A representation made as a principal or agent to a prospective purchaser of a promissory note secured by real property about the market value of the securing property without a reasonable basis for believing the truth and accuracy of the representation.

Illustration 10-1 (cont.)

Comm. Reg. 2785. (a)(10)

Knowingly making a false or misleading representation or representing, without a reasonable basis for believing its truth, the nature and/or condition of the interior or exterior features of a property when soliciting an offer.

Comm. Reg. 2785. (a)(11)

Knowingly making a false or misleading representation or representing, without a reasonable basis for believing its truth, the size of a parcel, square footage of improvements or the location of the boundary lines of real property being offered for sale, lease or exchange.

Comm. Reg. 2785. (a)(12)

Knowingly making a false or misleading representation or representing to a prospective buyer or lessee of real property, without a reasonable basis to believe its truth, that the property can be used for certain purposes with the intent of inducing the prospective buyer or lessee to acquire an interest in the real property.

Comm. Reg. 2785. (a)(13)

When acting in the capacity of an agent in a transaction for the sale, lease or exchange of real property, failing to disclose to a prospective purchaser or lessee facts known to the licensee materially affecting the value or desirability of the property, when the licensee has reason to believe that such facts are not known to nor readily observable by a prospective purchaser or lessee.

Comm. Reg. 2785. (a)(14)

Willfully failing, when acting as a listing agent, to present or cause to be presented to the owner of the property any written offer to purchase received prior to the closing of a sale, unless expressly instructed by the owner not to present such an offer, or unless the offer is patently frivolous.

Comm. Reg. 2785. (a)(15)

When acting as the listing agent, presenting competing written offers to purchase real property to the owner in such a manner as to induce the owner to accept the offer which will provide the greatest compensation to the listing broker without regard to the benefits, advantages and/or disadvantages to the owner.

Comm. Reg. 2785. (a)(16)

Failing to explain to the parties or prospective parties to a real estate transaction for whom the licensee is acting as an agent the meaning and probable significance of a contingency in an offer or contract that the licensee knows or reasonably believes may affect the closing date of the transaction, or the timing of the vacating of the property by the seller or its occupancy by the buyer.

Comm. Reg. 2785. (a)(17)

Failing to disclose to the seller of real property in a transaction in which the licensee is an agent for the seller the nature and extent of any direct or indirect interest that the licensee expects to acquire as a result of the sale. The prospective purchase of the property by a person related to the licensee by blood or marriage, purchase by an entity in which the licensee has an ownership interest, or purchase by any other person with whom the licensee occupies a special relationship where there is a reasonable probability that the licensee could be indirectly acquiring an interest in the property shall be disclosed to the seller.

Comm. Reg. 2785. (a)(18)

Failing to disclose to the buyer of real property in a transaction in which the licensee is an agent for the buyer the nature and extent of a licensee's direct or indirect ownership interest in such real property. The direct or indirect ownership interest in the property by a person related to the licensee by blood or marriage, by an entity in which the licensee has an ownership interest, or by any other person with whom the licensee occupies a special relationship shall be disclosed to the buyer.

Comm. Reg. 2785. (a)(19)

Failing to disclose to a principal for whom the licensee is acting as an agent any significant interest the licensee has in a particular entity when the licensee recommends the use of the services or products of such entity.

Comm. Reg. 2785. (a)(20)

The refunding by a licensee, when acting as an agent for seller, all or part of an offeror's purchase money deposit in a real estate sales transaction after the seller has accepted the offer to purchase, unless the licensee has the express permission of the seller to make the refund.

Illustration 10-1 (cont.)

(b) Unlawful Conduct When Soliciting, Negotiating or Arranging a Loan Secured by Real Property or the Sale of a Promissory Note Secured by Real Property. Licensees when performing acts within the meaning of subdivision (d) or (e) of Section 10131 of the Business and Professions Code shall not violate any of the applicable provisions of subdivision (a), or act in a manner which would subject the licensee to adverse action, penalty or discipline under Sections 10176 and 10177 of the Business and Professions Code including, but not limited to, the following acts and omissions:

Comm. Reg. 2785. (b)(1)

Knowingly misrepresenting to a prospective borrower of a loan to be secured by real property or to an assignor/endorser of a promissory note secured by real property that there is an existing lender willing to make the loan or that there is a purchaser for the note, for the purpose of inducing the borrower or assignor/endorser to utilize the services of the licensee.

Comm. Reg. 2785. (b)(2)

(a) Knowingly making a false or misleading representation to a prospective lender or purchaser of a loan secured directly or collaterally by real property about a borrower's ability to repay the loan in accordance with its terms and conditions;

(b) Failing to disclose to a prospective lender or note purchaser information about the prospective borrower's identity, occupation, employment, income and credit data as represented to the broker by the prospective borrower.

(c) Failing to disclose information known to the broker relative to the ability of the borrower to meet his or her potential or existing contractual obligations under the note or contract including information known about the borrower's payment history on an existing note, whether the note is in default or the borrower in bankruptcy.

Comm. Reg. 2785. (b)(3)

Knowingly underestimating the probable closing costs in a communication to a prospective borrower or lender of a loan to be secured by a lien on real property for the purpose of inducing the borrower or lender to enter into the loan transaction.

Comm. Reg. 2785. (b)(4)

When soliciting a prospective lender to make a loan 'o be secured by real property, falsely representing or representing without a reasonable basis to believe its truth, the priority of the security, as a lien against the real property securing the loan, i.e. a first, second or third deed of trust.

Comm. Reg. 2785. (b)(5)

Knowingly misrepresenting in any transaction that a specific service is free when the licensee knows or has a reasonable basis to know that it is covered by a fee to be charged as part of the transaction.

Comm. Reg. 2785. (b)(6)

Knowingly making a false or misleading representation to a lender or assignee/endorse of a lender of a loan secured directly or collaterally by a lien on real property about the amount and treatment of loan payments, including loan payoffs, and the failure to account to the lender or assignee/endorse of a lender as to the disposition of such payments.

Comm. Reg. 2785. (b)(7)

When acting as a licensee in a transaction for the purpose of obtaining a loan, and in receipt of an "advance fee" from the borrower for this purpose, the failure to account to the borrower for the disposition of the "advance fee."

Comm. Reg. 2785. (b)(8)

Knowingly making a false or misleading representation or representing, without a reasonable basis for believing its truth, when soliciting a lender or negotiating a loan to be secured by a lien on real property about the market value of the securing real property, the nature and/or condition of the interior or exterior features of the securing real property, its size or the square footage of any improvements on the securing real property.

Authority: Business and Professions Code Section 10080. Reference: Business and Professions Code Sections 10176 and 10177.

SUGGESTIONS FOR PROFESSIONAL CONDUCT

Note: The Real Estate Commissioner has issued Suggestions for Professional Conduct in Sale, Lease and Exchange Transactions and Suggestions for Professional Conduct When Negotiating or Arranging Loans Secured by Real Property or Sale of a Promissory Note Secured by Real Property.

The Purpose of the Suggestions is to encourage real estate licensees to maintain a high level of ethics and professionalism in their business practices when performing acts for which a real estate license is required.

The Suggestions are not intended as statements of duties imposed by law nor as grounds for disciplinary action by the Department of Real Estate, but as suggestions for elevating the professionalism of real estate licensees.

Illustration 10-1 (cont.)

Copies of the suggestions may be obtained from the Department.

As a part of the effort to promote ethical business practices of real estate licensees, the Real Estate commissioner has issued the following Suggestions for Professional Conduct as a companion to the Code of Professional Conduct (Section 2785, Title 10, California Code of Regulation):

(a) Suggestions for Professional Conduct in Sale, Lease and Exchange Transactions. In order to maintain a high level of ethics and professionalism in their business practices, real estate licensees are encouraged to adhere to the following suggestions in conducting their business activities:

(1) Aspire to give a high level of competent, ethical and quality service to buyers and sellers in real estate transactions.

(2) Stay in close communication with clients or customers to ensure that questions are promptly answered and all significant events or problems in a transaction are conveyed in a timely manner.

(3) Cooperate with the California Department of Real Estate's enforcement of, and report to that Department evident violations of, Real Estate Law.

(4) Use care in the preparation of any advertisement to present an accurate picture or message to the reader, viewer or listener.

(5) Submit all written offers in a prompt and timely manner.

(6) Keep oneself informed and current on factors affecting the real estate market in which the licensee operates as an agent.

(7) Make a full, open and sincere effort to cooperate with other licensees, unless the principal has instructed the licensee to the contrary.

(8) Attempt to settle disputes with other licensees through mediation or arbitration.

(9) Advertise or claim to be an expert in an area of specialization in real estate brokerage activity, e.g., appraisal, property management, industrial siting, mortgage loan, etc., only if the licensee has had special training, preparation or experience.

(10) Strive to provide equal opportunity for quality housing and a high level of service to all persons regardless of race, color, sex, religion, ancestry, physical handicap, marital status or national origin.

(11) Base opinions of value, whether for the purpose of advertising or promoting real estate brokerage business, upon documented objective data.

(12) Make every attempt to comply with these Suggestions for Professional Conduct and the Code of Professional Conduct and the Code of Ethics of any or-

ganized real estate industry group of which the licensee is a member.

(b) Suggestions for Professional conduct When Negotiating or Arranging Loans Secured by Real Property or Sale of a Promissory Note Secured by Real Property. In order to maintain a high level of ethics and professionalism in their business practices when performing acts within the meaning of subdivisions (d) and (e) of Section 10131 and Sections 10131.1 and 10131.2 of the Business and Professions Code, real estate licensees are encouraged to adhere to the following suggestions, in addition to any applicable provisions of subdivision (a), in conducting their business activities:

(1) Aspire to give a high level of competent, ethical and quality service to borrowers and lenders in loan transactions secured by real estate.

(2) Stay in close communication with borrowers and lenders to ensure that reasonable questions are promptly answered and all significant events or problems in a loan transaction are conveyed in a timely manner.

(3) Keep oneself informed and current on factors affecting the real estate loan market in which the licensee acts as an agent.

(4) Advertise or claim to be an expert in an area of specialization in real estate mortgage loan transactions only if the licensee has had special training, preparation or experience in such area.

(5) Strive to provide equal opportunity for quality mortgage loan services and a high level of service to all borrowers or lenders regardless of race, color, sex, religion, ancestry, physical handicap, marital status or national origin.

(6) Base opinions of value in a loan transaction, whether for the purpose of advertising or promoting real estate mortgage loan brokerage business, on documented objective data.

(7) Respond to reasonable inquiries of a principal as to the status or extent of efforts to negotiate the sale of an existing loan.

(8) Respond to reasonable inquiries of a borrower regarding the net proceeds available from a loan arranged by the licensee.

(9) Make every attempt to comply with the standards of professional conduct and the code of ethics of any organized mortgage loan industry group of which the licensee is a member.

The conduct suggestions set forth in subsections (a) and (b) are not intended as statements of duties imposed by law nor as grounds for disciplinary action by the Department of Real Estate, but as guidelines for elevating the professionalism of real estate licensees.

COST CONTROLS

Cost controls separate good managers from those who don't provide an appropriate yield for the property owner on invested capital. Cost effectiveness is derived through a thorough analysis of the various factors of cost and how they can be handled most efficiently. One of the important first steps in the process is to learn what cost items are offset in the form of rent if net leases are involved. If the lessees are being charged proportionately for utilities, maintenance, etc. through the lease document, they would be willing participants in a cost reduction process.

One of the frailties of real estate investment can also be its strength. When you are dealing with property outside of your immediate sphere of influence, there are many local aspects of property management that require a quick study. California investors who flocked to Texas as the bloom went off of the apartment rose in their home state didn't bargain for the fact that rents collected **included** utilities which were industrial strength during the hot summer months when air conditioning units were belching amperes like they were going out of style. That slight accounting faux pas created investment indigestion, since prices had been established on the basis of the tenants paying the utilities. The net result was a lot of loans going back to lenders. If investors had not only studied the **quantity** of income, but also its **quality**, this grievous error would have been detected.

In reviewing a cost reduction agenda, several factors have to be considered:

- Type of management - owner direct or professional property manager?

- Utilities - Included in the rent, or paid by the tenant? If included in the rent, various tenant incentives for efficient utility usage should be considered.

- Bookkeeping - Manual, automated or outside vendor used to prepare statements, reports, etc.

- Payroll - Internal control or external vendor - analyze on a cost/benefits basis

- Property taxes - Can the assessed valuation be challenged due to unusual purchase terms, thus reducing levies?

- Insurance - Think in terms of blanket, rather than individual, coverages. Be sure that the coverage is in accordance with lease arrangements made with the tenants. It is imperative to check the insurance company to determine that it has the financial stability to sustain claims. In recent years, failure to properly check the background of a casualty insurer has turned out to be a casualty for the insured.

- Maintenance - In-house staff or outside vendors should be considered on a cost/benefits analysis. Maintenance should be performed on a regular basis with regular property inspections, as opposed to a knee-jerk reaction to problems created by lack of it.

- Reserves for replacement - Bulk equipment purchases afford larger discounts.

- Supplies - Purchase in bulk, particularly if the ownership controls several buildings offers considerable savings.

- Vendor maintenance contracts - Office equipment, roofs, heating and air conditioning equipment, etc. that are under guaranty or service contract should be reviewed periodically to determine where cost savings might be effected. At some point in time it might be better to be self-insured for equipment maintenance than be under contract with the vendor.

The principal advantage of size in a organization is the ability to effect cost reduction through the exercise of purchasing power. One who owns 100 units of apartments has a much better chance of cost reduction than a single owner of a 10 unit building. It is the same way with office ownership. The same holds true of the owner of office space. The more square footage controlled, the greater the savings, whether it be for installation of tenant improvements or for building maintenance.

CREATING EFFECTIVE MARKET EXPOSURE FOR THE PROPERTY

In establishing a market for your particular property, one should be well aware of the competition. Long before any property is acquired, there should have been a rental survey performed on all of the competitive buildings in the vicinity of subject property to learn not only rent levels but the building features that may be lacking in subject. Extremely importance in this evaluation of competitive buildings is the determination of maintenance as a factor of occupancy. As a general rule, poorly maintained buildings enjoy the lowest level of occupancy. In this highly competitive world of selling space to office occupants, the race belongs to the observant, not the ignorant.

Strategy in the market place has been likened to the **AIDA** approach to selling.

- **A stands for attention** - The features of a particular building have to be exposed to potential tenants in order to arouse any further interest. This may be done through a variety of media devices, but many times it is observed that nothing beats the network of knowledgeable commercial/industrial brokers in the area who know all the players who are looking for space.

- **I stands for interest** - Interest is aroused once the benefits of subject property are exposed to potential space consumers.

- **D stands for desire** - Through the use of adroit salesmanship, the sales person, whether it be a professional property manager or a professional leasing agent, the client sees the benefits of leasing that particular property as opposed to its competition.

- **A stands for action** - When the client signs on the dotted line!

Due to the specialized nature of commercial/industrial property, the principal method of marketing, other than newspaper ads is for the property manager or leasing agent to prepare flyers concerning space availability which point out the salient features and benefits of this particular building. These should be distributed to the most active commercial/industrial realtors and large space users in the area. Utilities, financial institutions, professional firms, and government agencies are typical space users where these fliers would be directed. When inquiries are made to the building office, they should be handled in a prompt and courteous fashion.

Just as in any form of real estate, the property will have to be shown to prospective users or their agents. The property should be shown in its best light, just as in residential property. Avoid cluttering up the space by using it for storage not allowing the tenant to get the vast panorama of the space. It should also be kept clean and orderly for showing using the effectiveness of lighting if at all possible. Persons showing the property should have full knowledge of the benefits not only of the space, but the location of the property relative to shopping, transportation and other items of interest to potential tenants. Services within the building that might be of benefit to the tenant, such as mailbox, shipping, etc., should be indicated as well.

An effectively marketed space offered at a competitive price stands a much better chance of rental than one that is shoddy expecting top of the market rates. In addition, there are efficiencies to full floor tenants where attractive discounts can be offered for using hall space which could not otherwise be rented.

ADVANTAGES OF SPECIALIZATION

When property managers just specialize in office space, as opposed to retail space or some industrial applications, they are able to get a better feel for the market place and provide a higher level of service to tenants. This knowledge is then transmitted to the ownership in the form of higher yields and potential future appreciation on the basis of elevated occupancy levels.

Specialization allows the professional manager to interface with his peers through professional groups keeping track of trends in the business and taking advantage of them. One of the most apparent trends in office buildings today is the fact that the ground floor tenants were financial institutions in the past. With the vast degree of consolidations and failures in recent years, this type of tenant is slowly vanishing from the tenant agenda. A principal ingredient in the make up of an office structure is the nature of a ground floor tenant. If the ground floor tenant is a computer store, computer users might be strong candidates for the upper floors, and so on.

Adroit property management is the principal ingredient in realizing the potential of **any** real estate investment. Without it, the green foliage of capital is reduced to the dust of annihilation.

Anwar al-Sadat noted in his **In Search of Identity** that:

". . . land is immortal, for it harbors the mystery of creation . . ."

Real property ownership through means of judicious investment practices can provide the rewards of land's immortality through generous expansion of the investor's pocket book with minimal tax implications. Go for it!

EPILOGUE

American Capital Investments is proud to have had the opportunity of preparing this extensive examination of the decision process involved in seeking a proper dedication of investible funds. The devotion of capital to any enterprise is one to be approached with considerable thought and attention.

The staff of American Capital stand ready to be of service to the serious real estate investor by providing a host of potential investments, each possessing these unique qualities (as shown in Illustrations E-1, E-2, E-3, and E-4):

- Principal secured by a grant deed for the investor's percentage interest in the project.

- Cash flow projects with the ability to service debt based on terms of purchase.

- Liquidity concerns are assuaged by a guaranteed buy out from American Capital after the first year.

- Built-in profit from day one in the project plus participation in potential appreciation of the real estate.

- Monthly cash distributions from project cash flow.

- Interest reserve set asides to guarantee cash distributions.

- High return on capital to the investor.

- Experienced management devoted to maximizing investment potential through negotiations designed to maximize the utility of the property acquired with appropriate leverage that will not burden the syndication.

Additionally informative seminars are offered to the investment community showing the advantages of investing in real estate owned from financial institutions who are pressed by their regulators to dispose of these properties.

In order to gain more information on this exciting new investment vehicle and for seminar information, contact American Capital Investments, Inc. at (310) 822-0005.

"Knowledge, in truth is the great sun in the firmament. Life and power are scattered with its beams." These great words by Daniel Webster in his **Address on Laying the Cornerstone of the Bunker Hill Monument** in 1825 serve to summarize the thrust of this text. Our objective is to give you, the reader, the power, through knowledge, allowing your capital to sustain a vigorous life in the way of tax advantaged return in a revolutionary investment vehicle which the economic times of the early 1990s has afforded. Our country's future will be built on the foundation of capital growth. Be a part of it!

Illustration E-1

SORRENTO REO PARTNERS III
16% PLUS GRANT DEED PARTNERSHIP

100% 16% PLUS PROFIT PARTICIPATION

BENEFITS:

★*100% Secured Principal*   ★*One Year Buyout*

★*Secured 16% Plus Interest*   ★*Experienced Management*

★*Monthly Cash Distributions*   ★*Plus 45% Additional Built-in-Profit*

★*Interest Reserve Account*   ★*Limited Liability*

Illustration E-2

**GRAND NATIONAL PLAZA REO V
16% PLUS SPECIAL WARRANTY DEED PARTNERSHIP**

100% 16% PLUS PROFIT PARTICIPATION

BENEFITS:

★*100% Secured Principal*   ★*One Year Buyout*

★*Secured 16% Plus Interest*   ★*Experienced Management*

★*Monthly Cash Distributions*   ★*Plus 28% Additional Built-in-Profit*

★*Interest Reserve Account*   ★*Limited Liability*

Illustration E-3

100% PROFIT PARTICIPATION
16% PLUS

WILSHIRE PLAZA REO IV
16% PLUS SPECIAL WARRANTY DEED PARTNERSHIP

BENEFITS:

★*100% Secured Principal*   ★*One Year Buyout*

★*Secured 16% Plus Interest*   ★*Experienced Management*

★*Monthly Cash Distributions*   ★*Plus 23% Additional Built-in-Profit*

★*Interest Reserve Account*   ★*Limited Liability*

Illustration E-4

SORRENTO REO PARTNERS III
NEW REO 16% PLUS, ONE YEAR SECURED GRANT DEED PARTNERSHIP
EXECUTIVE INVESTMENT SUMMARY

Fifty years ago, Uncle Sam appeared on army recruiting posters, a tall man dressed in stars and stripes, pointing his finger and saying I WANT YOU! How do you think that poster artist would draw Uncle Sam today? Probably in a red blazer, white shirt, and star-studded blue tie, holding a ballpoint pen in one hand and a real estate contract in the other. Why? Because as of 1990, Uncle Sam is the world's biggest real estate seller!

REO = Real Estate Owned; REO is the banking acronym for real estate owned and it refers to properties that the lending institution has foreclosed upon because of mortgage default. Carrying foreclosed properties on their books costs banks and the RTC money and usually produces little or no income. As a result, lenders and the RTC want to sell their REO properties. In other words: THEY WANT OUT!

With new REOs coming into the bailout inventory almost every day and the old stuff generating more carrying costs every day, we have highly motivated sellers. In every real estate marketplace, highly motivated sellers set the stage for fabulous deals (for the buyers). To allow the sell/buy drama to unfold, all that's needed is a savvy buyer, like American Capital Investments Inc., "ACI" Inc.

ACI Inc. has created the most exciting, profitable, and secure financial investment since the post depression 1940s. ACI capitalizes with investors on the tremendous buying opportunities created by the S&L debacle in the commercial real estate arena. By designing a product that eliminates the traditionally negative aspects of a limited partnership, while at the same time providing the protection of limited liability, and emphasizing safety, 16% minimum annualized return, (paid monthly), liquidity, a built-in- profit, and 100% appreciation potential, you the investor benefit.

The Sorrento REO Partners III, features:

HIGHLIGHTS OF THE OFFERING INCLUDE;

100% SECURED PRINCIPAL: Full repayment of all principal is secured by a grant deed on the REO property. American Capital Investments Inc. has guaranteed it will return to the Partnership the aggregate amount of funds invested in the REO Partnerships.

SECURED INTEREST: The REO's cash flow also secures monthly payment of basic interest in the partnership. American Capital Investments Inc. has corporately guaranteed to insure against any shortfall in monthly income.

LIQUIDITY: American Capital Investments Inc., guarantees to buy out each investors equity interest at original cost, at the end of one calender year from date of investment.

100% PARTICIPATION IN REAL ESTATE UPSIDE: The Partnership's unique feature of allowing investors to be equity owners of the property under the protection of a limited liability partnership structure, gives each investor two exciting benefits: 1) 45% built-in-profit of $513,423.50 from the first day of investment, (i.e. partnership cost basis vs. current market appraisal, based on the current Net Operating Income and very recent sales comparables), and 2) a 100% participation in additional appreciation.

MONTHLY CASH DISTRIBUTIONS: Monthly cash distributions begin the month immediately following your investment, and are scheduled to arrive to each investor approximately on the 15th of each month. INTEREST RESERVE ACCOUNT: American Capital Investments Inc., has set aside, a partnership interest reserve account of 16% on $1,000,000.00 or $160,000.00 for the express and specific purpose to guarantee investors monthly distributions.

16% PLUS, SECURED RETURN: Investors are entitled to receive a minimum of 16% annualized return, paid monthly, plus 100% profit participation, on a pro rata basis, of net cash proceeds from sales.

EXPERIENCED MANAGEMENT: American Capital Investments Inc., (ACI) purchases commercial properties from banking and/or insurance institutions. All the properties involved had been taken back by the financial institutions involved through foreclosure. Currently, ACI, owns and operates more than fifteen commercial office buildings in Florida and California. ACI is now in negotiations for the purchase of eight more commercial office buildings and a real estate investment trust, which has a portfolio of over $56,000,000 of undervalued commercial real estate throughout Texas, California, Florida, Colorado, and New York, and a purchase cost basis of approximately $ .15 cents on the dollar.

BIBLIOGRAPHY OF SUGGESTED READINGS

Martin, Dr. Preston, **Real Estate Principles and Practice,** New York, Macmillan Publishing Co., 1949

Reyburn, Stanley S. and Morton, Thomas, **California Real Estate Finance,** Glenwood Illinois, Scott Foresman & Co. (Now in revised form from Dearborn Publishing in Chicago), 1988

Reyburn, Stanley S., **California Escrow Procedures, a Blueprint for the Nation,** Englewood Cliffs, New Jersey, Prentice-Hall, 1980

Reyburn, Stanley S., **Escrows, Principles and Procedures, Second Edition,** San Leandro, California, Anthony Schools, 1990

Schumacher, David with Bucy, Eric Page, **The Buy and Hold Real Estate Strategy,** New York, John Wiley & Sons, 1992

Freshman, Samuel, **Principles of Real Estate Syndication, 2nd Edition,** Los Angeles, Parker & Son, 1973

Ogden, Melvin B., **Real Estate Law in California,** Los Angeles, Parker & Son, 1956

California Residential Property Management, 3rd Edition, San Leandro, California, Anthony Schools, 1990

Black's Law Dictionary, 6th Edition, St. Paul, Minnesota, West's Publishing Company, 1990

Bartlett, John, **Bartlett's Familiar Quotations, 125th Anniversary Edition,** Boston, Little Brown & Company, 1980

Schachtman, Tom, **Skyscraper Dreams,** Boston, Little Brown & Company, 1991

Betts, Richard M. and Ely, Silas J., **Basic Real Estate Appraisal, 2nd Edition,** Englewood Cliffs, New Jersey, Prentice-Hall, 1990

Reyburn, Stanley S. and Hanvey, Robert S., **Real Estate Economics**, San Leandro, California, Anthony Schools, 1991

Ringsdorf, Royce, **The Basic Steps in Real Estate Exchanging,** Visalia, California, Moffit & Ringsdorf, 1975

Reno, Richard R., **Profitable Real Estate Exchanging and Counseling,** Englewood Cliffs, New Jersey, Prentice-Hall, 1965

Ivy G. Lester, Executive Editor, **Tax Reform Act of 1986 Manual,** Chicago, Illinois, Longman Financial Publishing, 1987

Sirota, David, **Essentials of Real Estate Investment, 4th Edition,** Chicago, Real Estate Education Company, 1991

Allen, Roger H., **Real Estate Investment Strategy, 3rd Edition,** Cincinnati, Ohio, South-Western Publishing Company, 1989

Hines, Mary Alice, **Real Estate Investment,** New York, Macmillan Publishing Co., 1980

Barrett, G. Vincent and Blair, John P., **Foundations of Real Estate Analysis,** Macmillan Publishing Co., Inc., 1981

Greylnolds, Elbert B., Jr., and Aronofsky, Julius S., **Practical Real Estate Financial Analysis Using the HP-12C Calculator,** Chicago, Real Estate Education Company, 1983

Seldin, Maury, **Real Estate Investment for Profit Through Appreciation,** Reston, Virginia, Reston Publishing Company, 1979

Ratcliff, Richard U., **Real Estate Analysis,** New York, McGraw-Hill Book Company, 1961

Maisel, Sherman J. and Roulac, Stephen E., **Real Estate Investment and Finance,** New York, McGraw-Hill Book Company, 1976

Shenkel, William M., **Real Estate Finance and Analysis,** Plano, Texas, Business Publications, Inc., 1988

Reyburn, Stanley S. and Farrell, William, Tech. Eds., Bond, Robert J., **California Real Estate Practice, 3rd Edition,** Glenwood, Illinois, Scott Foresman & Co., (now Chicago, Illinois, Dearborn Publishing), 1988

Fay, James S., Senior Editor, **California Almanac, 5th Edition,** Santa Barbara, California, Pacific Data Resources, 1991

United States Department of Commerce, **Statistical Abstract of the United States, 1991, 111th Edition,** Washington, D. C., Superintendent of Documents, 1991

Periodical References
Economic Indicators, a monthly by subscription publication available from the Superintendent of Documents, Washington, D.C.

Wall Street Journal, a week day business publication by Dow Jones & Co. from New York

Los Angeles Times, a daily newspaper available by subscription

Federal Reserve Bank of New York, Quarterly Review, available by subscription through contacting the Public Information Department, 33 Liberty Street, New York, New York 10045-0001

Orange County Register, available by subscription

Business Week, December 21st, 1992 edition

Fortune Magazine, November 2nd, 1992 Edition

Cycles, Membership Magazine of the Foundation for the Study of Cycles, Inc., published semi-monthly

Orlando REO Partners II, an offering by American Capital Investments, Inc.

Regulatory Matters

State of California Department of Real Estate - Real Estate Handbook and Real Estate Law

Depository Institutions Deregulation Act of 1982 (Garn - St. Germain Bill)

Foreign Investment in Real Property Tax Act - Federal and State levels

Financial Institutions Reform, Recovery and Enforcement Act of 1989 (FIRREA)

Various state and Federal Environmental Control Acts including Proposition 65 and the state and federal superfund legislation

Section 1031 of the Internal Revenue Code

Tax Reform Act of 1986

ABOUT THE AUTHORS

STEPHEN J. MURPHY — Author of numerous other leading educational books, magazines, and newsletters dealing with international trade, international banking, and used by many Fortune 500 companies, including: "Complete Export Guide," "Complete Import Guide," *International Trade News*; President, founder and CEO of American Capital Investments, Inc., a $50,000,000.00 REO Real Estate Vulture firm, with commercial properties in California, Connecticut and Florida. Graduate of U.C.L.A., Mr. Murphy is a Vietnam veteran and is very active in community affairs, being a member of the U.C.L.A. Chancellors Associates, U.C.L.A. Royce Two Seventy Association, the Finance Chairman of the Western Los Angeles County Council of the Boy Scouts of America, board member of New Directions, a non-profit rehabilitation program for homeless veterans organization based in West Los Angeles, and founder of the non-profit American Capital Foundation for the Homeless, a California non-profit corporation, which provides housing and rehabilitation programs for the less fortunate. In addition, Mr. Murphy has somehow found time to be a member of and financially assists the Universal Brothers of the Word, a branch of the Catholic Church working with Mother Theresa. Mr. Murphy is a renowned philanthropist having purchased two shelters for homeless veterans, one in Los Angeles, and the other in Connecticut. Mr. Murphy also supports these facilities financially. In 1992, the Los Angeles City Council adopted a resolution honoring Mr. Murphy for "his commitment to overcome adversity and despair and for his tremendous generosity in providing an opportunity for others to strive for a better quality of life." He has been featured in various newspapers, such as the Los Angeles Times, the Daily Breeze, and the Army Times, and an upcoming article in Reader's Digest. He has also been spotlighted on CNN and CBS and NBC for his successful business and humanitarian events. Mr. Murphy is a single parent, raising two beautiful daughters in Los Angeles.

DR. STANLEY S. REYBURN — Dr. Reyburn is a real estate consultant working with attorneys nationwide on litigation matters, college instructor at both College of the Desert and Los Angeles Valley College and writer with over 500 publications ranging from 11 texts to radio plays and technical articles. This Californian is the third generation of his family specializing in real estate and financing matters with over 40 years experience in the field. In his over thirty years of teaching experience in dealing with all aspects of real estate, he has been awarded the prestigious Norm Woest award from the California Real Estate Educators Association as the Most Outstanding Real Estate Teacher in California for the year 1992. Dr. Reyburn's writing talents have been recognized by both the California Escrow Association as well as Writer's Digest Magazine. He is the past president of the Palm Springs Writers Guild and is presently treasurer of the Desert Chapter of the National Press Women as well as a director of the California Real Estate Educators Association. He has written extensively on business matters for local and national publications.